SCM STUDYGUIDE TO ANGLICANISM

SCM STUDYGUIDE TO ANGLICANISM

Stephen Spencer

scm press

Published in 2010 by SCM Press
Editorial office
13–17 Long Lane,
London, EC1A 9PN, UK

SCM Press is an imprint of Hymns Ancient and Modern Ltd
(a registered charity)
13A Hellesdon Park Road
Norwich, NR6 5DR, UK
www.scm-canterburypress.co.uk

British Library Cataloguing in Publication data

A catalogue record for this book is available
from the British Library

978-0-334-04337-9

Typeset by Regent Typesetting, London
Printed and bound by
CPI Antony Rowe, Chippenham SN14 6LH

Contents

Part 4 Anglicanism as a Whole

Acknowledgements

Like Anglicanism itself, this book has evolved from the interaction of different points of view as they compete, check and redress each other. I am very grateful to the scholarship of many commentators, from different wings of the church, many of whom are listed in the Bibliography, for the resulting mix of these pages. However, the content of the text, describing a flock of different figures, movements and opinion, is inevitably selective, and I must offer my apologies in advance for the omission of those whom others would regard as essential. Nevertheless I hope that in broad terms this Studyguide can provide a suitable introduction to a rich and diverse subject.

Special thanks must go to the students of the Yorkshire Ministry Course (formerly the Northern Ordination Course), who through their commitment to learning and discussion have helped me develop the approach to the subject found in these chapters. Thanks are also due to Ben Gordon-Taylor who read sections of the book and made helpful suggestions. Stephen Platten has once again been generous with his time and attentiveness, reading all the chapters and making many invaluable critical and constructive comments. My wife Sally has gone through the text sentence by sentence making essential corrections. To all of these people I am greatly indebted. The errors and obscurities that remain are entirely my own responsibility. I would also like to thank Natalie Watson and the editorial board at SCM Press for giving me the opportunity to write on this subject.

My interest in Anglicanism was first awakened as a teenager by the enthused teaching and ministry of Alan Charters. In deep gratitude this Studyguide is dedicated to him.

Introduction

Different Ways of Being Anglican

A visitor to the city of Lancaster in the northwest of England cannot miss the medieval Priory Church. It sits on a small hill in the middle of the city next to the gaunt castle. The tower of the church is the highest point on the skyline and draws the eye to its weathered profile. The church itself is entered through an ornate porch with heavy wooden doors keeping the northern winds and rain out. Once inside, visitors find they are standing in a darkened space beneath a balcony with a free standing font ready for the baptism of those who take on the Christian faith. Then the eye is drawn up the length of the church, past the elegant gothic pillars and arches and towards the sanctuary at the east end. Light from the large stained glass east window fills this part of the building and illuminates the stone walls and polished floor. There, with space around it, is a major focus of the building, the point that the eye has been searching to settle upon, the altar. It is a long but well proportioned table, having a simplicity and presence and standing without candles or cross upon it. This draws attention to how this is a surface for plates and cups, for the serving of a meal: it shows that this whole building and its furnishings are there for a specific purpose – the celebration of the sacred meal of the Eucharist. In other words, the church is designed to draw the attention of people to the point where bread and wine become the body and blood of Christ and where those who receive them are united with one another in him.

To attend the main service at the Priory is to have this confirmed. The Eucharist is celebrated in a formal way, with robed choir, a large team of servers, incense and bells enhancing the movement of the liturgy towards the consecration of the elements and the distribution of communion. Preaching is valued within the service, but there is no doubt where its climax is meant to be, the procession of vessels and people toward the altar to receive Christ in bread and wine.

But Lancaster, like many other towns and cities in England, has other and contrasting examples of Anglicanism. Ten minutes walk down the hill and along one of the shopping streets is another parish church, St Thomas, which from the outside appears to offer another example of Gothic architecture and worship. But appearances can be deceptive! Entering the church on a Sunday morning one finds another large space with a balcony and a sanctuary. But comfortable chairs have replaced pews, large screens for overhead projectors hang above the nave and television screens are provided for those seats under the balcony with restricted views. In the sanctuary the altar has been replaced by a prominently placed modern lectern (though a table is still visible at the far end). Clearly the ministry of the Word through readings and preaching is central to the worship of this church.

This ministry is confirmed when worship takes place. The clergy and others lead from the lectern, with songs, prayers and readings leading toward a climactic moment in the service, which is revealed to be the sermon. This is not a ten-minute homily but a much longer exposition of the readings, in the language and idioms of the congregation: it is engaging, humorous, and the message is clear and practical. As the sermon unfolds, direct and powerful communication takes place between the preacher and the congregation: many are clearly moved and caught up in the thoughts of the preacher as he takes them on a journey from the text of scripture to its application in their own lives. But there is little interaction between the people themselves (apart from greetings which have taken place before the service): their attention is focused on the Word within their own lives. There is little formalized expression of belonging to a corporate body, such as through receiving communion. The focus and direction of the worship and sermon is towards the private lives of those who are present.

The Priory and St Thomas belong to the same church. This in itself is remarkable. But still it does not represent the full breadth of Anglicanism in Lancaster or other towns and cities. There is a third expression not so visible on a Sunday morning, but represented by a specific school uniform that is seen around the city during the week. This is the uniform of the pupils of Ripley School, a Church of England secondary school on the edge of the city centre. Ripley has over a thousand pupils and is housed in a mixture of Victorian and modern buildings sprawling over a large site that includes playing fields and a horticultural garden. Its Anglican identity is demonstrated by the presence of a large chapel, again built in the Gothic style, into which the pupils go for regular assemblies. Local clergy play a prominent part in leading these assemblies and also sit on the governing body, along with other church appointed governors, who together form a majority of members. The admissions policy places significant emphasis on church attendance for those who apply to the school. But the school is also open to those who do not attend Anglican churches and is committed, within these parameters, to serving the whole community.

Ripley School is an example of Anglicanism investing a significant proportion of its time and financial resources in the education of young people. While the school provides some explicitly Christian input within the regular timetable there is also a broader commitment to teaching the national curriculum for its own sake. The school measures its success not in the number of conversions or confirmations that take place (though these are valued) but ultimately in the academic performance of its pupils in public exams. Education, based on contemporary social and cultural norms and regulated by national government, is promoted for its own sake.

This portrait of a town and its expressions of Anglicanism opens up the subject of this book, a Christian church with a wide variety of traditions. It illustrates the diversity of Anglicanism and raises the question of why such diversity has come about: why does this church encompass churches and schools that are committed to such different objectives? Why does it encompass a sacramentally focused corporate expression of discipleship, a scripturally focused individualistic expression of discipleship, and a social and culturally focused educational expression of discipleship (and other variations on these themes as well)?

That the differences between these objectives can go very deep has been recently demonstrated by divisions between the bishops of the Anglican Communion. Their differences over the way to interpret and develop Anglicanism led a large number of them to decide not to attend the Lambeth Conference of 2008. Statements in the press revealed that those from Sydney viewed the church in a fundamentally different way from their colleagues in San Francisco, as did those from Cape Town compared to those from Kampala, as did those from Lagos compared to those from London.

The phrase 'unity in diversity' has often been used to describe Anglicanism. Recent events have emphasized how deep the diversity goes, to the extent of questioning whether there is still a real unity.

This Studyguide takes this diversity seriously. It does not attempt to paper over the cracks and project a non-existent uniformity onto the life of the Anglican Communion. It takes as its starting point the way that Anglicans have different views of the nature of Christianity and especially of the Christian life. It traces the way these differences have evolved historically through the lives and writings of key Anglicans, up to and including the twenty-first century. It especially focuses on discipleship because this is an aspect of Christianity which all share in, whether lay or ordained, male or female, rich or poor. Discipleship encompasses every aspect of the Christian life, from how we are saved through to the outward expression of faith in worship and engagement with society. It is a foundational element within the church and its changing nature and character over history reveals the changing nature and character of the church itself.

But Anglicanism is not simply a number of competing traditions. Surrounding and permeating this diversity are a range of 'instruments' and signs (theological and institutional) that (up to now) have held the different outlooks together. The final chapter of the book maps these out and seeks to uncover how far each one is a unifying force today.

Anglicans have usually described their discipleship as coming from three great authorities: *scripture*, meaning the books of the Bible, *tradition*, usually meaning the theology and practice of the ancient church, and *reason*, usually meaning the type of logic or rationality which shapes how people think and arrive at decisions. This last one is a different kind of source from the other two, not found in documents or books but in the culture of the day. (Some recent voices also add a fourth authority, the *experience* of salvation, which again is a different kind of authority and derives from the feelings of the heart rather than anything external.) These three (or four) authorities are seen as different streams that feed the Anglican river, or as different legs of the Anglican stool. But, as we shall see, different Anglican traditions place these authorities in different orders of priority. For some, scripture is the supreme authority and everything else needs to be tested against that. This was the view of the early Protestants represented by Thomas Cranmer and his Articles of Religion (printed in the back of the Book of Common Prayer). See, for example, Article VI, 'Of the Sufficiency of the holy Scriptures for salvation'. For the founders of the Oxford Movement, on the other hand, the tradition of the church was elevated to pole position, with scripture interpreted through the lens of Catholic tradition, rather than the other way round. Scripture, they pointed out, was itself the product of the early tradition of the church. Third, Anglicans inspired by the ideals of the eighteenth-century Enlightenment have argued that if the Christian faith cannot make sense in the terms, or 'reason', of the day and so carry authority among the people the church is seeking to win over, it should be re-thought and re-presented in a more reasonable way. For this point of view, 'reason' is primary. And then, from John Wesley and the Evangelical revival within the Protestant tradition, come those who believe that the emotional and bodily experience of salvation is a key touchstone in the Christian life, without which discipleship is not truly authentic. For this point of view, revived in the twentieth century by the Charismatic movement, experience stands alongside and even above the other authorities.

These fundamental differences concerning authority provide the underlying structure of this Studyguide, with each point of view having its own section within the book. Then, within each section, some of the key sub-themes of discipleship within that tradition are described, through portraits of the key people and ideas which promoted them. So, to begin with, we look at those who make scripture primary, which means starting with the Protestant reformers of the sixteenth century. We begin with their doctrine of justification by grace through faith because it was this doctrine, above all others, which underpinned their whole understanding of the Christian life and which launched the Protestant Reformation in Europe and in Britain. We examine their elevation of scripture over tradition in general, and especially examine its repercussions for worship. We also look at the Evangelical revival of the eighteenth and nineteenth centuries, which occurred within this tradition but which went beyond it in elevating the experience of salvation into a key authority within discipleship. The modern expression of this point of view by the Charismatic revival is also described.

We then turn to those who make the Catholic tradition primary, looking especially at the way the Western Catholic tradition of the Middle Ages was revived in the seventeenth century by the 'High Churchmen' and then by the Oxford Movement in the nineteenth century, with examples of how it received expression in the twentieth century. One of the chapters concentrates on the sacramental emphasis of this outlook, another at the way it showed how Anglicanism stood in the apostolic succession of the Catholic church, and a third at its effect on the externals of worship and churches in general.

Part 3 of the book looks at those who took inspiration from the European Enlightenment of the eighteenth century and who elevated human reason to be the arbitrating authority within the Christian faith. This point of view was very influential in the twentieth century. Its elevation of reason within Christian thinking in general is examined first, followed by its rethinking of the Christian life in the church and its attitude to scripture, and then its promotion of social reform and development in society at large.

This Studyguide is written in the conviction that concentrating on the common themes of scripture, tradition and reason within the different outlooks, along with the different ways they order them, is especially helpful in showing how Anglicans can share so much yet fundamentally and persistently disagree with each other. By using this approach it aims to open up the subject in a fresh way and hopefully make a contribution to intra-Anglican ecumenical understanding.

Such an approach is inevitably selective in its presentation of Anglican history and theology. It cannot present a complete account of the development of Anglican institutions or the phenomenon of Anglicanism around the world, or of every notable Anglican theologian or church leader. (For a concise and readable overview of that history see Chapman 2006; for an illustrated history of Anglicanism within the British Isles, alongside other traditions, written by a number of scholars, see Chadwick 2010.) Furthermore, it comes out of the British context and so draws many of its examples from that setting, which means other parts of the Anglican Communion do not receive the same attention. (For detailed treatments of worldwide Anglicanism see Ward 2006 and Kaye 2008.) Nor is it specifically about the clergy and their changing role (on this see, for example, Percy 2006). Nor is it a complete account of Anglican theology (for this see Sykes and Booty 1988; for Anglican ecclesiology see Avis 2002, and for a concise introduction to Anglican ecclesiology see Avis 2000). Nor is it an account of the current institutional life of the church (see Davie 2008 for the Church of England, and Kaye 2008 for worldwide Anglicanism). Nevertheless it does give an account of many key moments, people and theological developments in the unfolding drama of Anglican history, though always with the intention of uncovering what these meant for the discipleship of the ordinary member of the church. This is an approach that has been found to be helpful in the classroom and is now offered in print for a wider audience. It is also a didactic tool appropriate for entry into this subject at undergraduate level, and is offered as such.

To complete the picture, as already mentioned, a final chapter is provided on the theological and institutional structures and relationships that have kept the different viewpoints within one ecclesial framework. These also need to find a place in any introduction. It presents past and present 'instruments of unity', such as the role of the Archbishop of Canterbury and the Lambeth Conference, institutions like the parochial system, and more recent developments such as the Anglican Communion Covenant, exploring the importance of each in turn. It also explores whether there is an underlying core, as it were, that runs through the different viewpoints and holds them together whatever the apparent disagreements.

There are questions for reflection and discussion at the end of each chapter: these arise out of the stories told in the chapters and raise some live questions for the belief and practice of Anglicans today. Short book lists of further reading are also included to show where more detailed treatments of each topic can be found. This Studyguide is also written with an ecumenical readership in mind, which means distinctive features of Anglicanism are explained when they appear within the text.

As a whole, this kind of approach to Anglicanism will help readers make sense of the extraordinary diversity as well as the common structures and relationships within this rich yet puzzling branch of the Christian church. It will equip them with a detailed map, as it were, that will allow them to explore particular issues and questions with greater confidence.

Part 1

Protestant Ways of Discipleship

1

Justified by Grace through Faith

1.1 *Sin and Grace*: Luther's Theological Revolution

Anglicanism begins to emerge as a distinct communion within the Western Church during the Protestant Reformation of the sixteenth century. This century and its leading theologians, church leaders and official statements must be our first port of call as we explore key aspects of Anglican discipleship.

Many would expect the story to begin with Henry VIII and his marriage difficulties. Was it not his need to divorce Catherine of Aragon that made him break with the Roman Papacy? At one level, of the political realities of the time, this is undeniable. But if we ask why Henry was able to succeed in cutting England loose from the authority of the Catholic Church in a way that had never happened before, a different story must be told. This is a story about a broader range of cultural, economic and religious developments. And prominent among these was a theological revolution that had begun in the small German state of Wittenberg and which was rapidly spreading across northern Europe. It was this revolution that gave permission to Henry, as to other European monarchs at the time, to take the fateful step of ejecting the authority of the Pope from his lands in the Act of Supremacy in 1534. It is to the story of this theological revolution that we now turn.

To make sense of it, though, we must first examine the context out of which it came, the world of late medieval Catholicism. A description of this will throw into sharp relief what was new and distinctive about the new viewpoint.

In the pre-Reformation period the Catholic Church held sway in England as well as on continental Europe. In his authoritative survey of the period Euan Cameron points out that 'however greedy, vicious, grasping, or arrogant individual churchmen were, the Church was still "Mother Church" and the means to salvation'. This attitude was instilled into Europe's population 'in every aspect of religious life, where (in spite of the theologians' quibbles) the visible, institutional Church on earth and the Churches triumphant in heaven and suffering in purgatory were seen as indissolubly linked' (Cameron 1991, p. 79).

Cameron argues that this esteem held in check and balanced people's dislike of Catholic prelates and church taxation. The depth of the hold of Catholic religion on ordinary people's lives in England has been thoroughly and convincingly described by Eamon Duffy (see Duffy 1994, 2003).

In such an outlook the Christian life was all about making progress around a penitential cycle (Cameron 1991, pp. 79–83). Human living was understood to begin *in* God who ordains and presides over the whole cycle. As soon as a person is conceived in the womb, though, they become subject to original sin (as taught by Augustine of Hippo). This means they will end up in eternal damnation unless they can be absolved of their sins and brought into a state of grace in which entry into heaven becomes possible. The sacraments of the church, ministered through the office of the priest, provide the means for this to happen. A newborn baby must be brought to the church as soon as possible to be baptized so that most of the effects of original sin can be removed. As the baby grows into a child and then an adult it cannot avoid committing further sins. This means it must attend sacramental confession so that these ordinary sins of daily life can be absolved on a regular basis. The priest will give the believer some work of penance which allows the effects of their sins to be removed and for them to come into a state of grace once more. This process will continue throughout their lives until their death when, in most cases, there will still be a need to complete the requisite works of satisfaction. Purgatory, the liminal space between death and heaven, becomes the place where these works of satisfaction are finally completed and the Christian soul, as Dante classically describes it in *The Divine Comedy*, is able to pass through the gates of heaven.

An essential feature of this cycle is that the person during their earthly life is not yet a citizen of heaven but is only *on the way* to heaven. They must strive throughout their lives to confess and seek absolution, and they will not have final assurance that they are near or far from heaven: in fact it is possible they will never make it, especially if they commit serious or 'mortal' sins. For committed Christians this was a heavy burden, as the young Martin Luther (1483–1546) found when he endeavoured to do his utmost to reach a state of grace. As an Augustinian monk he became totally committed to the monastic disciplines to achieve this:

> I was indeed a good monk and kept the rules of my order so strictly that I can say: if ever a monk got to heaven though monasticism, I should have been that man. All my brothers in the monastery who know me will testify to this. I would have become a martyr through fasting, prayer, reading and other good works had I remained a monk very much longer. (Janz 1999, p. 77)

But the harder he tried the harder it became: 'my conscience could never give me certainty: I always doubted and said "You did not do that correctly. You were not contrite enough. You left that out of your confession"' (*ibid.*). In his famous Autobiographical Fragment he writes that

> Though I lived as a monk without reproach, I felt that I was a sinner before God with an extremely disturbed conscience. I could not believe that he was placated by my satisfaction. I did not love, yes I hated the righteous God who punishes sinners, and secretly, if not blasphemously, certainly murmuring greatly, I was angry with God . . . (*ibid.*, p. 75)

This was something of an existential crisis for Luther, and he describes how he 'raged with a fierce and troubled conscience'. Thankfully at around the same time he was also lecturing on the Psalms and Romans to students in the University of Wittenberg. His attention was drawn to Romans 1.17, 'In it the righteousness of God is revealed, as it is written, "He who through faith is righteous shall live."' Whereas before Luther had taken 'God's righteousness' to be all about just punishment for sins, he now began see that it might be about something else, God's forgiveness and acceptance of the sinner in his or her sinfulness. God, according to Paul, through the atoning death of Christ on the cross (as he makes clear in 3.25), may in fact be offering salvation as a free gift, not to be earned through endless works of penance but through simply accepting that gift through faith. Luther in his Autobiographical Fragment comes to the powerful conclusion that 'the righteousness of God is that by which the righteous lives *by a gift of God,* namely by faith' (*ibid.*, pp. 75–6, italics mine). E. P. Sanders has described this as the way a believer, for Luther, is 'at the same time righteous in God's sight but a sinner in everyday appearance' (Sanders 1991, p. 48). Or as Cameron put it, Luther saw that 'crucial parts of the New Testament could mean that God spontaneously, from simple mercy, and for Christ's sake, *forgives* people their faults *while they remain impure*' (Cameron in Chadwick, 2010, pp. 117–18).

The effect of this insight on Luther was immediate: 'Here I felt that I was altogether born again and had entered paradise itself through open gates' (Janz 1999, p. 76). He was now assured that he was justified and could live his life out of the shadows of the fear of death:

> Suddenly, it was no longer a struggle to become a purer, holier person through sacrament, prayer, and 'habits of grace', as in the medieval Church. It was the blissful release of accepting that God is generous, and calls on everyone to believe and trust in the forgiveness which they are offered. Once so forgiven, the believer would strive fervently to live a godly life of study, prayer and neighbourly charity: but out of serene thankfulness, not anxious solicitude for a soul perched between heaven and hell. (Cameron in Chadwick, 2010, p. 118)

This, then, is the heart of the new perception of discipleship: release, trust, gratitude and a desire to live a life worthy of the grace it had received. The Reformation swept all before it because it had this essentially liberating and life affirming approach to discipleship at its heart. No longer was the believer to be governed by the fear of not making the grade on judgement day: now there was to be a sense of assurance that justification had already taken place.

One of the first consequences of this emerging belief was Luther's pinning of his 95 Theses to the door of Wittenberg Cathedral. These were an attack on the practice of selling papal indulgences by the church. The Pope, Leo X, was raising money for the re-building of St Peter's in Rome by selling indulgence documents that cancelled a portion of the purchaser's sins, thus easing their passage through purgatory. This was preposterous, argued Luther: only God himself could forgive sins and the only human response was faith and godly living in gratitude for his mercy.

It may seem strange to devote the opening pages of a book on Anglicanism to a German monk but these events in Luther's life are the trigger for what

became the radical shift from medieval Catholicism to Reformation Protestantism in Britain as well as Europe. The doctrine of justification by faith (or, more
strictly the doctrine that the believer can be declared righteous and therefore
saved only through faith in the merits of Christ's death imputed to him or her,
with works or religious observance as irrelevant to this) was the foundation of
the new theological worldview: Cameron calls it 'the absolute crux of what was
shared in the thought of the different reformers' (Cameron 1991, p. 121). It was
not only the centrepiece of Luther's teaching (he himself calling it 'the summary
of Christian doctrine' and 'the sun which illuminates God's Holy Church'), but
for John Calvin, the greatest theologian of the Reformation, it became 'the main
hinge upon which our religion turns' (*ibid.*, for references).

Some Anglican voices confirm the importance of Luther for the Church of
England. John Jewel, Bishop of Salisbury from 1560 to his death in 1571, was one.
Writing after the Elizabeth Settlement in 1559, he looked back on the tumultu-
ous founding of Protestantism in England and described the crucial role of the
German monk. In response to Thomas Harding who vigorously defended the
Papacy and argued that before Luther the Church had lived in peace and unity,
Jewel wrote that 'Before the time that God's holy will was that Doctor Luther
should begin, after so long a time of ignorance, to publish the gospel of Christ,
there was a general quietness, I grant, such as in the night season, when folk are
asleep'! (Avis 2002, pp. 21–2). According to Paul Avis, Jewel goes on to state that
'in the midst of this death-like slumber of the church, Luther and Zwingli "being
most excellent men", were "sent of God to give light to the whole world"'. Like
the Old Testament prophets they were raised up to awaken the people of God
and reform the church. Their credentials may not always have been impressive.
Harding objects that the new teaching came not from Jerusalem or Rome but
from obscure Wittenberg. To which Jewel replies that Wittenberg was 'not more
simple than was the town of Nazareth', adding, 'Christian modesty would not
distain the truth of God in respect of place' (*ibid.*, see also Booty 1963).

It is important to add that Luther was not followed uncritically by the English Reformers: 'they are selective in what they adopt – justification by faith but
not Luther's sacramental doctrine, the freedom of the Christian man, but not
Luther's pervasive dialectic of law and gospel . . .' (*ibid.*, p. 29). Nevertheless
without Luther's formulation of the doctrine of justification by faith it is hard to
conceive of the English Reformation ever taking place, and with that the forming of Anglicanism. His insight into the way we are justified by grace through

faith in the cross of Christ launched the Protestant movement and has remained at its heart ever since (for a contemporary affirmation of the doctrine see Stott 1999, pp. 92–6).

1.2 *Faith then Works*: Cranmer's Founding Documents

The embedding of this doctrine at the heart of the Church of England is due to a very unlikely figure, a shy and retiring diplomat called Thomas Cranmer whom Henry VIII unexpectedly installed as Archbishop of Canterbury. But this embedding was far from straightforward. Some understanding of the broader political developments is necessary. Diarmaid MacCulloch has described several distinct phases in the political story, beginning with Henry's reforms (1533–47). These were initiated by the negotiations over the divorce of Henry and Catherine of Aragon in which Cranmer was recruited as a negotiator to find ecclesiastical justification for contradicting the wishes of the Pope and seeing the divorce through. It was Cranmer, when promoted to being Archbishop of Canterbury, who then annulled the marriage after Henry had already secretly married Anne Boleyn.

Anne was crowned queen in 1533 and this prompted the Pope to threaten the king with excommunication unless he returned to Catherine. Henry now took the fateful step of making Parliament pass the Act of Supremacy (1534) which declared that he was the 'supreme head' of the English Church, and a Treason Act which forbade denial of this supremacy. John Fisher, Thomas More and some leading monks who denied this supremacy were executed. The Catholic powers threatened to mount an invasion to reverse these changes and in response Henry began the violent dissolution of the monasteries in 1536, to acquire the wealth he needed to mount defensive preparations. The subsequent years of his reign showed a mood of religious equivocation, though, as he veered uncertainly between Protestantism and Catholicism. In many ways he retained a Catholic theology and spirituality (earlier in his life he had attacked Luther and in 1521 the pope had given him the title 'Defender of the Faith', a title the British monarch still retains). He sometimes found it hard to accept the views his Protestant ministers like Thomas Cromwell and his archbishop were promoting. MacCulloch describes this phase as 'a complicated matter': not 'Catholicism without the Pope' but 'Lutheranism without justification by faith' (Platten 2003, p. 23).

Cranmer

The retiring diplomat who would produce Anglicanism's founding documents, Thomas Cranmer (1489–1556), was born in Aslockton in Nottinghamshire and was ordained when he became a Fellow of Jesus College, Cambridge. In the 1520s he came under the influence of conciliar theory, which placed the papacy under the authority of general councils of kings and bishops, such as in the decree *Haec Sancta* of the Council of Constance of 1517, that 'this Council holds its power direct from Christ; everyone, no matter his rank or his office, even if it be Papal, is bound to obey it in whatever pertains to faith . . .' This theory was developed by Hugh of Pisa (d. 1210), John of Paris (d. 1306) and in the early writings of Nicholas of Cusa (1401–64) and allowed the Council to depose two popes and set in motion reform of the church. Cranmer began to want a new such council to do the same in his time (see MacCulloch 1996, pp. 29–30; see Avis 2006, Chapter 11, for the influence of Conciliarism on Anglicanism in general). He became convinced that the Pope had no jurisdiction over specifically English matters and so became willing to support Henry VIII in his search for a way of ending his marriage to Catherine of Aragon. When the king needed a new Archbishop of Canterbury and nominated Cranmer he was initially reluctant to take on the post. But Henry could not be refused. After being consecrated in 1533, Cranmer annulled the king's marriage and supported the break with Rome. Three years later, though, he had to also annul the marriage with Ann Boleyn, something which brought him private anguish because he was close to the Boleyn family and had come to share their Protestant theology. With Thomas Cromwell he was responsible for having the newly translated 'Matthew Bible' of 1539 printed and distributed around the parish churches of England, an act which initiated the slow but steady transformation of church life at local level.

Before becoming Archbishop, when on a diplomatic mission in Germany, Cranmer had followed the example of some of the continental reformers and had got married. But as a priest of the Catholic Church he was not allowed to do this and had to keep his marriage a secret. There was an apocryphal story that he secretly smuggled his wife into Lambeth Palace in a coffin. Now as arch-bishop he had to send her away for a while when the king, ever changeable, reverted to traditional views on clerical celibacy. But he retained the trust of the king and was one of Henry's few close advisers who were not later executed or imprisoned.

When Henry died in 1547 and was succeeded by his teenage son Edward VI, Cranmer at last had his opportunity to bring Reformation theology and prac-tice to England. He oversaw the translation and revision of services into English and published the first Book of Common Prayer in 1549. This was a book for all, laity as well as clergy, in which daily prayer and psalms were combined with the orders of different services. He came to believe, though, that the book did not go far enough. He invited the continental theologians Peter Martyr and Martin Bucer to come and live in England and under their influence published the second more radical Book of Common Prayer in 1552, in which the mass became 'The Lord's Supper', essentially a memorial meal. Cranmer was also largely responsible for its dignified and resonant prose, and for its extensive reli-ance on scripture for the content of the liturgy: 'The most frequently performed text in the English tongue, it has shaped the destiny of the world's dominant language' (MacCulloch in Chadwick 2010, p. 139). Cranmer also produced the 42 Articles (see below) and attempted a revision of Canon Law.

But when Mary Tudor, the daughter of Catherine of Aragon, came to the throne Cranmer's days were numbered. He was tried for treason, sentenced, imprisoned and then tried for heresy. He was sentenced to be burnt at the stake. Under duress he signed several recantations of his beliefs but when he came to be burnt at Oxford on 21 March 1556 he dramatically renounced his recanta-tions, thrusting his hand which had signed the recantations into the flames first saying 'This hand hath offended'.

Cranmer can appear a weak figure who was too quick to do Henry's wishes. Yet it is clear that throughout his life he acted in accord with his emerging Prot-estant convictions and that at the end he was prepared to stand by what he believed in. (See further MacCulloch 1996).

The Articles of Religion

The second phase of the Reformation swept away Henry's equivocation. This is the period when Edward VI was king (1547–53), a teenager who shared the Protestant convictions of his protectors and who supported and encouraged Cranmer to put in place the pillars of a Reformed Protestantism.

Henry may have been unsure about the doctrine of justification by grace through faith but Cranmer was not. In 1553 he was able to write and publish the Articles of Religion, a set of statements that committed the Church of England to the new discipleship. There were 42 articles, which would be re-configured as 39 articles under Elizabeth. They are not 'a complete statement of Christian doctrine, even less an Anglican systematic theology. They are in fact a response to matters of controversy in the sixteenth century. They make certain central affirmations directed against several specific targets: anti-trinitarianism, Roman Catholicism and radical Protestantism' (Avis 2000, p. 52). Nevertheless they reinforce some key theological commitments, notably giving the doctrine of justification by faith a prominent position. This comes after the general articles (describing what all Christians believe) and sounds a key note on the nature of salvation, with which to interpret the subsequent articles.

Article X describes the presupposition made by the doctrine, putting into formal words the kind of awareness we saw Luther acquire during his existential crisis:

> The condition of Man after the fall of Adam is such, that he cannot turn and prepare himself, by his own natural strength and good works, to faith, and calling upon God: Wherefore we have no power to do good works pleasant and acceptable to God, without the grace of God by Christ preventing us . . . (Article X)

Then Article XI, in typically understated fashion for Cranmer, announces the life-changing liberation of the new doctrine:

> We are accounted righteous before God, only for the merit of our Lord and Saviour Jesus Christ by Faith, and not for our own works or deservings: Wherefore, that we are justified by Faith only is a most wholesome Doctrine, and very full of comfort, as more largely is expressed in the Homily of Justification. (Article XI)

This last reference is to a homily found in a set of sermons written mainly by Cranmer for public reading in churches. They were distributed up and down the country in Edward VI's reign. After the Elizabethan Settlement a second collection was produced (which is listed in Article XXXV of the 1662 BCP). This homily is most likely to be the third in the first book, 'Of the Salvation of all Mankind'. In measured and yet moving prose Cranmer writes of the pure giftedness of justification:

> Justification is the office of God only, and is not a thing which we render unto him, but which we receive of him; not which we give to him, but which we take of him, by his free mercy, and by the only merits of his most dearly beloved Son, our only redeemer, Saviour, and justifier, Jesus Christ ... we must renounce the merits of all our said virtues, of faith, hope, charities and all other good deeds, which we either have done, shall do, or can do, as things that be far too weak and insufficient and unperfect, to deserve remission of our sins and our justification. (Janz 1999, pp. 306–7)

The importance of faith to justification, faith as simple trust in the cross of Christ, is made plain by Cranmer: 'And therefore we must trust only in God's mercy, and that sacrifice which our high priest and Saviour Christ Jesus, the Son of God, once offered for us upon the cross, to obtain thereby God's grace and remission' (*ibid.*, p. 307).

What of good works? Are they now irrelevant? Article XII makes clear that they still have a place in the Christian life, but not as any kind of qualification or payment that must be made in order to be justified. Rather they have their place *after* justification, when the disciple will practise them out of gratitude and in thanksgiving for being saved:

> Albeit that Good Works, which are the fruits of Faith, and follow after Justification, cannot put away our sins, and endure the severity of God's judgment; yet are they pleasing and acceptable to God in Christ, and do spring out necessarily of a true and lively Faith insomuch that by them a lively Faith may be as evidently known as a tree discerned by the fruit. (Article XII)

What this means in practice would be spelled out in the Catechism also printed in the Book of Common Prayer (see below).

The Articles also highlight the doctrine of predestination (Article XVII), the doctrine that God has predestined those who are justified to be saved, devoting more words to it than other doctrines. This helps to locate Cranmer and his agenda within the emerging Reformed tradition in Europe, for whom predestination was becoming a defining doctrine; this places him as distinct from the Lutheran tradition. It is important to note, however, that the Calvinist doctrine of double predestination, which teaches that God predestines some for damnation as well as others for salvation, appears to be missing. This shows that Cranmer was not going to explicitly follow the logic of Reformed Protestantism to this degree.

The Catechism

Catechisms had been part of the life of the church during the Middle Ages, but only for the few who could obtain and read a copy. Now with the advent of printing, and with Luther's emphasis on the importance of instruction of the faithful, it became possible and desirable to spread their use more generally. Luther had published his Shorter Catechism in 1529 and Cranmer followed suit, including one in the first edition of the BCP in 1549. This was the first time a body of teaching had been included in an officially authorized service book. The Catechism or 'Instruction to be learned of every person before he be brought to be confirmed by the bishop' adopted a question and answer format and included teaching on baptism, the Apostles' Creed, the Trinity, the Ten Commandments, duty to God and neighbour and the Lord's Prayer (other questions and answers were added in later editions of the BCP). It is not clear if Cranmer was the author of the words themselves: he may have simply adopted them from another writer. But they spell out clearly what the Articles of Religion mean when they talk of the 'good works' which are 'fruits of faith':

Question: What is thy duty towards God?
Answer: My duty towards God, is to believe in him, to fear him, and to love him with all my heart, with all my mind, with all my soul, and with all my strength; to worship him, to give him thanks, to put my whole trust in him, to call upon him, to honour his holy Name and his Word, and to serve him truly all the days of my life.

Question: What is thy duty towards thy Neighbour?

Answer: My duty towards my Neighbour, is to love him as myself, and to do to all men, as I would they should do unto me: To love, honour, and succour my father and mother: To honour and obey the King, and all that are put in authority under him: To submit myself to all my governors, teachers, spiritual pastors and masters: To order myself lowly and reverently to all my betters: To hurt no body by word nor deed: To be true and just in all my dealing: To bear no malice nor hatred in my heart: To keep my hands from picking and stealing, and my tongue from evil speaking, lying, and slandering: To keep my body in temperance, soberness, and chastity: Not to covet nor desire other men's goods; but to learn and labour truly to get mine own living, and to do my duty in that state of life, unto which it shall please God to call me.

Here, then, in words and phrases that recall the Ten Commandments and some of the teaching of Jesus, is a clear and practical guide to the Christian life, though with a strong dose of subservience to those in authority included in the mix. The disciple was to obey these prohibitions and prescriptions as a duty, and so live a godly life, but never forgetting that such obedience was not about gaining credit and forgiveness, but was to be given out of gratitude and thankfulness for the salvation that had already been granted through faith.

1.3 *Looking Within*: George Herbert

But is living the Christian life so straightforward? Can the disciple be sure of salvation? A different strand of Reformation thinking took an altogether more involved attitude to the Christian life, one which has resonated down the centuries and remains influential to this day. This is a strand of thinking and writing that comes to us through some early seventeenth-century poets. It lays emphasis on looking within, on the struggle for purity of faith and assurance of salvation.

George Herbert (1593–1633) was the foremost of these and one of England's greatest poets. He was a complex person who began his adult life as a successful academic at Cambridge. He could have become a courtier but instead, under the influence of Nicholas Ferrar (who had founded a community devout lay people at Little Gidding) was ordained and eventually became Rector of Fugglestone with Bemerton near Salisbury from 1630–3. He came from an aristocratic background but chose to live next to the smaller of the two churches he served. In one of his poems he contrasts a life of wealth and fame with a life devoted to prayer and shows he prefers the latter:

> I value prayer so,
> That were I to leave all but one,
> Wealth, fame, endowments, virtues, all should go;
> I and dear prayer would together dwell,
> And quickly gain, for each inch lost, an ell.
> (Sheldrake 2009, p. 4)

There is debate about whether Herbert should be seen as primarily a Protestant or Catholic. In some respects his attachment to the liturgy of the BCP and his respect for the threefold order of bishops, priests and deacons show Catholic sympathies. However, some of his poetry shows him standing light to Catholic Eucharistic theology. In 'Holy Communion – from manuscript W' he includes the following words addressed to the Lord:

> First I am sure, whether bread stay
> Or whether Bread do fly away
> Concerneth bread, not me.
> But that both thou and all thy train
> Be there, to my truth, and my gain,
> Concerneth me and Thee.
> (*Ibid.*, p. 141)

This statement shows a distinct lack of interest in the Catholic doctrine of transubstantiation, which states that when the bread and wine are consecrated by the priest in the mass they cease to be bread and wine (the bread does 'fly away') and starts literally to be the body and blood of Christ. For Herbert the Eucharist is about the presence of the Lord within the consciousness of the worshipper rather than in the elements. He seems to have no interest in the elements themselves containing the presence of Christ and it is this shows his affinity to Protestant doctrine (see below Chapter 2.2).

He published two very influential works. The first was *The Country Parson* in 1632, which was a prose portrait of a dutiful and caring vicar as he goes about his daily rounds. It is an idealized picture and, according to Sheldrake, was probably written with a rhetorical purpose in mind. Rhetoric, with roots in the Renaissance, 'sought to communicate much more than information or argument. Its purpose was to evoke love, feelings and imagination and thus to move the human heart to a response.' *The Country Parson* shares this purpose:

> In the first place the book is meant not simply to instruct but to move the reader to a deepening sense of call. In the second place the text portrays the priest as a rhetorician. That is, his fundamental task, in what he says, does and lives, is to move his parishioners to deeper faith and to greater involvement in the life of the Christian community. (Sheldrake 2009, p. 11)

The Christian life promoted by the priest and by Herbert in his book, then, was not to be one of just carrying out the kind of duties to neighbour described by the Catechism. Something deeper was needed, something to do with the interior life and the well springs of faith and love.

It is in Herbert's other book, a collection of poems published as *The Temple* of 1633 shortly after his death, that he reveals the inner struggle for purity of faith and assurance of salvation. Herbert's biographer, Isaak Walton, reports that when Herbert handed the poems to Nicholas Ferrar for safe keeping, he wrote that the poems are 'a picture of the many spiritual conflicts that have passed betwixt God and my soul before I could subject mine to the will of Jesus my Master; in which service I have now found perfect freedom' (*ibid.*, p. 11). Nevertheless modern commentators point out the poems also have a rhetorical purpose which shows they are not primarily autobiographical but have been written to move and encourage the reader. They are organized into three sections: 'The Church Porch', 'The Church' and 'The Church Militant', which broadly corresponds to the way a Protestant Christian moves from justification by grace (the Church Porch), through gradual sanctification and growth in personal holiness ('The Church'), and fulfilled sanctification in the next life ('The Church Militant'). It is the middle section that is the longest and most dynamic, revealing the inner struggle mentioned above.

The following poem is one of his most famous and expresses in a profoundly personal way the message of Articles X (on the fallen nature of humankind) and XI (on the grace of justification). It poignantly juxtaposes these two realities, with a profound sense of Herbert's unworthiness on the one hand, and the pure grace and affirmation of Christ's justification on the other:

LOVE bade me welcome, yet my soul drew back,
Guilty of dust and sin.
But quick-ey'd Love, observing me grow slack
From my first entrance in,
Drew nearer to me, sweetly questioning
If I lack'd anything.

'A guest,' I answer'd, 'worthy to be here';
Love said, 'You shall be he.'
'I, the unkind, the ungrateful? Ah my dear,
I cannot look on thee.'
Love took my hand and smiling did reply,
'Who made the eyes but I?'

'Truth, Lord, but I have marr'd them; let my shame
Go where it doth deserve.'
'And know you not,' says Love, 'who bore the blame?'
'My dear, then I will serve.'
'You must sit down,' says Love, 'and taste my meat.'
So I did sit and eat.

It would be hard to find a more beautiful yet profound description of the central doctrine of the Reformation.

Herbert's equally famous 'King of Glory, King of Peace' is also an evocative description of the response of the believer after they have been justified (as seen in the line 'thou hast granted my request'). It beautifully expresses the message of Article XII, that good works spring out of heartfelt response to God's grace and are summed up in gratitude and thanksgiving:

King of glory, King of peace,
I will love thee;
and that love may never cease,
I will move thee.
Thou hast granted my request,
thou hast heard me;
thou didst note my working breast,
thou hast spared me.

Wherefore with my utmost art
I will sing thee,
and the cream of all my heart
I will bring thee.
Though my sins against me cried,
thou didst clear me;
and alone, when they replied,
thou didst hear me . . .

The final verse shows how this thanksgiving and praise can hardly be contained by the justified believer:

Seven whole days, not one in seven,
I will praise thee;
in my heart, though not in heaven,
I can raise thee.
Small it is, in this poor sort
to enroll thee:
e'en eternity's too short
to extol thee.

Taken together Herbert's poems express a view of the Christian life that Rowan Williams has evocatively described as 'a clear-eyed and unconsoled awareness of the fragility of human thinking and motivation with an equally clear-eyed and deeply charged awareness of the terrible mysteriousness of God's grace, an awareness at once sweet and joyful and strange and frightening'. He then sums up the object of this dual perception (using Henry Vaughan's phrase) as 'a dazzling darkness' (Rowell, Stevenson, Williams 2001, p. 12).

But how did the Reformers defend this view of God's grace? To what authority did they appeal now that they had jettisoned the papacy? The answer lies in the way they elevated the place and role of scripture in the Christian life, for they had found this doctrine within its pages. The Bible would now become the sovereign authority lying behind everything they taught, and to its elevation within Anglicanism we now turn.

Discussion Questions

1 Do you agree that the doctrine of justification by grace through faith is 'a most wholesome Doctrine, and very full of comfort'? In what terms and language would you present it to a contemporary church congregation?

2 In the Declaration of Assent, that ordinands must make before or during an ordination service, it is stated that the Church of England 'led by the Holy Spirit . . . has borne witness to Christian truth in its historic formularies, the Thirty-nine Articles of Religion, the Book of Common Prayer and the Ordering of Bishops, Priests and Deacons'. In what ways do you think the Thirty-nine Articles of Religion have 'borne witness to Christian truth'?

3 What was the 'dazzling darkness', to use Henry Vaughan's phrase quoted by Rowan Williams, that George Herbert perceived within God? Does the way Herbert describes this perception speak to our own times?

Further Reading

Reformation history and theology in general

Cameron, Euan (1991), *The European Reformation*, Oxford: Oxford University Press.

Janz, Denis R., ed. (2002), *A Reformation Reader: Primary Texts with Introductions*, second edition, Minneapolis: Fortress Press.

MacCulloch, Diarmaid (2003), *Reformation: Europe's House Divided*, London: Allen Lane. This volume has many more suggestions for further reading.

MacGrath, Alister E. (2000), *Reformation Thought: An Introduction*, third edition, Oxford: Blackwell Publishing.

Thomas Cranmer and the English Reformation

MacCulloch, Diarmaid (1996), *Thomas Cranmer: A Life*, New Haven: Yale University Press.

MacCulloch, Diarmaid (2000), *Tudor Church Militant: Edward VI and the Protestant Reformation*, London: Allen Lane.

MacCulloch, Diarmaid (2003), 'The Church of England 1533–1603', in Stephen Platten, ed., *Anglicanism and the Western Christian Tradition*, Norwich: Canterbury Press.

O'Donovan, Oliver (1986), *On the Thirty Nine Articles: A Conversation with Tudor Christianity*, Exeter: The Paternoster Press.

George Herbert

Sheldrake, Philip, ed. (2009), *Heaven in Ordinary: George Herbert and His Writings*, Norwich: Canterbury Press.

Williams, Rowan (2004), 'Inside Herbert's *Afflictions*' in *Anglican Identities*, London: Darton, Longman and Todd.

2

The Word Above All

2.1 *Attending to the Word in English*: Tyndale's Bible

An emphasis on scripture as the primary authority within the Christian life is a defining theme within Protestantism. It is almost as important as the doctrine of justification by grace through faith. Some commentators see it as *the* defining feature of the Protestant view of the Christian faith (for example McGrath 2007). However, it was because of the doctrine of justification, with its assurance that salvation did not depend on the mediation of the church, that Luther and others felt able to elevate the authority of scripture over that of the church in the first place: the doctrine showed that the Christian needed neither priest nor sacramental absolution to be justified; he or she had already received justification directly from God in the hidden chambers of their heart. So the doctrine of justification is primary. But the fact that it came to Luther through his study of scripture and especially of Paul's letter to the Romans (or at least a certain reading of that letter), meant that the Bible acquired a major significance within this tradition. Furthermore, for many of the Reformers scripture became the only decisive authority in the Christian life, summed up in the oft repeated slogan 'sola scriptura' ('by scripture alone') (McGrath 1999, pp. 152–4).

Luther himself demonstrated his veneration of scripture by devoting his considerable energies to translating the Bible into German. This happened while he was under house arrest at the Wartburg castle near Eisenach, from June 1521. He published the New Testament in September 1522, a translation which came to have a huge impact in German speaking areas of Europe and which helped to lay the foundation of the modern German language.

The translation of the Bible into English was not far behind. The pioneer was William Tyndale (1494(?)–1536), a native of Gloucestershire and brilliant linguist of Magdalene Hall, Oxford, who had started to translate the New Testament in 1523. He based his translation on Luther's German translation (he probably met Luther at Wittenberg in 1524) and on Erasmus' 1516 scholarly edition of the Greek text, a major resource that embodied the aspiration of Renaissance scholarship to get back to the original version of ancient texts. (It is hard to imagine the Reformation taking place without Erasmus, who in 1509 was the first to attack in print widespread corruption in the church.) Tyndale sought the patronage of Cuthbert Tunstall, the Bishop of London, but was turned down, and, fearing he might be arrested, had to flee to Hamburg in 1524. It was in Germany, in Worms in 1526, that he was able to publish his first edition of the complete New Testament. This was a key moment in the English Reformation, when access to the word of God in the common tongue of the people (rather than in the Latin of the medieval church) was opened up. Subsequent editions of the NT were printed in the Netherlands and copies soon began to reach England.

Tyndale had now settled in Antwerp and here he worked on the Pentateuch, using the Latin Vulgate version as well as Luther's German translation, and this was published in 1530. He then translated the book of Jonah, and in 1534 a revised version of the New Testament. He included many marginal notes in his translation which expressed his strongly Protestant theological views. Henry VIII was not impressed with these and called them 'pestilent glosses'! This showed that Tyndale was acquiring many enemies who saw the revolutionary implications of his work. The Catholic authorities in the Netherlands arrested him in 1535 and then condemned him to death. He was strangled and burnt at the stake by order of Charles V the Holy Roman [German] Emperor, who was a nephew of the slighted Catherine of Aragon and a dedicated opponent of Protestantism.

Tyndale, however, had left behind a draft translation of the books of Joshua to 2 Chronicles, and these as well as his published books contributed to the first complete edition of the Bible printed in English, the one prepared by Miles Coverdale and published in the same year that he died, 1535. Coverdale cleverly dedicated it to the king. (This version also contained Coverdale's sparkling translation of the Psalms, which is still printed in the BCP.) This forced Henry, under pressure from his Lutheran political allies in Germany, to order that a copy of the

English Bible be placed in every church in the land. And although later, in 1543, he tried to restrict its public reading, the cat was out of the bag. MacCulloch comments that 'one cannot overestimate the impact of Tyndale's translation' (Platten 2003, p. 22). This is because the people of England, and soon across the British Isles as a whole, were being given access to an eternal salvation, no less, that did not depend on the priesthood and sacraments of the Church. This was an access through the word of scripture, as already mentioned, presented in the vernacular and interpreted through the lens of Paul's theology (in Luther's reading), which assured those with faith that they were justified before God and therefore freed from the fear of eternal damnation. No longer would they have to live under the uncertain and heavy burden of the Church's penitential cycle: they were free, and could now live lives of gratitude and thanksgiving. In other words an important shift was beginning to take place, a shift in the whole way the Christian faith was to be understood and expressed.

Tyndale the translator

The opening of the Sermon on the Mount in the Authorized Version of King James from 1611 is lifted directly from Tyndale's translation:

> And Jesus seeing the multitudes, went up into a mountain; and when he was set, his disciples came unto him. And he opened his mouth, and taught them, saying, Blessed are the poor in spirit: for theirs is the kingdom of heaven. Blessed are they that mourn: for they shall be comforted. Blessed are the meek: for they shall inherit the earth. Blessed are they which do hunger and thirst after righteousness: for they shall be filled. Blessed are the merciful: for they shall obtain mercy. Blessed are the pure in heart: for they shall see God
> . . .

David Daniell, the most recent biographer of Tyndale, writes that these familiar words 'sing with an English rhythm, making a poem which reflects the poetic, shaped quality of the original Greek. A case can be made throughout the Sermon on the Mount for Tyndale's dependence on the Greek alone, on the Vulgate Latin alone, the German [of Luther's translation] alone, or all three together. What is characteristic of Tyndale, and what matters, is his clarity, his determination to put nothing in the way of being understood' (Daniell 1994, pp. 112–13).

But Tyndale's translation is not only notable for its clarity:

> the English into which Tyndale is translating has a special quality for the time, being the simple, direct form of the spoken language, with a dignity and harmony that make it perfect for what it is doing. Tyndale is in the process of giving us a Bible language . . . In his Bible translations, Tyndale's conscious use of everyday words, without inversions, in a neutral word-order, and his wonderful ear for rhythmic patterns, gave to English not only a Bible language but a new prose. (*Ibid.*, pp. 115–16)

Another commentator, Rowan Williams, has described Tyndale as the true theological giant of the English Reformation and has written of his achievement in the following glowing terms: Tyndale

> spent his greatest energies in framing a vernacular language for speaking of God – or rather for God to speak. He is searching for words that will be capable of being owned by the poor and dispossessed as words of promise and of transfiguration. By common consent, he achieves a vigour and a music in his work as a translator which no one has really rivalled in our language. (Williams 2004, p. 23)

2.2 *Scriptural Services*: The Book of Common Prayer

The second phase of the Reformation, under Edward VI (1547–53), began to put in place for worship some of the radical implications of this elevation of scripture. Edward was a teenager who shared the Protestant convictions of his protectors and who supported and encouraged Cranmer to construct a Reformed Protestantism within the life of the Church of England.

Some key dates in the reform of worship

1547 Death of Henry and accession of Edward VI. The Chantries Act abolishes financing of prayers for the departed; clergy are allowed to marry, regular confession is made optional; religious images (statues, wall paintings) are destroyed.

1549 First Book of Common Prayer published and authorized.

1550 Stone altars are replaced by wooden tables in many churches. Cranmer publishes the Ordinal (the orders for making deacons, ordaining priests and consecrating bishops)

1552 Second Book of Common Prayer published. (Cranmer also begins the process of reforming the canon law of the English church, though this would not be completed until 1604.) All in all MacCulloch concludes that 'The short reign of Edward VI created many of the institutions of the Church of England which survive to the present day' (Platten 2003, p. 25).

1553 Death of Edward VI and accession of Mary Tudor.

Cranmer's reforms arise from the elevation of scripture within the life of the believer. This elevation is described in the Articles of Religion, first published in 1553, such as in Article VI:

> Holy Scripture containeth all things necessary to salvation: so that whatsoever is not read therein, nor may be proved thereby, is not to be required of any man, that it should be believed as an article of the Faith, or be thought requisite or necessary to salvation. (Article VI)

Here was a startling inversion of the authority of church and scripture. The church was now being given a subservient role in the economy of salvation: no longer were the sacraments and ministry of the Church to be seen as the means of access to salvation. That access lay directly between the believer and God, with scripture as the channel of grace. So the Church had no right to go against the word of scripture, as Article XX makes clear:

> The Church hath power to decree Rites or Ceremonies, and authority in Controversies of Faith: And yet it is not lawful for the Church to ordain anything

contrary to God's Word written, neither may it so expound one place of Scripture, that it be repugnant to another. Wherefore, although the Church be a witness and a keeper of holy Writ, yet, as it ought not to decree any thing against the same, so besides the same ought it not to enforce any thing to be believed for necessity of Salvation. (Article XX)

There were some important implications of this inversion of authorities. One of the most far reaching was a redefinition of the nature of the church itself. If it was no longer the gateway to heaven, and its priests the key holders of the gates of heaven, what was its purpose? Here, in broad terms, following Luther, the Reformers made a distinction between an invisible church, made up of those justified by God and known only to himself (because that justification takes place in the secret chambers of the heart and cannot be known by anyone else), and the visible church, the church which meets in buildings at the end of streets, with its services and clergy and lay people of all kinds. This visible church belongs to this world and, like the field in Jesus' parable, with both wheat and weeds. It is a place where scripture can be read and the good news about justification by grace announced to the community. It is a herald, like John the Baptist, pointing to something else, to the invisible church, which is the body of Christ, and which is not the same.

This theology comes to expression within Anglicanism, implicitly, in Article XIX: 'The visible Church of Christ is a congregation of faithful men, in the which the pure Word of God is preached, and the Sacraments be duly ministered according to Christ's ordinance . . .' The implication is that there is also an invisible church, the church of those justified and known only to God.

What does all this mean for the services of the church? If they no longer are the means of access to salvation, what is their purpose? Answers to this question are found in the ways Cranmer revised different liturgies and drew them together in the Book of Common Prayer.

Daily Prayer

In his revisions of the Divine Office, in which Cranmer reduces the monastic offices into two services – Morning and Evening Prayer (or Mattins and Evensong) – he is concerned above all to let Scripture speak in its own unhindered voice. This is clear from his original preface to the book, now reprinted as the second preface entitled 'Concerning the Service of the Church', where he begins by saying that he believed the ancient tradition of the church 'was not ordained but of a good purpose, and for a great advancement of godliness' (p. viii). But he does not want to uphold this ancient tradition for its own sake but because

> they so ordered the matter, that all the whole Bible (or the greatest part thereof) should be read over once every year; intending thereby, that the Clergy, and especially such as were ministers in the congregation, should (by often reading and meditation in God's word) be stirred up to godliness themselves, and be more able to exhort others by wholesome doctrine . . . and further, that the people (by daily hearing of holy Scripture read in the Church) might continually profit more and more in the knowledge of God, and be the more inflamed with the love of his true Religion. (BCP, p. viii)

The point then, was for the Christian to be given the opportunity to hear all of scripture, book by book and chapter by chapter, in a continuous reading, and so have their discipleship renewed through this encounter with God's word from within. The offices were to be a show case for the Bible, as it were, rather than a vehicle for tradition.

From Mass to Lord's Supper

What of the sacraments, if they are no longer the instruments of grace? When Cranmer was writing the Articles he had already come under the influence of the Swiss reformer Ulrich Zwingli (1484–1531) and his followers Jan Laski (1499–1560) and Martin Bucer (1491–1551), the last two of whom were invited to come and live in England by Cranmer. They thought that Luther had not followed through the logic of his insights, especially over the governing role of scripture within church life. For example, they looked in scripture for a warrant for a doctrine of the real presence of Christ at the Lord's Supper, and could *not* find it. Zwingli therefore taught that the Lord's Supper was a memorial meal, recalling an event (the death of Christ on the cross) that had happened long ago. Christ's sacrifice was not somehow re-created at the altar but was simply remembered in the minds and hearts of the faithful, with the bread and wine being mere tokens or badges of his body and blood. He rejected Luther's doctrine of consubstantiation (that Christ becomes present alongside and with the bread and wine) and argued it is only *within* the believer who receives the bread and wine with faith that Christ becomes present: 'the spiritual presence of Christ ... is not to be in any way identified with the element [the bread and wine] itself' (Cameron 1991, p. 164). The unconsumed bread and wine therefore could be thrown out or taken home by the curate for his breakfast after the end of the service.

Zwingli and Luther clashed in public over this issue at the Colloquy of Marburg in 1529, when Luther dramatically refused to budge by writing in chalk on the table of the room where they were meeting the words of John 6.63, 'This is my body'. He insisted that he was staying faithful to these words. The failure of the colloquy cemented an increasingly important division between his followers, the Lutherans, and the followers of Zwingli and later Calvin, who became the Reformed tradition within Protestantism.

What of Cranmer and the Eucharist within the Church of England? He was given permission by Edward's government to re-write the liturgies to reflect Protestant doctrine. He produced two successive forms of the Eucharist. The first, in the Book of Common Prayer of 1549, took the major step of translating the rite and seasonal variations from Latin into English and collecting it together in one volume. This was radical enough but it pleased no one. The traditionalists did not care for the loss of the Latin, and the Reformers objected to the presence of a liturgy that still looked like the mass. The second form, in the Book of Common Prayer of 1552, included a thorough revision to the liturgy itself, with many aspects of the mass removed and the whole rite refashioned to become a memorial meal in keeping with Zwingli and especially Bucer's teaching (see below). Prayers for the dead were also removed, as was any suggestion that the people could pray to the communion of saints. So in the prayer for the church, which previously had been understood to be prayers for the church in heaven as well as church on earth, Cranmer inserted the definite words 'militant here in earth' after the words 'Let us pray for the whole state of Christ's church'. The funeral liturgy was also changed, so that the focus was no longer on the body of the deceased and on praying for their soul, but on teaching and encouraging the faith of those who remained.

The 1552 changes to the 'canon of the mass' (the priest's prayers over the bread and wine) clearly show the influence of Zwingli's literal reading of scripture. Following Zwingli, Cranmer's overriding concern was to stop what he saw as the idolatry of the mass in which the bread and wine were thought to become the physical flesh and blood of Christ. For Cranmer, Christ was present in the hearts and minds of the people, received through faith, and the bread and wine were mere signs of this, not the thing itself. So he revised the order of the prayers and changed some of the wording. He removed the 'epiclesis', the prayer asking the Holy Spirit to turn the bread and wine itself into the body and blood of Christ, and substituted words which emphasized what was happening within the soul of the believer:

> grant that we, receiving these thy creatures of bread and wine, according to thy son our Saviour Jesus Christ's holy institution, in remembrance of his death and passion, may be partakers of his most blessed body and blood . . .

He also removed the rubrics telling the priest to hold the bread and wine during the words of institution (the words from the gospels that describe what Jesus did at the Last Supper). Again he was severing the connection between the bread and wine and 'the real presence' of Christ.

Most dramatically of all he shifted the position of the Prayer of Oblation (which is when the bread and wine are offered to the Father as Christ's body and blood on the cross) to a position *after* the communion of the people. In doing this he made sure that any link between its words and the bread and wine was severed, so that it became an offering of only the hearts and minds of the worshippers. The bread and wine could thereby retain their character as emblems or tokens of something that happened a long time ago, rather than becoming hosts for the real presence of Christ crucified. For Catholics this resulted in a liturgy that was now clumsy and disjoined; but for Protestants Cranmer had produced an order that had a new structural integrity, leading the worshipper from the readings and sermon to penitence and then to communion and praise.

Cranmer also removed the words 'The body of Christ' and 'The blood of Christ' from the words of distribution at communion. When the priest gave the communion he would now simply say 'Take and eat this in remembrance that Christ died for thee . . .' The bread and the wine were to be just tokens to remind the worshipper of another reality in another place, namely the death of Christ on the cross and what it achieved for the believer.

It is worth noting, however, that in the Articles of Religion, Cranmer goes beyond a Zwinglian definition of sacraments as just tokens:

Sacraments ordained of Christ be not only badges or tokens of Christian men's profession, but rather they be certain sure witnesses, and effectual signs of grace, and God's good will towards us, by the which he doth work invisibly in us, and doth not only quicken, but also strengthen and confirm our Faith in him. (Article XXV)

These words come from the Lutheran Augsburg Confession of 1530 and describe how the bread and the wine are being given an important role in bringing into effect the body and blood of Christ within the heart and life of the believer. They are not just signs but *effective* signs. Cranmer and the Church of England, then, were embracing a moderated form of Reformed Protestantism, one which leaned towards a doctrine of the real presence of Christ in the elements without actually stating as much. This was still very different from a Catholic definition, however: sacraments are there to quicken, strengthen and confirm faith in a prior salvation, rather than to quicken, strengthen and confirm salvation *itself* (see O'Donovan (1986), Chapter 10).

2.3 *Under a Monarch under Scripture*: Elizabeth's Settlement

The reign of Queen Mary (1553–58), the third phase of the English reformation, was a dramatic interruption of the Protestant programme (see Duffy 2009). Mary restored Roman Catholicism as the state religion and re-introduced heresy laws for those who would not subscribe to it and give their obedience to the Pope. Some 284 Protestants were burned (more in number and over a much shorter period than those executed by Elizabeth; and in Elizabeth's case they were executed for treason rather than heresy). Many of the Reformers fled to the continent, including those like Bucer and the Polish Jan Laski who had been invited to England in the first place by Cranmer. Cranmer himself, as well as Hugh Latimer (a popular preacher and bishop) and Nicholas Ridley (scholar and Bishop of London), were dramatically burned at the stake: a bitter experience that became 'a central part of English consciousness in succeeding Protestant centuries' (MacCulloch in Platten 2003, p. 26).

Mary's reign, however, was only a temporary restoration of Catholicism. When she died in 1558 the throne reverted to her younger half-sister Elizabeth, who had been raised as a Protestant, her mother being the highly intelligent and committed Protestant Ann Boleyn (the only one of Henry's wives whose time as his queen was described as her 'reign', MacCulloch 2003, p. 287). Elizabeth had the intelligence of her mother but also the experience as a young girl of living through the dramatic ebb and flow of power as one regime replaced another in England. She developed acute political antennae among the population in England as well as abroad and knew that she had to retain the loyalty of her subjects while keeping the great Catholic powers of Europe at bay. She knew that her people (especially the population of the South East) would welcome back Protestantism after the traumas of Mary's reign (and against the wishes of most of the nobility and clergy) but she also knew she could not impose the kind of campaigning Protestantism that Edward had sponsored. So it was in her long and ultimately triumphant reign (1558–1601) that Reformed Protestantism, with its commitment to the supremacy of scripture over Catholic tradition, became firmly established as the state religion, but in a moderated form that became quite distinct from the religion of the Swiss reformers.

This fourth phase of the English Reformation was initiated by Elizabeth's Act of Settlement of 1559. This re-established the royal supremacy over the Church of England, though Elizabeth described herself not as 'Supreme Head' but as 'Supreme Governor', leaving space (at last) for God's headship. Her moderated Protestantism is seen in the way that when she restored the 1552 Book of Common Prayer she came under pressure from the House of Lords (and possibly from her own inclinations) and revised it slightly, allowing use of some vestments (in the famous 'Ornaments rubric' at the start of Morning and Evening Prayer – see below pp. 84–9), and through combining the words of administration from the 1549 liturgy with those of the 1552 book ('The body/blood of Christ' with 'take and eat this'), which strengthened the possibility of reading into the words the doctrine of the real presence of Christ in the bread and wine (see below pp. 95–6).

She re-introduced the Articles of Religion in 1563, re-formatted as 39 Articles but still essentially the same. She came under pressure from Reformed Protestants, who were now being called Puritans, to go further than this and replace the threefold order of ministry, of deacons, priests and bishops, with an order that more closely reflected the kinds of minister described in the New Testament, namely an order of pastors, doctors (for example teachers), elders (who were to be disciplinarians) and deacons. This and further reforms she disallowed: enough was enough and Elizabeth pinned her colours to the mast of a conservative Protestantism that some believe was closer to Luther's Wittenberg than Calvin's Geneva. However, MacCulloch is quite clear, as already quoted, that the Elizabethan Settlement, which has formed the basis of the Church of England (and therefore of world-wide Anglicanism) to the present day, was not a religious compromise but a swift and decisive setting up of 'an unmistakably Protestant regime in Westminster' (Platten 2003, p. 27). This saw itself as part of the international Reformed Protestant family of churches, rather than the Lutheran family (*ibid.*, p. 31), though following Zwingli and Bucer over Calvin (*ibid.*, pp. 37–9).

The Protestant character of Elizabeth's faith is confirmed by her own public and private prayers, which show a genuine Protestant piety based on scripture, a hatred of superstition, and commitment to the doctrine of justification by grace through faith. A good example of this is her prayer delivered at Bristol on 15 August 1574. In ringing Tudor English she mentions not only her determination to 'render up . . . a perfect reformed church' but also her wish that her subjects be obedient to God's word and commandments:

> Stretch forth, O Lord most mightie, Thy right hand over me, and defend me from mine enemys, that they never prevayle against me. Give me, O Lord, the assistance of Thy Spiritt, and comfort of Thy grace, truly to know Thee, intirely to love Thee, and assuredly to trust in Thee. And that as I do acknow-ledge to have received the government of this Church and Kingdom at Thy hand, and to hold the same of Thee, so grant me grace, O Lord, that in the end I may render up and present the same again unto Thee, a peaceable, quiett, and well-ordered State and Kingdome, as also a perfect reformed church, to the furtherance of Thy glory. And to my subjects, O Lord God, grant, I beseech Thee, faithful and obedient hearts, willingly to submit themselves to the obedience of Thy word and commandments, that we altogether being thankfull unto Thee for Thy benefitts received, may laud and magnifie Thy Holy Name world without end. Grant this, O merciful Father, for Jesus Christ's sake, our only Mediator and Advocate. *Amen.* (Elizabeth I, 1574)

MacCulloch points out that Elizabeth could be disconcertingly inconsistent about her faith on occasions. For example, she retained a vested communion table that looked like an altar with candlesticks and silver cross in her Chapel Royal. But he states that overall, we might place her religious outlook as close to the discreet evangelicalism displayed by her stepmother Catherine Parr amid the splendours and continuing ceremonial worship of Henry VIII's Court in its last years: Protestantism indeed, but not in the uncompromising form prevailing in the Church of Edward VI. (MacCulloch 2001, pp. 25–6; see also MacCulloch 2003b, pp. 286–91)

It is also worth noting that in the second half of her reign she turned decisively against Roman Catholicism, partly because she herself became the object of plots on her life and also because Protestantism was at last becoming popular among ordinary people in the country at large. She had already been excommunicated by the pope (in 1570) and when in 1588 her navy defeated the Spanish armada, which was the Catholic superpower of the day, it was taken by many as confirmation of divine favour on this female ruler. She was now seen as the 'protectress' of the Protestant faith. Church and state were now deeply wedded and infused with Protestantism and its devotion to scripture above tradition. It would be a relationship that would persist through some profound challenges in the seventeenth century and become seemingly unassailable in the eighteenth century.

The Bible in the Church

This sixteenth-century Reformation resulted in a decisive shift in the focus of worship in parish churches up and down the country. This was not just the revision of the mass into the Lord's Supper, but a physical shift of focus away from the altar (now called the table) as the centre of worship. No longer was the mass or even the Lord's Supper to be the main act of worship. Instead it would become an occasional rite, celebrated once a month or even just on major festivals through the year. Instead the main act of worship would now become Morning Prayer ('Mattins') in which psalms and canticles would be said or sung in Genevan chant and readings from the Bible placed at the heart of the service. And the proclamation of the Word in the sermon was now to be the climax of the service, coming near the end before the final prayers.

Christopher Haigh has described the way this broad shift took place in English parish churches during the reign Elizabeth. It arose out of the re-introduction of the English Bible into church, and also through the spread across the country of Protestant minded clergy from the Protestant dominated universities of Oxford and Cambridge. This was accompanied by the rise of a Bible-based spirituality in the homes of the up-and-coming merchant class, especially in the South East, made possible by the availability of relatively inexpensive printed editions of the Bible. Scripture was found to provide a wealth of images and stories that could amply replace the statues, stained glass and rituals of medieval piety. The Book of Common Prayer, itself infused with the language and imagery of scripture, helped to consolidate this radical shift in piety (see Haigh 1993).

This change meant that the pulpit replaced the altar as the central *locus* of worship. Its position and dominance within the church building was enhanced, sometimes by increasing its height and decoration, sometimes by moving it into the very centre of the sanctuary. The altar, on the other hand, now became a table which could be moved around the sanctuary and pushed to one side when not needed for Holy Communion.

There are still a few examples of this once dominant arrangement in the Church of England today. One can be found in Whitby Parish Church in North Yorkshire and another in Slaidburn Parish Church in Lancashire. At Whitby there is a pulpit (constructed in the eighteenth century) which reflects this theology. It is a very elevated construction, with the preacher placed high above the people in the pews below. There is a second tier below this, for the reading of scripture, and a third tier at ground level for the parish clerk, who leads the congregation in their responses to the priest's versicles. The table for Holy Communion, on the other hand, is placed in the sanctuary which is partially hidden from view by one of the galleries (built to accommodate more people around the pulpit). When the worshipper enters the building it is not the table that catches the eye and draws it on, but this impressive pulpit (see further Yates 2001).

The elevation of word over sacrament is seen in many other aspects of Anglicanism. Rowell, Stevenson and Williams describe the way the whole religious culture of sixteenth and seventeenth-century England was infused and affected:

> The availability of English Bibles must equally be noted as a crucial factor in Reformed English devotion; appeal to scriptural example becomes wider in reference than in the Middle Ages, and the images and idioms of scripture penetrate devotional writing and, of course, preaching (you can see one

simple effect of all this in the quantity of plain expository sermons by some-one like Jewel, for instance). (Rowell, Stevenson, Williams 2001, p. 11)

More recent examples of this scripturally based religion can be found in eighteenth-century hymns. One of the most famous must be the fourth verse of John Newton's 'Amazing Grace':

> The Lord has promised good to me,
> His Word my hope secures;
> He will my Shield and Portion be,
> As long as life endures.

From the nineteenth century a well known example comes from the 1861 hymn of Sir Herbert Baker (1821–77), which makes an explicit link between scripture and salvation.

> Lord, Thy Word abideth,
> And our footsteps guideth;
> Who its truth believeth
> Light and joy receiveth.

> When our foes are near us,
> Then Thy Word doth cheer us,
> Word of consolation,
> Message of salvation . . .

John Stott provides a twentieth-century description of this scriptural form of discipleship within Anglicanism (and other churches). In many ways it sums up the type of Christianity we have traced in this chapter:

> The primary question in every religion relates to the topic of authority: by what authority do we believe what we believe? And the primary answer which evangelical Christians (whether Anglican, Lutheran, Presbyterian, Baptist or other) give to this question is that supreme authority resides neither in the church, nor in the individual, but in Christ and the biblical witness to him. (Stott 1999, p. 43)

While many within Protestantism would agree with Stott, a different point of view has come to gain more and more influence within that world, one which says authority comes not just from the words of scripture but from a personal experience of salvation within the life of the believer: without the authenticating testimony of this experience scripture on its own cannot guide the Christian life. In the next chapter we trace the birth and growth of this increasingly influential point of view.

Discussion Questions

1 Tyndale translated the New Testament into 'the simple, direct form of the spoken language, with a dignity and harmony that make it perfect for what it is doing' (Daniell). Much of his translation was retained in the King James version of 1611. Should Anglicanism retain the use of this incomparable translation today?
2 What do you see as the strengths of the theology of the 1552 version of the Lord's Supper? What do you see as its weaknesses?
3 Should teaching and learning about the Bible always be at the heart of Christian worship?

Further Reading

William Tyndale

Daniell, David (1994), *William Tyndale: A Biography*, New Haven: Yale University Press.

Daniell, David (1995), *Tyndale's New Testament, modern spelling*, New Haven: Yale University Press.

Williams, Rowan (2004), 'The Christian Society' in *Anglican Identities*, London: Darton, Longman and Todd.

The Book of Common Prayer

Cuming, Geoffrey (1983), *The Godly Order: Texts and Studies relating to the Book of Common Prayer*, London: Alcuin and SPCK.

Jeanes, Gordon P. (2008), *Signs of God's Promise: Thomas Cranmer's Sacramental Theology and the Book of Common Prayer*, London: Continuum.

Procter, Francis and Walter Howard Frere (1965), *A New History of the Book of Common Prayer*, London: Macmillan and Co.

Elizabeth and the Reformation

MacCulloch, Diarmaid (2001), *The Later Reformation in England 1547–1603*, Basingstoke: Palgrave.

The Bible in Anglicanism

Haigh, Christopher (1993), *English Reformations: Religion, Politics and Society under the Tudors*, Oxford: Clarendon Press.

Yates, Nigel (2001), *Buildings, Faith and Worship: The Liturgical Arrangement of Anglican Churches 1600–1900*, Oxford: Oxford University Press.

3

Personal Experience as the Touchstone

3.1 *Feelings Within*: the Witness of the Wesleys

This chapter is about the rise of the authority of experience within Protestant discipleship, an authority not derived from an external source like the text of scripture or the teachings of the church but from the inner feelings of the heart. This informal kind of authority came to prominence in the modern period and its rise can be traced back to the decade 1734 to 1744. David Bebbington, a widely respected historian of these events, writes how those years 'witnessed in the English-speaking world a more important development than any other, before or after, in the history of Protestant Christianity: the emergence of the movement that became Evangelicalism' (Bebbington 1989, p. 20). (This use of the word 'Evangelicalism' is different from its use in Germany, where it describes the German Lutheran tradition in general.) This movement has played and continues to play an influential role in Anglicanism, not least in drawing attention to the importance of experience. In some of its forms it has elevated experience over scripture as the primary source of authority (such as in Charismatic Evangelicalism: see below). There are many events and personalities who would need to be included if a complete history of the movement was being presented (see Noll 2003 for such an overview). This is not being attempted here: instead this chapter presents 'windows' onto characteristic features of the movement using a range of different examples from across the period and from around the world.

The Evangelical movement began with the conversion of a number of key individuals, starting in Wales with a young schoolmaster living near Brecon called Howel Harris, and a curate from Carmarthenshire called Daniel Rowland. They both had intense experiences of forgiveness and began to travel around South Wales gathering large audiences and preaching 'the arresting message that salvation could be known now' (Bebbington 1989, p. 20). England followed two years later when George Whitefield, who had been converted early in1735, began preaching to large audiences in Bristol and London 'exhorting his hearers to seek the new birth' (*ibid.*).

At the same time, in New England, the Presbyterian minister and theologian Jonathan Edwards helped to lead a revival in Northampton, Massachusetts, the town where he was a minister. Whitefield, an Anglican, would soon travel to New England to help fan the revival into something much bigger, a spiritual tidal wave which became known as 'the Great Awakening' (see section 3.2 below). And then it was the turn of the Wesley brothers, first Charles (who had helped to mentor Whitefield and whose hymns helped mould the doctrinal understanding of Methodism as well as many Anglicans), who had a strong experience of spiritual renewal in May 1738, and then his older brother, the strong willed and charismatic John, who three days later had a similar experience. John Wesley is usually remembered for his role in founding the Methodist Church, but his impact on Anglicanism was equally significant and he demands our attention in this chapter.

John Wesley's Life

1703 Born the son of Samuel Wesley the Church of England Rector of Epworth, a 'High Churchman' (see below 5.2), and his wife Susanna, who instilled a devout faith in him.

1726 After education at Charterhouse School and Christ Church College, Oxford, he was ordained and elected to a fellowship at Lincoln College, Oxford, where he gathered together a 'Holy Club', nicknamed 'Methodists', because they were serious minded and methodical in their approach to discipleship. The group included his brother Charles and George Whitefield.

1735 John became a missionary to Georgia in the American colonies but fled home in 1737 after a scandal with a woman. On the rough voyage home he was deeply impressed with German Moravian Christians and their sincere Pietistic faith.

1738 24 May. His 'awakening' at a meeting at Aldersgate Street, London, followed by the start of his evangelistic work among the urban and rural poor of Britain. When churches were closed to him he began preaching in fields. He is alleged to have travelled over 200,000 miles during his life and preached 40,000 times. He had a close rapport with the poor and was wary of riches, though in politics remained a Tory.

1741 A rift developed with Whitefield over the doctrine of predestination. Wesley was an Arminian: following the teaching of the Dutch Reformed theologian Jacobus Arminius, he believed justification was open not just to some ('the predestined') but to everyone. He started commissioning lay preachers (including women) and organizing the class system (home groups for Christian instruction) across the British Isles. He gradually helped to organize 'the connexion' – an organized network for the local groups ('societies') that sprouted up in the wake of his and other people's preaching.

1751 Wesley instituted an annual conference of lay preachers.

1784 He 'ordained' Thomas Coke to be a superintendent or bishop of the Methodists in America. He wished Methodism to remain within the Church of England, but the organization was increasingly independent and formally split in 1795. Wesley himself died in 1791 before this happened.

At his death there were already 294 local preachers and 72,000 members of the Methodist societies in Britain. There were also 198 local preachers and 43,000 members in America, and over 5000 members on mission stations. His evangelistic ministry, then, was one of extraordinary scope.

There seems little doubt that his awakening provides the key to understanding where his ministry came from. His experience of inner salvation became the wellspring of his desire to preach and convert people across the country.

It is important to listen to Wesley's own account of the experience from his Journal:

> In the evening I went very unwillingly to a society in Aldersgate Street where one was reading Luther's *Preface to the Epistle to the Romans.* About a quarter before nine, while he was describing the change which God works in the heart through faith in Christ, I felt my heart strangely warmed, I felt I did trust in Christ, Christ alone for my salvation, and an assurance was given me that he had taken away *my* sins, even mine and saved *me* from the law of sin and death. I began to pray with all my might for those who had in a more especial manner despitefully used me and persecuted me. I then testified openly to all these what I now first felt in my heart. (Turner 2002, pp. 27–8)

This passage is now regarded as one of the classic descriptions of an evangelical conversion experience and shows how the receiving of the merits of Christ's death on the cross was not meant just to inform the mind but to bring about an awakening of the heart, of the feelings, of the emotions. It shows how such an awakening is an individual experience that is based on a deep awareness of the sinfulness and inadequacy of the believer, and results in an awareness of their own specific salvation. It is an interior experience rather than a corporate one. The passage also demonstrates the sources of this tradition, for it was a reading of Luther's writing on Paul's letter to the Romans, at the meeting at Aldersgate Street, that prompted the experience.

A few days later Wesley was preaching at the University Church in Oxford (11 June 1738), and his sermon provides a clear insight into the kind of theology Wesley now espoused. It was later placed as the first of his collected 44 sermons to be studied by local preachers, so is a very significant text. Revealingly, the sermon is entitled 'Salvation by Faith'. It begins with a series of assertions that recall Luther's train of thought in his monk's cell: there is a sharp contrast between the corruption of humankind and its efforts to atone for its sins ('having nothing, neither righteousness nor works, to plead, his mouth is utterly stopped before God'), and the grace of God: 'All the blessings which God hath bestowed upon man are of His mere grace, bounty, or favour; His free, undeserved favour; favour altogether undeserved; man having no claim to the least of his mercies' (Paragraphs 1–2).

He then provides a clear assertion of the doctrine of justification by grace through faith: '"By grace" then "are ye saved through faith." Grace is the source, faith the condition, of salvation' (paragraph 3). Then, crucially, Wesley defines the nature of this faith in a personal way:

> it is not barely a speculative, rational thing, a cold, lifeless assent, a train of ideas in the head; but also a disposition of the heart . . . a full reliance on the blood of Christ; a trust in the merits of His life, death, and resurrection; a recumbency upon Him as our atonement and our life, *as given for us,* and *living in us*; and, in consequence hereof, a closing with Him, and cleaving to Him, as our 'wisdom, righteousness, sanctification, and redemption', or, in one word, our salvation. (I.5)

Here, then, is the way that Wesley and, around him, the Evangelical revival as a whole brings the heart of Protestant discipleship into modern Evangelicalism, including Anglican Evangelicalism: through a new emphasis on the *feeling* of justification in the emotions of the heart, where in a physical way the believer can experience the salvation that the cross of Christ provides.

Charles Wesley had had his own awakening three days before this, writing his great hymn 'And can it be' in response to this (he would eventually write some 6000 hymns). It is likely that John sang this hymn soon after his own awakening to 'vital religion'. It expresses the liberating nature of the inner experience of salvation. The first verse gives a compact summary of justification by grace through the atoning death of Christ on the cross. It is significant that the hymn uses the singular 'I' rather than the plural 'we', showing an individualistic approach to salvation:

> And can it be that I should gain
> An interest in the Saviour's blood?
> Died He for me, who caused His pain—
> For me, who Him to death pursued?
> Amazing love! How can it be,
> That Thou, my God, shouldst die for me?

The second and third verses dwell on the mystery of this grace revealed on the cross, and then the fourth verse describes the moment of justification with the imagery of Peter's release from jail in Acts 12. It also recalls the way Martin Luther recounted his 'tower experience' which led to the development of the doctrine of justification by grace through faith:

Long my imprisoned spirit lay,
Fast bound in sin and nature's night;
Thine eye diffused a quickening ray—
I woke, the dungeon flamed with light;
My chains fell off, my heart was free,
I rose, went forth, and followed Thee.

For our purposes the key verse is the fifth, which is often omitted in modern hymn books because of its reference to 'the wrath of hostile heaven' (which seems to contradict the notion of a loving God). It is the verse as a whole which is illuminating:

Still the small inward voice I hear,
That whispers all my sins forgiven;
Still the atoning blood is near,
That quenched the wrath of hostile Heaven.
I feel the life His wounds impart;
I feel the Saviour in my heart.

These words clearly emphasize not just knowledge of justification in the mind but the feeling of justification within the heart of the believer. In verse form, for a popular audience, this strikingly shows an elevation of the importance of inward bodily experience within the Christian life.

3.2 *Feelings Without*: From Whitefield to Alpha

Neither did it remain just an inner experience. George Whitefield (1714–70), who followed Wesley to Georgia and then returned to England to be ordained and to raise money for an orphanage in the colony, was the first to begin to preach in the open air and to draw large and enthusiastic crowds. He saw his role as an 'awakener' serving all the churches. He again travelled across the Atlantic to preach up and down the American colonies. It was here that he became an improbable celebrity. In his mid-twenties, slightly built, middling height, he seemed diffident, even affected. He was also permanently cross eyed, a result of childhood measles, which earned him the nickname Dr Squinton. And the prospect of speaking in public often made him feel physically sick. Yet he 'became transformed in the pulpit into a charismatic preacher, a "divine dramatist"' (Reynolds 2009, p. 45). He became renowned across all the colonies in the 1740s, being one of the main spurs for the Great Awakening, part of a fundamental and enduring transformation of American life which shook up the social order and reached across the racial divide between white landowners and black slaves.

When Whitefield preached in the open air he made a dramatic impression. One Connecticut farmer, Nathan Cole, who travelled with his wife on horseback to Middletown to hear Whitefield, wrote in 1740 that to him Whitefield 'Lookt almost angelical; a young, Slim, slender youth before some thousands of people with a bold undaunted Countenance . . . as if he were Cloathed with authority from the Great God; and a sweet sollome solemnity sat on his brow. And my hearing him preach, gave me a heart wound' (*ibid.*, p. 46).

The crowd that day was estimated at 3–4000. In Boston and Philadelphia his open air preaching would frequently draw 7–10,000, which meant he spoke to more than half the population. Reynolds writes that 'Much of this was due to Whitefield's personal magnetism as he conjured up the torments of Hell and called on his hearers for a "New Birth" in the Spirit. He acted out his biblical stories with mimicry and pathos, tears rolling down his cheeks, and could project his beautifully modulated voice over a remarkably large area' (*ibid.*, p. 46). Whitefield in his Journal provides the following account of one of his sermons in Savannah, Georgia:

> When we came to public prayer, the Holy Ghost seemed to come into the congregation like a mighty rushing wind carrying all before it. I had not long begun before several fell a weeping sorely and the number still increased till young men and maidens, old men and children were all dissolved in tears and moaning after Jesus. I believe there were scarcely half a dozen in the whole congregation that were not deeply affected. I never saw the like before. An effectual door is opening in America and in trust the time is coming when the Earth shall be filled with the knowledge of the Lord as the water cover the sea.

But there were other preachers who also contributed to the religious awakening of the 1740s. Historians now talk not of a one-off Great Awakening but of a series of religious revivals right across America that continued into the nineteenth century. The hallmarks of these revivals were dramatic conversion experiences and a fervour within communities of believers which often became very egalitarian in nature, thus challenging the hierarchy within the Anglican and other older established churches of New England and the Southern states. And these revivals laid the ground for dynamic new congregations such as the Methodists and Baptists, which takes us to a story beyond the scope of this Studyguide.

There was a similar kind of impact among working people on this side of the Atlantic. Compelling evidence is provided by letters written to Charles Wesley. He encouraged those who had recently been converted to write to him and describe what they had experienced. The letters are mostly unpublished and stored in the John Rylands Library at Manchester. They provide a moving insight into what this new Evangelicalism meant for ordinary men and women. One example is the letter from a joiner by trade, Joseph Carter, who wrote to Charles Wesley in November 1741. He wrote in a colloquial but fluent English (presented here with his own spelling). He described how he had been praying to God 'for his grace and holy spirit' and how he found 'a deale of satisfaction in it; so that I was moved to pray again and again'. Then he started to attend meetings of 'religious societies' in London and reports how, after hearing one speaker, 'I was powerfully persuaded thro' him that religion was not anything outward, but that it was a thorough change of the heart . . . but could not find it in myself.' After some time he met an apprentice who had come to ask for some wood shavings from his carpentry shop. Carter was impressed that this apprentice, unlike most others, took no more than what he had asked for. So they got into conversation and were quickly talking about matters of faith and about a 'new religion'. The apprentice then asked Carter if he had

> any notion of this new religion? Which new religion replyed I. Why salvation thro faith only. No I told him; I had heard nothing of it. What did you never hear Mr Wesleys said he? (no, I never heard them). Mr Charles is in town, and he'll preach a Sunday at this church well I think to goe to hear him. Mr John is coming from abroad and he is a very fine man likewise said he.

Carter replied that he knew that he believed 'in all the articles of religion', referring to the Articles in the Book of Common Prayer, though adds 'I believe at that time I never had read them all over nor hardly knew of what was in them', and likewise 'in the scriptures of the Old and New Testament [and] in all the creeds'. Then the apprentice asked him directly if his belief influenced all his life and actions and Carter had to admit that it did not: 'He told me then my faith was of the head and not of the heart'.

This conversation plunged Carter into a period of self examination and questioning and a renewed fear of judgment and hell because of his own sinfulness:

> These terrors followed me hard and close and even almost to desperation, but I strove to get rid of them by amusing myself at my work and working harder and harder ... Then was I at as great a loss about that, that I could find no comfort, for about an hour or an hour and a half.

Finally the light began to dawn for Carter:

> At last there came into my inmost soul a voice, that thro' the mercy of God in Christ Jesus my sins were forgiven me; I burst out acrying, and laughing, and dancing, and jumping about the room; that anyone if they had seen me would have thought me craze. I then knew that God was my father, and I could cry Dear Father, my father abba father! I then say that he had mercy upon me purely and only for the sake of Jesus Christ my saviour, then did I plainly see my own vileness, my own nothingness, and I saw nothing upon the face of the earth so vile as myself, and in particular I saw myself worse than the dirt I trod on, and for this reason Jesus Christ died. Then I cryed out, o my dear Saviour, have I all my life time been rumiging over so many books to find salvation, and at last have found it in thee!

Later in the letter Carter adds that 'in this full assurance of faith and love of God I went on in for about six months, in which time I never had any occasion to pray for anything, but only rejoyceing in him, and especially giving him thanks for his great love and mercy' (Carter 1741).

This letter not only demonstrates the manner in which the Protestant doctrine of justification by faith was received and expressed by working men and women in eighteenth-century England, but shows how it took hold with an emotional strength of expression untypical of the earlier Reformation. It shows how for some the affective dimension of justification was not just as a gentle warming of the heart but a dramatic outward overcoming of the whole body.

John Wesley's preaching also induced strong outward expressions in the crowds he addressed. One report tells of how 'emotion swept the crowd, some confessed themselves sinners; some shouted that they were kings; some broke into songs of thanksgiving; some were seized with convulsions. "While I was preaching", records Wesley, "one before me dropped down as dead, and presently a second or a third. Five others sank down in half an hour, most of whom were in violent agonies. We called upon the Lord and he gave us an answer of peace"' (Cragg 1966, p. 144).

This emphasis on the outward expression of salvation has come down to the present through Pentecostalism, which had a major impact on Anglicanism through the Charismatic movement from about 1960 onwards. The Pentecostal movement spread from a revival in a multi-racial congregation in Los Angeles in 1906 (for an overview of its development see McGrath 2007, especially Chapter 15). As David Martin (2002) has argued, Pentecostalism is an extension of the type of church life found in early Methodism, especially in the Holiness tradition, because it shares an emphasis on scripture, on the doctrine of justification by faith, and on the experiential dimension of conversion and Christian living, magnifying this into a concern with a whole range of physical manifestations of faith, such as speaking in tongues (glossolalia) and healing (as described in 1 Corinthians 12.8–10 and 12.14).

The Charismatic movement was initially promoted within worldwide Anglicanism by Michael Harper, who was a curate at the leading Evangelical church of All Souls, Langham Place in London, under the influential vicar and writer John Stott. Stott, though, opposed the idea of post-conversion baptism in the Spirit and Harper resigned his curacy, pursuing his ministry elsewhere. A split has existed within Evangelicalism ever since, between those who promote the Charismatic movement and those who do not, symbolized by the divergent styles of worship and ministry at All Souls and the other leading Evangelical parish church in London, Holy Trinity in Brompton.

Harper formed the Fountain Trust which produced the magazine *Renewal* and organized ecumenical conferences that grew in size in the 1970s. His aim was to promote renewal in local churches rather than to create new churches or communions. And whereas Pentecostal churches describe the gifts of the Spirit as 'baptism in the Holy Spirit', implying that all genuine Christians *will* experience them, the Charismatic movement more recently has given them a more general description of 'being filled with the Holy Spirit', which implies they are not strictly necessary to salvation but do enhance the Christian life. One commentator describes its achievements in the following terms:

> The movement has brought a deepening of faith to many and a greater expectancy in Bible study and prayer. New forms of music and a fuller participation in worship, including gesture, dance, drama and the gift of prophecy have been introduced to many congregations. In particular it has helped to break down denominational and theological barriers, for though it began in Evangelical circles it has influenced all sections of the Church and is particularly strong in Roman Catholicism . . . It may come to be seen as the most significant movement in British Christianity in the second half of the [twentieth] century. (Worral 2004, p. 294)

Most recently it has found wider expression within Anglicanism (and far beyond) through the Alpha Course, especially through its 'Holy Spirit' residential weekend, energetically promoted by Holy Trinity, Brompton, which itself drew inspiration from the American Charismatic teacher John Wimber and from the Toronto Blessing movement of the 1980s. A typical Alpha meeting begins with a meal or refreshments and social time, followed by an expository talk and then open discussion in small groups. The content of the teaching is tightly controlled, so that the essentials of an evangelical faith are presented, but all questions and discussion are welcomed and participants are given the space to think through what they have heard. The Holy Spirit weekend then provides an extended opportunity to respond to the teaching in a variety of ways, shifting the emphasis away from intellectual assent to emotional and physical expression. The 'filling of the Holy Spirit' is awaited and expected and often takes place, in powerful and life changing ways. The weekend becomes the turning point in the course for many.

The Alpha Course has been remarkably popular not only in Britain but around the world. Leaders of the course from eighty three nations were present at the 2008 international gathering at Holy Trinity, and it was reported that 192,000 people in Britain and 1.5 million people around the world took the course in 2007. From its beginnings in the 1980s to 2009 it has been estimated that thirteen million people in 163 countries have taken the course! Within Anglicanism its impact is set to be equally significant, both in Britain and around the world, though there is debate over whether its primary impact will be one of renewing already existing congregations or of drawing new believers into the church (see Hunt 2004 and Heard 2010).

What cannot be denied, however, is that the course has strengthened the wider church's awareness of the importance of personal inner and outer experience in receiving and responding to salvation: in other words it has massively strengthened an experiential form of discipleship within Anglicanism. Some would go further and argue that it has helped to encourage the growth of a fourth major authority in Anglicanism – this personal experience of salvation, especially through charismatic forms of worship – alongside scripture, tradition and reason, even replacing scripture as the primary authority. Some evangelical leaders are worried that scripture is no longer being given the attention and honour it once held because of the popularity of charismatic forms of worship. While Methodism has often claimed to supplement scripture, tradition and reason with personal experience, this is something more: a moving of such experience to the centre of the Christian life. Whether in the long term this proves to be the case is another matter. The Alpha course has only been prominent for around twenty years and it may be losing influence in Britain as it gains strength in other denominations around the world. However, the question of the changing authority of scripture in Anglican Evangelicalism is a live one.

3.3 *What, then, of Baptism?* The Gorham Case

If the personal experience of justification is the touchstone, without which one cannot be sure if one has crossed the threshold into the true church, what does this imply about the rite of baptism? Is baptism still strictly necessary, or is it just a sign of something else? Does Anglican Evangelicalism, in other words, have a high or a low view of the church's sacraments, implying a high or low ecclesiology?

To answer this question it is necessary to go back to the sixteenth-century reformers and their theology of the church. They generally believed in a distinction between the visible and the invisible church. The visible church, which practised the sacraments, belonged to this world; the invisible church was the true church and only God knew its membership. Richard Field (1561–1616), Dean of Windsor and then Gloucester, who spanned the end of Elizabeth I's reign and the beginning of James I's reign, gave classical expression to this doctrine from an Anglican perspective:

> Hence it cometh that we say there is a visible and invisible Church, . . . to distinguish the diverse considerations of the same Church; which, though it be visible in respect of the *profession* of supernatural verities revealed in Christ, use of holy Sacraments, order of Ministry, and due obedience yielded thereunto, and they discernible that do communicate therein; yet in respect of those most precious effects, and happy benefits of saving grace, wherein only the elect do communicate, it is invisible; and they that in so happy, gracious and desirable things have communion among themselves are not discernible from others to whom this fellowship is denied, but are known only to God. That Nathaniel was an Israelite all men knew; that he was *a true Israelite, in whom was no guile*, Christ only knew. (More and Cross 1935, p. 41)

This means that the visible church (as already seen in connection with Article XIX on p. 34 above), is like the field with the wheat and the tares: it contains within it those who have been justified as well as those who have not. The justified are known only to God and they comprise the true yet invisible church. There are others among them who have not been justified and do not belong to this church. Membership of the visible church therefore does not of itself give salvation, and this implies that reception of the sacraments cannot of itself give salvation. It comes in other ways. And, put the other way round, this means that it is possible to be justified by faith and never to have been baptized or receive communion.

The Baptist tradition has always been clear that conversion and justification by faith is the primary requirement, so that the baptism rite should only take place after someone has had the experience of salvation in this way: baptism is the sign of justification, rather than a means toward justification. The question now is whether the Anglican Evangelicalism of the Wesleys and Whitefield and their successors would follow the logic of this doctrine. Did it also adopt a low view of the church and its sacraments, or did it retain a place for a higher view in which participation in the sacraments of the church facilitates salvation? The question is especially pressing because The Book of Common Prayer of 1662, which in other respects has been the touchstone of Anglican Evangelical doctrine, confusingly muddied the waters. At the start of 'The Ministration of Publick Baptism of Infants' the following unequivocal statement is made by the priest:

> Dearly beloved, forasmuch as all men are conceived and born in sin, and that our Saviour Christ saith, none can enter into the kingdom of God, except he be regenerate and born anew of Water and of the Holy Ghost: I beseech you to call upon God the Father, through our Lord Jesus Christ, that of his bounteous mercy he will grant to *this child* that thing which by nature he cannot have; that *he* may be baptized with Water and the Holy Ghost, and received into Christ's holy Church, and be made *a lively member* of the same.

This statement describes the doctrine of baptismal regeneration, which is the belief that the service of baptism itself brings the infant into the salvation of the kingdom. This regeneration clearly cannot depend on the *experience* of salvation by the infant. Such regeneration is confirmed at the end of the service when the priest categorically states that 'this Child is by baptism regenerate'. Furthermore the Catechism in The Book of Common Prayer, an 'instruction to be learned of every person before he may be brought to confirmation by the bishop' states that baptism is 'the occasion of our new birth'.

Would modern Evangelicals accept this? The question, according to David Bebbington, probably qualifies as the chief theological controversy of the early and mid-nineteenth century in England (Bebbington 1989, p. 9). Controversy began in 1812 when Richard Mant, a traditional High Churchman, criticized Evangelicals for rejecting this Prayer Book doctrine. Evangelicals made a variety of replies:

> The order of infant baptism, some held, expresses a charitable hope about the future regeneration of the child; or, according to others, the service is designed for believers who could pray with confidence for the salvation of the child. Others again felt that they had to embrace a doctrine of baptismal regeneration, going on to redefine regeneration to mean not 'becoming a Christian', but something less decisive. This was the course taken, for instance, by J. B. Sumner, later Archbishop of Canterbury. It is a shaky answer, a sign that Evangelicals found this apparent discrepancy between their doctrine and their liturgy embarrassing. (*Ibid.*)

Henry Ryder (1777–1836), the first of the Evangelical leaders to become a bishop (becoming Bishop of Gloucester in 1815 and Bishop of Lichfield in 1824), kept the issue alive by complaining against the 'most serious error of contemplating all the individuals of a baptized congregation, as converted' (Chapman 2006, p. 63). Conversion was necessary to salvation, so if some had been baptized but not converted it was clear they would not be saved, thus contradicting the Prayer Book.

The issue came to a head in the Gorham case of 1847–51. George Gorham was an Evangelical clergyman who had been a fellow of Queens' College, Cambridge and a curate at Clapham. He served in Cornwall and was a determined opponent of the Oxford Movement and its advocacy of Catholicism within the Church of England. While in Cornwall he once advertised for a curate 'free from Tractarian error', which shocked his bishop, the High Churchman Henry Philpotts (Chadwick 1971, p. 251). Gorham had a large family and for their education needed to move from the extremities of Cornwall to a parish nearer a town. In 1847 the Lord Chancellor, the patron of the parish of Bramford Speke near Exeter offered the parish to Gorham. But Philpotts had to agree to the appointment and he insisted on interviewing Gorham: he was not going to institute a clergyman into a new parish if he did not agree with the doctrine of the Prayer Book. So for thirty eight hours, over five days, and then another fourteen hours over three more days (!), he questioned Gorham closely and especially over the doctrine of baptismal regeneration. Gorham did not believe that regeneration was always given in baptism, though it could be given when there was a prior faith among those present. 'Baptism was made truly efficacious when regenerating grace was given' (*ibid.*, p. 254), not the other way round. Philpotts believed, in line with medieval Catholic teaching as well as with the wording of the Prayer Book, that because infants 'having committed no actual sin, were incapable of putting a bar to the entry of grace ... therefore that with the baptism of infants "regeneration" was linked indissolubly' (*ibid.*). He found therefore Gorham's views to be 'unsound' and refused to institute him to his new living.

Gorham then appealed to the ecclesiastical Court of Arches to compel the bishop to institute him. After a delay and then lengthy hearings, together lasting a year, the Court made its pronouncement: that though the meaning of regeneration in the Prayer Book was imprecise, the infant *was* regenerated at baptism. The bishop had been in his rights to refuse Gorham because the latter had contradicted the teaching of the Church of England. To many Evangelical clergy this decision, if upheld, would be catastrophic. It would mean they would in all conscience no longer be able to conduct baptisms in the parishes where they lived and would either have to abandon their Evangelical convictions or leave the Church of England!

Gorham appealed to the judicial committee of the Privy Council (which included Archbishop Sumner), and finally on 9 March 1850 it gave its judgment on Gorham: the members of the committee 'were not satisfied that this single clergyman contradicted the formularies of the Church of England' (*ibid.*, p. 261). Evangelicals (and liberals) were delighted, but supporters of the Oxford Movement were horrified. Here was a secular court deciding a key point of ecclesiastical doctrine. Controversy raged in the press and over 60 tracts and books were published in the months and years ahead. A number of the Catholic party decided that enough was enough and that they must leave to become Roman Catholics, including Henry Manning (later Cardinal Manning) and Robert Wilberforce (the Archdeacon of the East Riding and son of William Wilberforce). Petitions were drawn up to stop the Archbishop from allowing Gorham to be instituted. Sumner, having been on the judicial committee, was not inclined to accede to this. Bishop Philpotts then solemnly 'excommunicated' anyone who should institute Gorham. But this did not stop Sumner issuing the document that Gorham needed and 'on 10 August 1850, after finding (as was alleged) the lock of the church door blocked with mortar, and breaking in, Gorham was inducted to the parish of Bramford Speke by commission, and on 15 September preached his first sermon to a vast devout congregation, on justification by faith' (Chadwick 1971, p. 268, see pp. 250–71 for a full account of the whole crisis).

It was a defining moment for modern Anglican Evangelicalism: its adherents were being allowed to continue to retain their low view of the sacraments and, by implication, of the church as a whole. Even though the Prayer Book appeared to require belief in the doctrine of baptismal regeneration this did not have to be taken at face value: it could be interpreted more loosely, including allowing the belief that baptism is a sign of something else, of the regeneration that comes through justification by faith.

This does not mean that Evanglicals abandoned infant baptism or treated it casually. It has retained its place in many Evangelical parishes, though with an emphasis on testing and nurturing the faith and commitment of the parents and godparents, so that when the rite is conducted there is a clear sense that the baptism rite is a sign of the more important 'regeneration through faith' present in the baptism party. Many recent revisions of the baptism services in the Anglican Communion have supported this by removing the language of baptismal regeneration and laying more emphasis on the parents and godparents declaring their repentance and commitment to the Christian faith before the baptism itself takes place. These changes have made it easier for Evangelical clergy to promote infant baptism in their parishes.

Nevertheless it is hard to deny that the visual message of the rite is powerful in its own right. It continues to suggest that the baby, as it is taken into the arms of the priest and has the water poured over its forehead, in the name of the Trinity, is somehow being washed and welcomed into the salvation of the kingdom, well before he or she has had any opportunity to come to faith. In Bebbington's phrase, infant baptism continues to be something of an 'anomaly' that has remained 'to trouble twentieth-century Evangelical Anglicans'. In 1965 the *Church of England Newspaper* asked its largely Evangelical readership whether the church should cease baptizing infants altogether. While a clear majority of the clergy said no, over a third of the laity said yes: 'Clearly a high proportion of the respondents were worried about what infant baptism was supposed to signify' (Bebbington 1989, p. 10). This led to the National Evangelical Congress at Keele in 1967 insisting on conversion among the parents before a child could be baptized:

> only the children of parents who profess to be Christians are fit subjects for this rite. Indiscriminate baptism, as commonly practised in England, is a scandal ... We must be welcoming to little children, as Jesus was. But we deny the propriety of baptizing the infants of parents who do not profess to be Christians themselves and who cannot promise to bring up their children as Christians. (Crowe 1967, pp. 34–5)

This anomaly, within a low view of the sacramental life of the church, remains an integral part of modern Anglican Evangelical discipleship alongside commitments to the doctrine of justification by faith, the primacy of scripture within the Christian life, and the importance of personal experience of salvation, the last of these being a touchstone for many. There is, however, another defining feature of Evangelicalism (for both Charismatic and non-Charismatic strands) that demands attention: a profound commitment to evangelism.

Discussion Questions

1 'I feel the life His wounds impart; I feel the Saviour in my heart'
    (Charles Wesley). Is this a necessary experience within the Christian
    life?
2 At his conversion Joseph Carter describes how 'I burst out acry-
    ing, and laughing, and dancing, and jumping about the room; that
    anyone if they had seen me would have thought me craze'. Should
    Anglicanism encourage this extrovert form of religious expression?
3 How is it possible for Evangelical Anglicans to promote the baptism
    of infants?

Further Reading

The Evangelical Revival in general

Bebbington, David (1989), *Evangelicalism in Modern Britain: A History from the 1730's
    to the 1980's*, London: Unwin Hyman.
Noll, Mark (2003), *The Rise of Evangelicalism: The Age of Edwards, Whitefield and the
    Wesleys*, Leicester: InterVarsity Press.

John and Charles Wesley

Newport, Kenneth and Ted Campbell (2007), *Charles Wesley: Life, Literature and
    Legacy*, Peterborough: Epworth Press.
Rack, Henry (1989), *Reasonable Enthusiast: John Wesley and the Rise of Methodism*,
    London: Epworth Press.
Turner, John Munsey (2002), *John Wesley: The Evangelical Revival and the Rise of
    Methodism in England*, Peterborough: Epworth Press.

From Whitefield to Alpha

Anderson, Allan (2004), *An Introduction to Pentecostalism: Global Charismatic
    Christianity*, Cambridge: Cambridge University Press.
Heard, James (2010), *Inside Alpha: Explorations in Evangelism*, Milton Keynes:
    Paternoster.

Hunt, Stephen (2004), *The Alpha Initiative: Evangelism in a Post-Christian Age*, Aldershot: Ashgate.

Pollock, John (1986), *George Whitefield and the Great Awakening*, London: Lion Hudson.

4

The Necessity of Evangelism

4.1 *Evangelism for all*: Mr Grimshaw's Circuit

The identity of Anglican Evangelicalism, from Whitefield and Wesley onwards, is closely related to its commitment to evangelism. Wherever the one has appeared the other has taken place. This chapter presents a portrait of the different ways it has done this, with examples from Britain, North America, West Africa and East Africa. There are other parts of the world where Anglican Evangelicals have proclaimed the gospel in striking ways, but these examples give a broad cross section of the range and dynamism of what has taken place.

After his awakening John Wesley became committed to travelling the country 'to promote as far as I am able vital practical religion and by the grace of God to beget, preserve, and increase the life of God in the souls of men'. He did this first through preaching in churches and then, when increasingly denied access by hostile incumbents, from 1739 in fields and market squares, up and down the country, covering over 200,000 miles on horseback or in a carriage over the course of his life. He regularly rose at four in the morning, preached at five, and spent his days in a full round of preaching, counselling, exhorting, correcting, organizing and encouraging. He went round England annually, paid twenty visits to Scotland, and the same number to Ireland. He was sometimes attacked by hostile mobs but was not deflected. He was influenced by Arminianism, as already noted, and did not accept Calvin's teaching on predestination but believed that everyone on the planet could be justified and therefore needed to be given the opportunity to hear the gospel and respond with faith: it was not only 'the elect' who could be saved. Wesley disregarded the parochial boundaries of the Church of England, ranging widely and freely, famously declaring that 'I look upon all the world as my parish' (*Journal* 3 July 1759).

He did not see evangelism taking place just through preaching, however: his genius was to recognize that the support and fellowship that believers receive from other church people *after* their conversion was just as important as the preaching itself. He therefore established a system of 'class meetings' for the teaching and support of converts, some 60 per cent of whom were women. Each convert was put into a class of twelve or so members who met under a leader, normally another lay person, for mutual help, fellowship and instruction. The small group was crucial in allowing members to learn the faith in an interactive way, for unlike in a large meeting there was opportunity for questions and discussion involving everyone. The teaching, in other words, was being presented and being heard in the idioms of that locality: it was the Word being spoken and heard in the vernacular. Wesley organized the Methodist movement so that this interactive form of evangelism would be embodied in its structures. He would later inspire Charles Simeon, the leader of Anglican Evangelicalism in the next generation, to adapt these principles for new home groups in his parish in Cambridge.

This evangelistic ministry with its congregational 'follow-up' shows a distinct emphasis that the Evangelical revival gives to modern Protestantism in the English-speaking world (drawing it closer to Catholic forms of evangelism with their emphasis on incorporating the believer into the life of the church). At the time of Luther and Calvin it was assumed that everyone in Europe was Christian and belonged to the church. The need was for reformation, not conversion. But from the time of the Evangelical revival onwards, with industrialization creating vast new conurbations of the unchurched, the need for an evangelism that included incorporation into the fellowship of the church was increasingly apparent. Wesley and the Methodist laity provided an impressive and influential example of how Evangelicalism rose to this challenge.

Wesley lived and died an Anglican, and thus his life and work have an appropriate place in this book. He believed, for example, that every Methodist should continue to attend the local parish church where the sacraments would be received. They were to be as much part of the full sacramental life of the Catholic Church as other Anglicans. In this way he believed they would be led from justification to sanctification or, as he controversially termed it, 'perfection', where

'He that is, by faith, born of God sinneth not' (Wesley 1944, *44 Sermons,* II.6). However, after his death the Methodist movement was shunned by the bishops and became committed to its own denominational structures and life, so losing contact with the Church of England. (Nor did the bishops recognize Wesley's ordinations of Methodist ministers.) Our story needs to continue with those who worked within Anglicanism and, in particular, with the first Evangelical incumbents.

The earliest is also the most impressive. William Grimshaw was rector of a straggling grey village on the West Yorkshire moors, a village that would later be made famous by the Brontë family: Haworth. Grimshaw was incumbent from 1742 until his death in 1763. He had a conversion experience just before arriving at Haworth and began his ministry there with a commitment to spreading the gospel. But the historian Kenneth Hylson-Smith reports that Grimshaw found the parishioners

> mostly sullen, rough, superstitious people, unsympathetic to the Christian message and suspicious of strangers. The situation demanded a man with courage, who would be forthright and declare a simple message in plain and unambiguous language, with a demonstrable concern for the local residents which would be expressed in an unsentimental but compassionate manner.

Hylson-Smith continues, 'Grimshaw provided these qualities and this approach, with the addition of an earnestness and persistence which demanded attention' (Hylson-Smith 1997, p. 176).

John Newton, the ex-slave trader turned hymn writer, visited Haworth and some years later wrote the following about Grimshaw's preaching:

> The desire of usefulness to persons of the weakest capacity, or most destitute of the advantages of education, influenced his phraseology in preaching . . . he chose rather to deliver his message in what he used to term *market language*; and though the warmth of his heart, and the rapidity of his imagination might sometimes lead him to clothe his thoughts in words which even a candid critic could not wholly justify, yet the general effect of his 'plain' manner was striking and impressive, suited to make the dullest understand, and to fix for the time the attention of the most careless. (Newton 1799, p. 126; quoted in Cowie 1973, p. 11)

There is a connection here with Tyndale and his work to translate the gospel into the vernacular. While Tyndale sought to provide access to scripture through an imaginative and engaging style of translation, Grimshaw sought to provide it through an imaginative and engaging style of preaching. Both sought to provide access to the saving truth of the gospel for ordinary people in the language they used and understood.

But Grimshaw did not only preach. Newton also describes how he would leave church, while the psalm was being recited and before the sermon, and go to the churchyard and street and ale-house and gather together the absentees and bring them into church. (Some would try to make their escape by jumping out of lower windows or over walls.) This dramatic and unconventional pastoral ministry appealed to the people and produced results: Grimshaw gained a huge influence not only in his own parish but in the surrounding parishes as well. When he arrived at Haworth there were only twelve communicants. After several years of his ministry he could count three to four hundred communicants in winter and in the summer 'near twelve hundred' (Hylson-Smith 1997, p. 178).

His wider significance for the Evangelical revival is shown by the way he undertook itinerant preaching in other parts of Yorkshire, Lancashire, Cheshire and north Derbyshire. He would preach between twenty and thirty times a week and justified this work as a response to the way many incumbents were absent through having multiple livings or simply living elsewhere. He also worked with the Methodists and assisted John Wesley, who spoke of 'Mr Grimshaw's circuit'. He visited Methodist classes, made his parsonage a centre for Methodist preachers and trained and encouraged them. He was committed both to the ministry of the Church of England, believing it 'to be the soundest, purest most apostolic Christian Church in the world' (*ibid.*), and to the wider Evangelical revival beyond the four walls of the established church.

But Grimshaw was only the first of a string of passionate and hard working Anglican clerical and lay leaders who moved out of church buildings to make contact with and evangelize people in their own localities and language. John Fletcher (1729–85) was another, the incumbent of the industrial town of Madeley in Shropshire, in which he ministered until his death (he had turned down a wealthier living because there was not enough work). Fletcher was also a keen supporter of local Methodist societies and a right hand man to Wesley and moved around the district and the country on preaching journeys. Wesley thought he might succeed him as leader of the whole movement, but Fletcher died before Wesley.

Henry Venn, the Vicar of Huddersfield between 1759 and 1771, is another dramatic example. Venn preached and ministered to the weavers and farmers of that growing town. The much travelled Wesley wrote of them in 1757 that 'a wilder people I never saw in England'. But Venn was able to reach them and he drew vast crowds to his services. The parish church was not big enough and he had to preach elsewhere. He also supported the Methodist societies and their local preachers, especially concerned about the follow-up that converts received. Like Grimshaw and Fletcher he preached around the country, aware of the national dimension as well as the local dimension of the revival. He even paid for the construction of a Methodist chapel in Huddersfield so that he could be sure the revival would continue after his incumbency (there was no guarantee the next Vicar of Huddersfield would be of the same persuasion). In 1771 he had to resign his living because of exhaustion and moved to a parish near Cambridge, where he became a mentor to the next generation of Evangelical leaders who included Charles Simeon among others.

Kenneth Hylson-Smith has described the secret of the power of these early Anglican evangelists in the following way:

> The pioneer Evangelicals of the eighteenth century shared with all their fellow evangelicals a belief in original sin, justification by faith and the new birth, which was not merely a cerebral acknowledgment of a set of doctrines, but was a deep-seated, and indeed passionate, part of the very fabric of their personalities, because it was born out of experience. They knew that the doctrines were true, because they had found them to be so in their own lives. And such knowledge was like a fire burning within them. They had to share the good news; they could do no other.

Hylson-Smith recalls that scripture remained key to their outlook alongside the personal experience of salvation:

> The message which had transformed their lives was contained in the Bible; and the Bible, therefore, was precious to them. It was their meat and drink; their authority; and the basis for all their faith and practice. And at the very centre of the biblical message was the cross. They proclaimed a person; a

saviour and redeemer … it was all to do with relationships: man alienated from God because of sin; man restored to God because of the life, death and resurrection of Christ; new birth; a new and living relationship with God arising out of the conversion experience; a new life in Christ and with the Holy Spirit. (Hylson-Smith 1997, p. 183)

4.2 *Evangelism from Below*: West and East Africa

Grimshaw, Fletcher and Venn were educated and wealthy preachers who came into poor communities from the outside and conducted their evangelism as out-siders. John Wesley, though, had seen the importance of evangelism coming from the people themselves, from the grass roots up, in the class meetings and through the local preachers. It was Venn's grandson, also called Henry Venn, who worked hard to put this principle into practice within nineteenth-century Anglicanism. He did not do this in England, however, but through the Church Missionary Society, of which he was secretary, and specifically in its work in Nigeria.

Henry Venn (1796–1873) was the son of John Venn who was the Rector of Clapham and one of the founders of the Church Missionary Society (CMS). Henry was brought up in the rectory at Clapham and came to work for CMS, being its secretary from 1841 to 1872. He believed that churches planted by Anglican missionaries should raise up clergy and leaders from among the people they converted. These churches should be national churches responsive to their local conditions. He espoused what he called the 'three selfs' for these local churches: self-extension, self-support, and self-governance. In contrast to the Society for the Propagation of the Gospel (SPG), a 'High Church' mission-ary society that believed bishops should be sent as the pioneer missionaries who would then build a church around themselves, Venn believed that bishops arrived at the end of the process, after a church had come into being and was already self-supporting.

A major example of this approach occurred in West Africa, which was an in-hospital place for European missionaries (most died from malaria) and where it was imperative there was a local church leadership. A group of well educated African clergy was sent to start work along the Niger river, and with knowledge of the local languages they would evangelize in the vernacular and set about establishing the church. 'Progress was slow, but the policy gradually changed from the planting of small mission stations to that of "native churches", which emerged from the bottom up. Venn sought what he called the "euthanasia" of the mission and the "full development of the native African church". The CMS became a self-extending agency pushing out from its bases' (Chapman 2006, p. 108; for a full account see Ward 2006, Chapter 7). This work has produced what is now the largest and arguably most self-confident church in the Anglican Communion, the Church of Nigeria. The crowning achievement of Venn's strategy was the consecration of Samuel Ajayi Crowther as bishop in 1864, the first black bishop in Anglicanism. This appointment has been described as 'one of the most far-sighted ecclesiastical decisions in African church history' (Bishop Bengt Sundkler in Yates 2004, p. 76).

Ajayi was born in Osugun in the Yoruba state of Oyo around 1806. He was enslaved in 1821 but his boat was captured by the British. He was released in Freetown, Sierra Leone, and took advantage of the educational opportunities there, also becoming a baptized Christian in 1825. He came to England in 1826 and soon returned to train as a teacher at Fourah Bay College. He married a fellow teacher, Susan Thomson (also a freed slave), and took part in the Niger expedition of 1841. He again came to England and was trained by CMS for ordination. He was ordained in 1843 and joined the Yoruba mission, where he played a large part in translating the Bible into Yoruba. He developed a system of writing down the tones in the Yoruba language. His exceptional gifts were recognized in 1864 when he was consecrated in Canterbury Cathedral as Bishop in West Africa (excluding Sierra Leone and Lagos). He worked hard to establish churches up and down the Niger and encouraged his African clergy to translate the Christian message into the vernacular. But after Venn's departure from CMS he was not supported by the society. A group of young European missionaries arrived in 1887 and bypassed his authority, objecting to the way Crowther earned a living from trading alongside his church work. These European missionaries superseded his staff and effectively dismantled his African Niger mission. He died in 1891. The next Nigerian bishop would not be consecrated until 1952.

Venn's scheme has been criticized for imposing European patterns of church life on an African context. However, it was the African leadership that itself decided to embrace and promote these patterns in its own life. Despite the disruption to Venn's strategy in the 1880s the Nigerian church has continued to grow and today clearly has an independence of life and views that could re-shape worldwide Anglicanism. This must in part be due to Venn's initial strategy and its reception in West Africa.

East African Revival

Twentieth-century Anglican Evangelicalism provides more examples of this grass roots pastoral evangelism. One of the most influential comes from the East African Revival or 'Balokole'. This had roots in classical Evangelical revivalism and the interdenominational Keswick Movement of the late nineteenth century (Ward 2006, p. 175). Aspects of the movement were relayed by CMS missionaries to Uganda, Rwanda, Kenya and Tanganyika (Tanzania) in the first half of the twentieth century. The Revival itself started in the mid-Thirties in Rwanda, where an English CMS doctor, Joe Church, shared an experience of deep personal forgiveness and renewal with a Ugandan orderly, Simeon Nsimbambi, in the hospital where they worked. This experience of renewal then spread through other orderlies in the hospital: 'Great emphasis was placed by the *balokole* ("saved ones") on forgiveness through the saving blood of Christ, on personal confession of sin and testimony to personal salvation' (Yates 2004, p. 175).

This European-African movement spread to Uganda itself in 1935–36 when a deacon called Blasio Kigozi addressed the synod of the Church of Uganda (which was already well established among the ruling elite of Buganda and other regions of the country). He made a fervent plea for Anglicans to reject the mixing of African customs with Evangelical Christianity, to stop the clericalism of the church's institutional life and to change its stifling approach to 'orthodoxy'. Instead Anglicans were to 'Awake!' (Ward 2006, p. 176).

In response to this rallying call

> [r]evival fellowships began to emerge throughout Buganda and southern Uganda. Members of the fellowship called themselves *ab'oluganda* (brothers and sisters), and saw themselves as belonging to a new clan, a new expression of African communal values and solidarity. They denounced paganism and unchristian compromises (particularly with regard to sexual practice) and espoused a strict monogamy, a puritanical life style and a fierce honesty. The public confession of sin within the fellowship resulted in the singing of the great Revival hymn of absolution, 'Tukutendereza Yesu' ['We Praise You,

Jesus, Jesus the Lamb'], which became the characteristic song of the Revival. (*Ibid.*)

Ward comments that 'preaching a radical message of equality, including the equality of white and black, the Revival movement played a significant part in freeing the Gospel from its association with colonialism' (*ibid.*, p. 177). It divided the church and schism became a possibility, though never actually happened. Its influence then spread across the border to Kenya and Tanganika, where Christians from many different denominations were affected.

Many of the future church leaders were touched and inspired by the revival. The kindly and prayerful Janani Luwum is one example. He was ordained into the Anglican Church of Uganda and became provincial secretary in the 1960s and a bishop in 1969. In 1977 he became Archbishop of Uganda when Idi Amin's regime was reaching the height of its lawlessness and terror. Luwum and the other bishops criticized the regime and became targets of Amin's enmity and vengeance. Luwum was arrested and then put to death by Amin's henchmen in the same year. Luwum and other martyrs, such as a number of Kikuyu Christians put to death in the Mau Mau uprising in Kenya, 'showed the Christian depth and constancy of many of those [the Revival] had reached' (Yates 2004, p. 176).

All of this is especially relevant for this chapter because the Revival put great emphasis on lay witness, on the ability of women as well as men to testify and preach, a true vernacular evangelism coming from the grass roots up. Eventually East African Anglicanism as a whole would become 'deeply influenced by the values and ethical standards of the Revival, though the extent to which it became intertwined with the church varied from place to place' (Ward 2006, p. 178, see pp. 175–9 for an overview of the whole East African Revival).

3.3 *Evangelism in Deed*: from Wilberforce to Stott

But is evangelism about more than preaching the gospel? Going back to the late eighteenth and early nineteenth century, it is possible to see that the second generation of Evangelical leaders thought so, and their stories introduce another important dimension of Evangelical discipleship, one which widens the scope of its evangelism.

There are three key individuals who in different ways did this. Charles Simeon (1759–1836) was educated at Eton and King's College, Cambridge and then became a fellow of the college and incumbent of Holy Trinity, Cambridge, where he remained for the rest of his life, 54 years in all. The churchwardens initially tried to lock him out, because they had wanted the curate to become vicar. But Simeon's theatrical yet intense preaching attracted large numbers of undergraduates from the university and by the end of his life he had inspired whole generations. They then went out to spread the Evangelical faith in parishes up and down the country.

Simeon, though, saw a need not only to influence the hearts and minds of people but to gain control of parish appointments so that evangelical clergy could always be appointed to them. He founded the Simeon Trust in 1817 to purchase the rights of appointment ('the patronage') from whichever members of the aristocracy had them to sell (and were willing to sell). He encouraged wealthy friends to donate funds to the trust and by the time of his death he had acquired the right to appoint incumbents to 42 churches including Bath Abbey, Bradford, Bridlington, Cheltenham and Derby. Macaulay said of him, 'If you knew what his authority and influence were . . . you would allow that his real sway over the Church was far greater than that of any primate.'

William Wilberforce (1759–1833) came from a wealthy family in Hull and attended St John's College, Cambridge, but spent an idle time there. He became the MP for Hull in 1780, and soon after for Yorkshire as a whole. In 1784–85 he was travelling in Europe with the theologian Isaac Milner and spent much of the time studying his Greek New Testament. After a period of inner turmoil he experienced a joyful conversion. John Newton persuaded him not to be ordained but to stay in Parliament and work for the Evangelical cause there, and Thomas Clarkson persuaded him to campaign for the abolition of the slave trade, for as well as humanitarian considerations how could men and women freely respond to the gospel if they were in the shackles of slavery? In 1797 Wilberforce started living at Clapham and became a leading member of the 'Clapham Sect', a group of Evangelical reformers gathered together by the rector John Venn, the son of Henry Venn of Huddersfield.

In 1797 Wilberforce published his *Practical View of the Prevailing Religious System of Professed Christians*, which argued that religious faith was not just about living an ethical and benevolent life but was based on revealed truths that changed the whole person. It was very popular and established him as an important leader of the Evangelical group in the Church of England. He donated large sums to Hannah Moore's charities and was part of the group that founded the Church Missionary Society in 1799 and the British and Foreign Bible Society in 1804, and he advocated the sending of missionaries to India. He also defended Catholic Emancipation in 1813 (allowing Catholics to worship openly and hold public office including sitting in Parliament), and he also campaigned for Sunday observance (making Sunday a day of rest for everyone). Meanwhile he continued to speak and campaign against the slave trade and in 1807 at last secured its end in Parliament. He then supported the movement for the complete abolition of slavery in British dominions, which was finally put into law just before his death in 1833. His sons Robert, Samuel and Henry, surprisingly, became keen supporters of the Oxford Movement and Robert and Henry eventually became Roman Catholics. But William showed that the evangelism of the Evangelicals did not just involve sharing words with others but also campaigning for justice in political life.

The third of the three is Hannah More (1745–1833), who was born at Stapleton in Avon and as a young adult had contact with David Garrick and Samuel Johnson, who encouraged her to publish plays and poems. She moved towards Evangelicalism and in 1788 published *Thoughts on the Importance of the Manners of the Great to General Society*, which was widely read. She joined the circle of William Wilberforce and John Newton, who became her spiritual adviser. Wilberforce visited her and her sisters in 1789 in the Mendip Hills and commented that while he found the scenery delightful he found the spiritual degradation of the inhabitants appalling. 'The redoubtable Miss More needed no further encouragement to embark on the redemption of the people among whom she had come to live' (Bradley 1976, pp. 43–4). By the turn of the century she and her sisters had set up over a dozen day schools and Sunday Schools for adults and children in an area where there had been no educational provision for the poor. 'The Mendip schools became a model for the development of voluntary schools throughout the country. Other Evangelical ladies quickly followed the More sisters' lead. Within a few years Mrs Trimmer had established schools at Brentford and Lady Spencer had set up Sunday schools and adult classes at St Albans' (*ibid.*, p. 44). More also wrote tracts to counteract the influence of the French Revolution, and from 1802 was part of the Clapham Sect with Venn and Wilberforce.

John Stott's leadership

Evangelism, then, was also about evangelization, the forming of the right social conditions, through working within the established church as well as engaging in political and educational reform, so that the gospel message could take root in church and nation and transform peoples' lives. It was about *deed* as well as word. In the first half of the twentieth century this broader approach receded for a time in Anglican Evangelical circles, but was revived in the 1960s through the influence of John Stott, the Rector of All Souls, Langham Place. It began to be apparent when he was chairing the National Assembly of Evangelicals in 1966, a convention organized by the Evangelical Alliance at the Methodist Central Hall in Westminster. He opened the meeting by describing his own conscientious, continuing membership of the Church of England: 'Its formularies are biblical and evangelical. Evangelicals are therefore the Anglican loyalists, and non-Anglicans the deviationists.' But in the main address the influential Free Church preacher Martyn Lloyd-Jones made an unexpected call for Evangelicals to leave their 'mixed' denominations and form an Evangelical church. While he was speaking John Stott looked 'flushed, rattled, and annoyed' (Steer 2009). Then in his concluding remarks as chairman Stott stated that 'We are here to debate this subject, and I believe history is against Dr Lloyd-Jones, in that others have tried to do this very thing. I believe that Scripture is against him, in that the remnant was within the Church and not outside it' (*ibid.*). These remarks were controversial and divided opinion within the Evangelical Alliance as a whole. The national assembly had to be cancelled the following year. But Stott remained convinced that he was to remain in his 'mixed denomination' and 'bear witness to the truth as we have been given to understand it' (*ibid.*). The evangelism of Evangelicals, then, was to continue to include the evangelization of Anglicanism. But these remarks were only a hint, and said little about the political and educational dimensions promoted by Wilberforce and More.

The first National Evangelical Anglican Congress, held at Keele University in 1967, made his position much clearer. Stott chaired the committee which meticulously prepared the conference. Over 1000 people attended and it was reported that '"the atmosphere was as exhilarating as on Derby Day". Youth and ability were to the fore among "the bright, thrusting, unsquashable men and women . . . who gave this congress an unmistakeable glitter"' (Bebbington 1989, p. 249). Stott opened the conference by distancing himself and the conference from the negativity of earlier twentieth-century Evangelicalism: 'Evangelicals have a very poor image in the Church as a whole . . . We have acquired a reputation for narrow partisanship and obstructionism. We have to acknowledge this, and for the most part we have no one but ourselves to blame' (Hastings 2001, p. 553). Now, at a time when the Church of England was in institutional flux, with canon law, liturgy and church government all in the melting pot, the conference and its constituencies resolved to take part in its remodelling. One of the sections of the resulting Keele statement was devoted to 'The Church and its Structures'. Bebbington comments, 'No longer would other [denominational] traditions be able to determine the terms of the debate within the church' (Bebbington 1989, p. 249). This was illustrated in the way Archbishop Michael Ramsey, coming from a very different wing of the church, was asked to open the conference. It was then most clearly seen in the closing statement, especially concerning the Eucharist: 'we determine to work towards the practice of a weekly celebration of the Sacrament as the central corporate Service of the Church' (Crowe 1967, p. 35). Hastings comments that 'Evangelicals were here at last re-entering, instead of battling against, the central worshipping development of the century – embracing the principal positive contribution of Anglo-Catholicism, the liturgical movement, Parish and People. Just as Vatican II [the 1960s council of all Roman Catholic bishops] was making it possible for non-Roman Catholics to be on the same wavelength as Catholics, so Keele made it possible for non-Evangelicals to be on the same wavelength as Evangelicals' (Hastings 2001, p. 554).

There were also commitments to become involved in ecumenical dialogue and social involvement:

> Evangelism and compassionate service belong together in the mission of God. There was a commitment to give serious attention to the problems of society. No longer would Evangelicals be able to regard their task as withdrawal from the world in the company, if possible, of other souls to be snatched from it. A decade later the significance of Keele was summed up as a symptom of a 'release from the ghetto'. (Bebbington 1989, p. 250)

Bebbington adds that this was not a movement of liberal Evangelicals, but of conservatives: 'The postwar Evangelical renaissance was in fact a movement among those of firmly orthodox belief. Keele represents the triumph of the conservatives in the Evangelical party of the Church of England' (*ibid.*).

One participant at the conference, David Atkinson, a future Church of England bishop, has described the impact that it made on him. He writes how the conference

> was a transforming experience. I was there as a potential ordinand ... Dr Stott's response [to Martyn Lloyd-Jones], and particularly the Keele Congress, helped me to see not only that the Church of England was a proper home for Evangelicals; but, much more, that to belong to a Church rooted in the scriptures and the creeds, framed by the Articles, and open in ministry and mission to everyone, was a wonderful privilege ... Keele turned Evangelical Anglicans churchwards: we understood that we belonged within the Church of England, and had a part to play in its life. It also turned us outwards: there was a recognition that Evangelical Anglicans had some hard work to do in the world of work, mission, ethics and education. (Atkinson 2003)

John Stott's role is underlined by Atkinson:

> Dr Stott's towering leadership over the years lies behind the tremendous significance of Keele and Nottingham [the second national congress ten years later]. He was once described by David Edwards as 'more than a bishop'. His leadership – perhaps because he was not a bishop – managed to hold a disparate coalition firmly together, though there were divisions: Charismatic and formal; open and conservative (often of a 'preservative' sort). He inspired us to continue to play a fully engaged part in Church and world, in evangelism, and in concern for social justice. (*Ibid.*)

Evangelism, then, was to include action, not least action for justice. Countless practical initiatives have sprung from the Keele Congress, prominent among them the growth of Tearfund as an agency for development in the Third World. This has shown that Evangelicalism at the close of the twentieth century had returned to the tradition of Wilberforce and More and was recognizing the importance of deed alongside word in its great work of evangelism.

* * *

But what of the other major strands within the Anglican inheritance? It is time to return to the sixteenth and seventeenth centuries to see how Catholic forms of discipleship emerged and developed within a Protestant context.

Discussion Questions

1 John Wesley, Grimshaw, Fletcher and Venn paid little attention to parish boundaries in their revivalist evangelism. What are the strengths and weaknesses of this kind of approach?
2 Henry Venn of CMS believed in 'three selfs' for new churches: self-extension, self-support, and self-governance. Was this a wise policy for CMS in the nineteenth century? Is it a wise policy for missionary work today?
3 Preaching or social action: which should be primary in evangelism?

Further Reading

The Evangelism of the Evangelicals

Bebbington, David (1989), *Evangelicalism in Modern Britain: A History from the 1730's to the 1980's*, London: Routledge.
Hylson-Smith, Kenneth (1989), *Evangelicals in the Church of England 1734–1984*, Edinburgh: T and T Clark.
Steer, Roger (2009), *Inside Story: The Life of John Stott*, Leicester: InterVarsity Press.
Wesley, John (1944), *Sermons on Several Occasions (44 Sermons)*, London: The Epworth Press.

Social action

Bradley, Ian (1976), *The Call to Seriousness: The Evangelical Impact on the Victorians*, London: Jonathan Cape.
Hague, William (2008), *William Wilberforce*, London: HarperCollins.
Tomkins, Stephen (2004), *William Wilberforce*, London: Lion Hudson.
Warner, Robert (2007), *Reinventing English Evangelicalism, 1966–2001: A Theological and Sociological Study*, Carlisle: Paternoster Press.

Overseas evangelism

Sanneh, Lamin (1983), *West African Christianity: The Religious Impact*, London: C. Hurst and Company.

Ward, Kevin (2006), *A History of Global Anglicanism*, Cambridge: Cambridge University Press.

Ward, Kevin and Brian Stanley, eds (2000), *The Church Missionary Society and World Christianity, 1799–1999*, London: Routledge.

Yates, Timothy (2004), *The Expansion of Christianity*, Oxford: Lion Publishing.

Part 2

Catholic Ways of Discipleship

5

Sacraments above All

5.1 *Traces of Catholic Liturgy*: the Book of Common Prayer

Word or sacrament: which is the primary point of contact between the believer and their God? In the first part of this Studyguide we have looked at those who were quite firm in their conviction that the word, in scripture and preaching, is the primary point of contact. Now it is time to look at those who had a different outlook. Their story must begin with Henry VIII and the old religion which nurtured him. In this, the Catholic Church through its sacraments provided the means of grace and hope of glory: Cyprian of Carthage's dictum *extra ecclesiam nulla salus* ('there is no salvation outside the church'), re-iterated by Augustine of Hippo, still held sway. In practice this meant that the Christian must take part in the worship of the church and especially the penitential cycle if he or she was to gain access to the salvation of heaven (see Chapter 1.1). But Luther, and then more so Zwingli and Calvin, had insisted that the word of Scripture was the primary authority in the Christian life, and so participation in the sacramental life of the church was a secondary matter (though still desirable). For the ordinary lay person, the reading of the Bible at home was to replace the saying of confession in church as the most important act of personal devotion.

This supremacy of scripture is in many ways reflected in the foundation documents (sometimes called the 'historic formularies') of the Church of England. The Articles of Religion, first published by Thomas Cranmer in 1553, reflect this belief, with their statement that scripture contains 'all things necessary to salvation' (see above p. 33). However, what is interesting about the Articles is that this statement occurs only after earlier articles (five in all) have carefully set out the Trinitarian and Christological doctrines of the ancient Catholic Church (the church prior to its division between Roman Catholic West and Eastern Orthodox at the first millennium). Then, after the affirmation of scriptural supremacy, in Article VI, and guidance on how to interpret the Old Testament in Article VII, the three creeds of the ancient church – the Nicene, the Athanasian and the Apostles' creeds – are named with the statement that they 'ought thoroughly to be received and believed' (Article VIII). Catholic tradition, then, is given some recognition.

This moderation of scriptural supremacy is found to a greater extent in the Book of Common Prayer (BCP) itself, so much so that it can be read as opening the door to a different view of where authority lies. Cranmer's original preface to the book (moved to being the second preface in 1662 and now entitled 'Concerning the Service of the Church') makes it clear that he believed the ancient tradition of the church 'was not ordained but of a good purpose, and for a great advancement of godliness' (p. viii). This respect for ancient tradition is found at many points through the book. For example, it can be traced in the way the BCP was compiled: Cranmer was not, by and large, the author of the words but the compiler, translator and editor of a range of different texts, some from the continental Reformers but many from the medieval and ancient church. He melded them together in a remarkable synthesis. Rowan Williams, Kenneth Stevenson and Geoffrey Rowell, in their preface to their own compilation of Anglican spiritual writings, have this to say about the BCP:

> Its evolution is remarkable. Beginning in piecemeal translations and adaptations of liturgical material, it was already, by the time of its second (1552) version, providing a consistent style of reflection and public prayer that consciously set out to mould an entire religious sensibility. Cranmer, architect though not exclusive author of the 1549 and 1552 books, can be credited with the extraordinary achievement of expressing a fairly radical Protestant doctrine of dependence upon grace at all points in a language not only weighty and authoritative in itself but also evocative of ancient and medieval piety. Protestant theology is made to speak a dialect deeply rooted in Greek and Latin liturgy, and so acquires an added depth and seriousness; this, it seems to say, is what the true tradition of the Church has been saying all along. (Rowell, Stevenson and Williams 2001, p. 10)

Seasons and Calendar

Specific traces of Catholic liturgical tradition are seen in a number of features of the book. One is the retention of the seasons of the Christian year (sometime called 'the temporale' in Catholic liturgical texts) associated with Sundays and other 'Holy Days'. Advent is placed first, followed by Christmas, Epiphany and Sundays 'after Epiphany', then Sundays before Lent, Ash Wednesday and Lent, the days of Holy Week, Easter, Whitsunday, Trinity and Sundays after Trinity. Each is given its own collect, epistle and gospel for Holy Communion, and lessons and psalms for Morning and Evening Prayer. The congregation's encounter with scripture, then, is to be channelled through this traditional seasonal framework that forms and guides the expectations of the worshipper. The Swiss Reformed tradition, which Cranmer followed in many other respects, had little time for this aspect of medieval Catholicism. Worship was to be guided by direct engagement with the text of scripture, with no intermediary seasonal framework coming between preacher and Word.

Another retention is the Calendar (pp. xxi–xxxii, originally spelt 'Kalendar'), with its adherence to and its recognition of specific saints' days (sometimes called 'the sanctorale' in Catholic liturgical texts). In the 1552 book Cranmer followed Reformed Protestantism by removing many of the saints and their associated readings from the calendar. He retained, though, collects and readings for those saints mentioned in the New Testament, such as the apostles and John the Baptist, and had their names printed in red ink in the book (which led to the coining of the phrase 'red letter days' for these feast days). And he retained two festivals for Mary the mother of Jesus: her 'purification' on 2 February, and the annunciation on 25 March. A key feature of medieval Catholic devotion, one rejected by most of the continental reformers, therefore continued, surprisingly, to find a place in Anglicanism's historic formularies.

Furthermore he retained the naming of four other saints' days, St George, Lammas, St Lawrence and St Clement, in the Calendar. These are called the black letter saints' days, because they were printed in black ink. So even though large numbers of other saints had been evicted, the principle of keeping a temporale was retained.

Later editions of the BCP would expand the numbers of saints named in the calendar, with fifty seven names being added in Elizabeth I's edition of 1561, and in the 1662 edition Alban and the Venerable Bede also having their names added.

In the run up to the publication of 1662 the Puritans attacked the retention of these days, but the bishops defended them on the grounds (among others) that these commemorations 'are useful for the preservation of their memories' (quoted in Procter and Frere 1951, p. 341), again showing deference to church tradition. Furthermore in 1662 the commemoration of the visitation of Mary to Elizabeth was reinserted in the calendar (2 July), and in the table of proper lessons for holy days, the title of the Annunciation became 'The annunciation of our ladie' (printed as 'lady' on p. xix of the Cambridge edition). This was a popular title within a strand of Anglican devotion within the seventeenth century and here draws the BCP marginally closer to Catholic tradition.

Solemnization of Matrimony

Another specific example of medieval Catholic tradition making an overt appearance in the BCP is the marriage service and especially the marriage vows. The more radical 1552 book made few changes to the 1549 book, and the form of the service in this book followed closely the pattern and much of the wording of the Sarum version of the Catholic rite, which with other rites and ceremonies had been drawn up near the beginning of the thirteenth century for use in the cathedral at Salisbury and which by the start of the Reformation had become very widely used across England. Furthermore much of the Sarum version was spoken in English so that the parties to the marriage would understand what was happening (Procter and Frere 1951, p. 611) This continuity is most clearly seen at the heart of the service, the marriage vows and the plighting of troth, where there is mostly a word for word correspondence between the Sarum rite (printed here) and the 1549/1552 rite:

> *N:* 'Wylt thou have this woman to thy wife and love her and wirschipe her (*to the woman* and to be buxom [obedient] to him, luf hym, obeye to him and wirschipe hym, serve hym) and kepe her in sykness and in helthe and in all other degrees be to her as husbande sholde be to his wife, and all other forsake of her, and holde thee only to her to thy lyves ende?'
> *Ans:* 'I will.'

> 'I N take thee N to be my wedded wife (husband) to have and to hold from this day forward for better for worse, for richer for poorer, in sickness and in

health, (to be bonere and buxom [faithful and obedient] in bed and at the board) till death us departe, if holy Church it will ordain; thereto I plight thee my troth.' (*Ibid.*, p. 614)

Confession

Traces of medieval Catholicism are also seen in the BCP's Visitation of the Sick. Medieval Catholicism had stipulated that there were five other sacraments (confirmation, confession, marriage, last rites and ordination). The Reformers had been emphatic that there were only two sacraments – baptism and Holy Communion – because only these were mentioned in scripture. The Articles of Religion uphold this doctrine (see Article XXV) but the rite of the Visitation of the Sick is surprising because it includes the words of the sacrament of confession and absolution. Half way through the service the rubrics stipulate that '*the sick person shall be moved to make a special confession of his sins, if he feel his conscience troubled with any weighty matter. After which confession, the Priest shall absolve him (if he humbly and heartily desire it) after this sort*'. The form of words which the priest then uses comes directly from the Catholic rites and, according to Procter and Frere (*ibid.*, p. 625), is the principal form of absolution used in the Western Church up to the twelfth century. In these words the priest is not simply reminding the penitent person of the forgiveness they receive directly from God, but somehow of his own volition bringing into effect that forgiveness:

> Our Lord Jesus Christ, who hath left power to his Church to absolve all sinners who truly repent and believe in him, of his great mercy forgive thee thine offences: And by his authority committed to me, I absolve thee from all thy sins, In the name of the Father, and of the Son, and of the Holy Ghost. Amen. (BCP, p. 317)

The appearance of this sacramental approach within the rite can be explained by the reliance of the service as a whole on the old service from the Sarum Manual. Nevertheless it is surprising that Cranmer should allow one of the five disallowed Catholic sacraments to make this furtive appearance within the BCP. It is one more way in which Anglicanism's historic formularies *moderated* the Protestant agenda of the Swiss reformers.

Ornaments of Worship

There is evidence that this moderation went a step further in Elizabeth I's edition of the BCP. This appeared in 1559 and made some changes which implicitly elevated the traditional role of the Church in the economy of salvation. One set of changes were to the rite of Holy Communion (see section 5.3 below) and another were to the outward appearance of worship.

The 1559 book contained the following rubrics at the start of Morning and Evening Prayer, with the second often called the 'Ornaments Rubric':

> And the Chancels shall remain as they have done in times past.

> And here is to be noted, that such Ornaments of the Church, and of the Ministers thereof at all times of their Ministration, shall be retained, and be in use, as were in this Church of *England* by the Authority of Parliament, in the Second Year of the Reign of King *Edward* the Sixth. (p. lxvi)

The year referred to here is 1549, two years after Edward's accession in 1547. This, significantly, is the same year as the publication and authorization by parliament of the first Book of Common Prayer. This is significant because it is *before* the introduction of Cranmer's radical reforms in the 1552 prayer book, when much of the visual paraphernalia associated with Catholic worship was disallowed. Elizabeth's prayer book is seeking to restore aspects of pre-Reformed Protestant Anglicanism. (On the rubric in general see Proctor and Frere, pp. 360–3.)

What 'ornaments' could be kept? Here is one common interpretation of the rubric:

> The ornaments of the church referred to are such things as the Bible, Prayer Book, altar, chalice and paten, linens, font, bell, chair, and pulpit. All these are mentioned in the First Prayer Book; besides them we have, by implication, credence, cruets, pyx, lectern, litany desk, etc. The ornaments of the minister include, of course, the vestments ordered by the First Prayer Book, that is to say, alb, chasuble, cope, surplice, customary habit of the bishop, and no doubt the usual vestments of choristers and acolytes. (Daniels)

The Puritans in Elizabeth's reign were wanting all these items to be disallowed because they were inherited from medieval Catholicism and in tangible ways signified continuity between the pre- and post-Reformation Church of England.

This rubric is overriding these wishes. It allows the use of the ornaments of medieval Catholicism in the worship of the Church of England from this point onwards. This did not mean that a Catholic interpretation of their meaning was being enforced on the church: the BCP does not go this extra step. But it does mean that worshippers who were used to seeing these ornaments and interpreting their meaning in traditional ways were not prevented from doing so. Neither Catholic nor Protestant minded Anglicans could use this rubric to enforce their point of view on the other party, but it did allow the possibility of such an interpretation for those drawn in that direction.

This 'Catholic moderation' of Cranmer's Reformed Protestantism gathered pace in the seventeenth century. It was focused above all on revisions to the order for Holy Communion, and in the way this sacrament came to be regarded within the devotional life of the Christian (at least in some quarters). But to understand these changes it is necessary to know the background story of the 'high churchmen' who promoted these changes, and this story is intertwined with the politics of the period.

5.2 *A High Church*: James I and his Successors

It was King James VI of Scotland, who succeeded to the English throne as James I in 1603, who launched the ascendancy of the high church party. Our story must begin with him and the way that when he became King of England he was immediately put under pressure by the Puritans to extend the Reformation and allow the Church of England to become more like the Reformed Church of Calvin's Geneva (as was happening in Scotland with the rise of Presbyterianism under the influence of John Knox). James called the Hampton Court Conference, which met in 1604, and made a few concessions to the Puritans but rejected the idea of the Church of England taking on a Presbyterian polity. He wanted to keep the episcopacy because he saw the fate of the bishops and his own crown as indissolubly linked: he believed in a link between the Apostolic succession of the church's ministry and the doctrine of the divine right of kings to rule (the doctrine that it is God's will that kings rule over their people). Against the Puritans he is reported as stating 'no bishop, no king!'

The following 'Premonition' was published by James in 1609. It was written to other European monarchs and represents a benchmark statement of how he wished his religion to be understood. In the English of the time it provides a ringing overture to the themes of this chapter:

> I will never be ashamed to render an account of my profession and of that hope that is in me, as the Apostle prescribeth. I am such a CATHOLIC CHRISTIAN as believeth the three Creeds, that of the Apostles, that of the Council of Nice [Nicaea], and that of Athanasius . . .
>
> I reverence and admit the Four First General Councils as Catholic and Orthodox. And the said Four General Councils are acknowledged by our Acts of Parliament, and received for orthodox by our Church . . .

The statement mentions many different subjects and with each James argues that he is upholding the faith of the ancient Catholic Church (the church as it was before the division of East and West at the first millennium). He upholds episcopacy and asserts that 'I ever maintained it as an Apostolic institution and so the ordinance of God – contrary to the Puritans, and likewise to [the Jesuit cardinal] Bellarmine, who denies that Bishops have their jurisdiction immediately from God.' This allows James to accuse the Jesuits of being 'Puritan-Papists'. His main point is that he is more Catholic than the Roman Catholics, holding the ancient faith more consistently than them. He concludes with a rhetorical flourish:

> And I will sincerely promise, that whenever any point of the Religion I profess shall be proved to be new, and not Ancient, Catholic, and Apostolic (I mean for matter of faith), I will as soon renounce it . . . I will never refuse to embrace any opinion in divinity necessary to salvation which the whole Catholic Church with an unanime [unanimous] consent have constantly taught and believed even from the Apostles' days, for the space of many ages thereafter without any interruption. (More and Cross 1935, pp. 3–8)

It is hard to imagine Elizabeth speaking in these terms and James' words represent an notable shift in the outlook of the supreme governor of the Church of England. To be a member of this church was now to be a member of the Catholic Church, and more Catholic than the Church of Rome. (Though it should also be noted that James was not repudiating Calvinism, and he gave more leeway to Puritans than Elizabeth had done. In 1604, for example, he sanctioned the 'propheysing' meetings that Elizabeth had banned in the 1570s; see Doerkson 1997.)

There were a number of churchmen who followed James' lead in promoting this Catholic understanding of Anglicanism. Their leader was Lancelot Andrewes (1555–1626) who became an influential bishop in the reign of James I. He was a brilliant linguist and preacher who was made Bishop of Chichester and then Bishop of Winchester, becoming a key translator of the Authorized or King James version of the Bible. He was also a person of deep piety whose book of personal prayers (*The Preces Privatae*) has provided inspiration for many over the centuries. He often preached before James I at Whitehall (see Chapman 2008). As the following sermon from 1623 shows, he elevated the sacraments above preaching within the Christian life. Speaking of how we gather for the Eucharist he wrote how

> we do not gather to Christ or of Christ, but we gather Christ Himself; and gathering Him we shall gather the tree and fruit and all upon it. For as there is a recapitulation of all in Heaven and earth in Christ, so there is a recapitulation of all in Christ in the holy Sacrament . . . And even thus to be recollected at this feast by the Holy Communion into that blessed union, is the highest perfection we can in this life aspire unto. We then are at the highest pitch, at the very best we shall ever attain to on earth, what time we newly come from it; gathered to Christ, and by Christ to God. (pp. 55–6)

To describe Holy Communion as the highest perfection that we can aspire to is a very strong statement and suggests the rite is no longer a mere sign but somehow embodies the very thing it represents. Andrewes is therefore recovering a Catholic view of the altar being more important than the pulpit and, with that, a 'high' view of the importance of the sacramental life of the church. The sermon as a whole reveals a great devotion to the sacrament, and this was also reflected in the way Andrewes led worship in his private chapel at Winchester, using altar lights and incense and mixing water with wine in the chalice, a practice of the ancient church that had been discontinued in the 1552 BCP. In a strong but covert way, then, Andrewes demonstrated a revival in a certain section of the church of a deeply sacramental piety that hardly fits within Reformed Protestantism.

However, in an age when the Puritans were increasing their influence in the country at large this revival would soon be checked. The high church party would suffer a great fall before rising to a position of supremacy within the Church of England. There are two acts in this dramatic story:

Act 1: Fall

1603   Death of Elizabeth and accession of James VI of Scotland, who becomes James I of England.

1604   James calls the Hampton Court Conference to address the grievances of the Puritans.

1605   The discovery of the Gunpowder plot leads to strong measures to curb the activities of Roman Catholics.

1607   Jamestown in Virginia is founded, England's first permanent colony in North America.

1611   The Authorized Version of the Bible is published.

1625   Death of James I and accession of Charles I.

1629   Charles dissolves Parliament and rules without it for the next 11 years.

1633   William Laud is appointed Archbishop of Canterbury by Charles. A small and determined man, he is a high churchman, which means he has a 'high' understanding of the divine authority underpinning monarchy, episcopacy and the sacraments, and he sees the Church of England as a branch of the Catholic Church. When Bishop of St Davids (in 1622) he argued with a Jesuit, Mr Fisher, that he 'never did grant [believe] of the Roman Church, or ever mean to do' that it was 'the only true Church' or 'the root and ground of the Catholic'. In other words it was perfectly possible to be a rooted and grounded Catholic outside of the Roman Church. The latter was merely 'a member of the whole. And this I never did nor ever will deny, if it fall not away absolutely away from Christ' (More and Cross 1935, pp. 56–7). In other words, Laud was provocatively arguing that the Roman Catholic Church and the Church of England were both parts of the same Catholic Church. No wonder the Puritans were enraged by his views and would later exact their

---

revenge. When he was consecrated bishop he made sure that those who consecrated him were undisputedly in the apostolic line (some in the Irish and others in the Italian line of bishops deriving from the early church).

As Archbishop of Canterbury he is now given significant civil powers and sets about imposing high church practices on parish churches, such as putting candlesticks and a cloth on 'the altar', making this, rather than the pulpit, the centre of worship. This incenses the Puritans. Laud also promotes the doctrine of the 'divine right of kings', that God had appointed Charles to rule. The division between king and archbishop on the one side, and Puritan members of Parliament on the other, becomes unbridgeable.

1640   Charles is forced to call Parliament in order to raise taxes (the 'short' and then the 'long' Parliament).

1641   The Puritan parliamentarians seize their opportunity to pass bills that will abolish episcopacy and other church powers. Laud is arrested and imprisoned in the Tower of London.

1642   The King decides to fight the parliamentarians and 'raises his standard' at Nottingham. The Civil War begins.

1645   Laud is executed at Tower Hill, London, protesting that he is no papist but believes in the Protestant Church of England. Parliament orders the abolition of the Book of Common Prayer and its replacement with the Puritan *A Directory of Church Government*, which had originally been compiled by Walter Travers and was meant to pave the way for the introduction of Presbyterianism into England.

1646   Parliament abolishes the episcopate.

1649   Charles I is tried and executed in Whitehall.

1651   Charles II is defeated by Oliver Cromwell at Worcester and goes into exile on the Continent.

1653   Cromwell is installed by Parliament as Lord Protector.

Act 2: Rise

1658 Death of Cromwell.

1660 Parliament dissolves itself and orders new elections. Charles II returns to England on a wave of royalist popularity and is restored to his throne. Episcopacy is reinstated.

1661 Parliament passes the Corporation Act which excludes 'Dissenters' from local government. The Savoy Conference also takes place in the Strand, London, to review the Book of Common Prayer. There are 12 bishops and 12 Presbyterian divines present, as well as other assessors. The Presbyterians resist the idea that ministers need to be episcopally ordained, but Gilbert Sheldon, a high church Bishop of London (soon to be Archbishop of Canterbury), works behind the scenes to secure their defeat. The BCP is re-introduced into the Church of England by the 1662 Act of Uniformity with few changes. Many clergy cannot accept this and are deprived of their livings (2000 in all between 1660 and 1662).

1673, Parliament passes the Test Acts which exclude Dissenters
1678 from central government. This cements the exclusion of Puritans from the centre of national life, which is now controlled by 'Churchmen'. Puritans have to form their own gathered churches for worship.

1685 James II, who is already a Roman Catholic, comes to the throne and becomes deeply unpopular. Fears of a Mary Tudor style reconversion of England mean that when James is challenged by William of Orange very few are willing to support him.

1688 James flees and William, unexpectedly, takes the throne (claiming legitimacy through his wife Mary who is James II's daughter). Nine bishops, including Thomas Ken of Bath and Wells and Richard Sancroft the Archbishop of Canterbury, as well as some 400 clergy, cannot accept that their oaths of loyalty to James have been annulled and they refuse to give their allegiance to William and Mary. They are deprived of their livings but are not deprived of their orders as clergy. These 'Non-Jurors' continue to live and worship in schism for a number of decades.

> **1701** Parliament passes the Act of Settlement, which amongst other things makes it a requirement that the monarch 'join in communion with the Church of England as by law established'. The monarch, in other words, must be a member of the Church of England. When William, who was a Dutch Calvinist Presbyterian, attempts to make the BCP and Canons more Presbyterian, he is thwarted by Convocation (the clergy in their assembly), who remain predominantly High Churchmen: 'England henceforward practised its virtues of moderation within a framework to a large degree set by High Churchmen, though not to the degree they wished' (Jonathan Clark in Chadwick 2000, p. 177).
>
> It was the theology of these High Churchmen which came to influence the revision of the Book of Common Prayer, not least in seventeenth-century Scotland, and this process now demands its own examination.

5.3 *Real Presence*: from Cosin to the Scottish Liturgy

We have already seen how Cranmer's 1552 order for Holy Communion turned the mass into a memorial meal (see Chapter 2.2). But we also noted how Article XXV gave sacraments a fuller and richer role in the life of the disciple than the revisions themselves might suggest, for the sacraments are described as the means whereby 'he doth work invisibly in us, and doth not only quicken, but also strengthen and confirm our Faith in him'. There was the bare possibility, therefore, of believing in a real presence of Christ in the rite, the one who works invisibly, thus keeping the door open to an Catholic interpretation.

This 'door' was nudged a little more widely in Elizabeth's BCP of 1559. Her edition was essentially a re-issue of the 1552 book, but in the words of administration for communion the formula from the 1549 book, 'The body of our Lord Jesus Christ, which was given for thee, preserve thy body and soul unto everlasting life', which implies the real presence of Christ within the bread (and the wine), was added to the 1552 formula, 'Take and eat this in remembrance that Christ died for thee, and feed on him in thy heart by faith with thanksgiving', which had been formulated to deny a theology of the real presence! The historian Patrick Collinson describes how this 'accommodated anyone, perhaps including the Queen, still attached to belief in some sort of real presence' (Chadwick 2000, p. 146). MacCulloch calls it 'a masterpiece of theological engineering' (MacCulloch 2001, p. 27)!

The revisions within the 1662 book, approved at the Savoy Conference of 1661 (against the wishes of the Puritan delegates) continued this approach and in a few ways strengthened the hand of those who wanted to interpret the rite in a Catholic way. The words of institution, recalling what Christ did and said at the Last Supper, were now given some new rubrics which directed what the priest should do as he recited the words. The first rubric sets the tone:

> When the Priest, standing before the Table, hath so ordered the Bread and Wine, that he may with the more readiness and decency break the Bread before the people, and take the Cup into his hands; he shall say the Prayer of Consecration, as followeth. (p. 255)

This rubric directs the attention of the priest and the congregation not to each other but to the elements themselves: clearly something important is going to happen to them, underlined by the way the whole section is now called the prayer of consecration. Then, as Christ's words are recited, the priest is directed 'to take the patten into his hands', 'to break the bread', 'to lay his hand upon all the bread', 'to take the cup into his hands', and 'to lay his hand upon every Vessel (be it Chalice or Flagon) in which there is any Wine to be consecrated' (p. 256). This is very far from a memorial service of an event from the past: something dramatic and holy is happening within the vessels and the rubrics draw the attention of everyone to them. Furthermore, if the bread and wine runs out, more must be consecrated in the same way (p. 257), and if any consecrated bread and wine remain at the end it must be 'revently' consumed immediately after the blessing. (p. 262). It is no wonder that the Puritans could not accept the 1662 book.

John Cosin

A figure who begins to draw out this theology from these hints in the 1662 BCP is John Cosin (1594–1672). He had the good fortune to be twenty years younger than Laud and to reach the pinnacle of his career at the point when the tide turned against the Puritans and Cromwell's Commonwealth, and Charles II was restored to the throne in 1660. He was made Bishop of Durham in 1660 and had an important influence on the revising of the Book of Common Prayer in 1661–62. Many of his writings were directed against Roman Catholic teaching, so he was no papist, but nor was he in sympathy with the Puritans. He had been a personal friend of William Laud and had followed Andrewes in using candles, vestments and incense in worship. He believed firmly in the Catholic identity of the Church of England, as his 'Last Will' makes clear. In this document he revealingly writes of 'the Church of England, or rather the Catholic Church'. He denounces 'Separatists, the Anabaptists, and their followers, (alas) too many, but also the new Independents, and Presbyterians of our country, a kind of men hurried away with the spirit of malice, disobedience, and sedition, who by a dis-loyal attempt (the like whereof was never heard since the world began) have of late committed so many great and execrable crimes, to the contempt and despite of religion and the Christian Faith: which, how great they were, without horror cannot be spoken or mentioned.' He then produces this ringing description of the church that he believes in and has membership of, the worldwide Catholic church:

> But in what part of the world soever any Churches are extant, bearing the name of Christ, and professing the true Catholic Faith and religion, worship-ping and calling upon God, the Father, the Son, and the Holy Ghost, with one heart and voice, if any where I be now hindered actually to be joined with them, either by distance of countries or variance amongst men, or by any other let whatsoever, yet always in my mind and affection I join and unite with them . . . (More and Cross 1935, pp. 13–14)

Such a Catholic understanding implies a high view of what takes place in the church's sacraments and especially in the Eucharist. Cosin gives expression to this high view in his 'First Series of Notes' on the BCP (discussed in Cuming 1983, pp. 127–9). Cosin holds firmly that the Church of England through the

BCP teaches 'the presence of Christ's body and blood in the sacrament . . . It is confessed by all divines that upon the words of consecration the body and blood of Christ is really and substantially present, and so exhibited and given to all that receive it'. Cosin adds, however, a qualification which shows he is not following the teaching of the Church of Rome: 'and all this, not after a physical and sensual, but after a heavenly and invisible and incomprehensible manner' (*ibid.*, p. 128).

Jeremy Taylor

This way of viewing Holy Communion is more prominently stated in the writings and career of Jeremy Taylor (1613–67). He was a Cambridge scholar and 'High Churchman' who early in his career wrote a pamphlet that argued that the table where the Eucharist is celebrated should be reverenced even when there is no sacrament upon it:

> shall not the Christian Altar be most holy where is present the blessed Body and bloud of the Sonne of God? I but, what when the Sacrament is Gone? The relation is there still, and it is but a relative Sanctity we speake of, it is appointed for his Tabernacle, it is consecrate to that end, and the destination of man, the Presence of the Sone of God, the appointing it to a most holy end, the employment in a most sacred worke, and the Presence of Angels (which, as S. Peter saith, desire to looke into these mysteryes,) if all this be not enough to make a thing most holy, there is no difference, nor can be any in the world betweene Sacred and prophane. (Taylor, late 1620s)

This is a strongly Catholic statement and it did not go down well with the Puritans. Taylor's association with Archbishop Laud also did him no favours with that party. During the Civil War he was imprisoned four times (he supported the Royalists) and had to retire to Wales where he became a chaplain to a noble family. It was here that he wrote his great books on *Holy Living* of 1650 and *Holy Dying* of 1651, works described as having a 'balanced sobriety and an insistence on a well-ordered piety which stresses temperance and moderation in all things'. The first of these, *Holy Living*, 'deliberately builds up to the eucharist, as if it were what Christianity is all about. Indeed, he says as much, time and again, for example: "The celebration of the holy sacrament is the great mysteriousness of the Christian religion'" (Stevenson 1994, quoting IV, x, 1). The last few pages of the book contains this fervent and evocative prayer focused on the elements of the sacrament:

> O blessed Jesus, who art my Saviour and my God, whose body is my food, and thy righteousness is my robe, thou art the priest and the sacrifice, the master of the feast and the feast itself, the physician of my soul, the light of my eyes, the purifier of my stains; enter into my heart and cast out from thence all impurities, all the remains of the old man; and grant I may partake of this holy sacrament with much reverence, and holy relish, and great effect, receiving hence the communication of thy holy body and blood, for the establishment of an unreprovable faith, of an unfeigned love, for the fulness of wisdom, for the healing my soul, for the blessing and preservation of my body, for the taking out the sting of temporal death, and for the assurance of a holy resurrection; for the ejection of all evil from within me, and the fulfilling all thy righteous commandments; and to procure for me a mercy and a fair reception at the day of judgment, through thy mercies, O holy and ever-blessed Saviour Jesus.

Taylor published many other writings, including *Ductor Dubitantium, or the Rule of Conscience* (1660) which became one of a number of authoritative guides to casuistry (resolving problems of conscience and duty) for seventeenth-century Anglicans. Other 'Caroline divines' (teachers of theology in the reigns of Charles I and Charles II) who promoted this approach to moral theology were Robert Sanderson and John Sharp. It was broadly based on an older pre-Reformation Catholic tradition of casuistry, especially drawing on Thomistic categories, but instead of looking to the priest in the confessional as the one to resolve moral dilemmas, it looked to the conscience of the ordinary believer and 'wished to assist people as far as possible to resolve their own moral problems with confidence and safety' (Wood 1986; Kenneth Kirk, Robert Mortimer and Lindsay Dewar are twentieth-century exponents of this approach).

After the restoration of Charles II in 1660, Taylor and other high churchman were brought back into the establishment and Taylor became Bishop of Down and Connor (where he continued to clash with Puritans) and vice-chancellor of Dublin University, which he revived and restored. In general the Restoration allowed Taylor's sober kind of sacramental piety to be openly practised and promoted within the Church of England. However, it needs to be recognized that there is nothing within the 1662 rite that *explicitly* encourages a Catholic doctrine of the real presence of Christ in the bread and wine. For that we must cross the border into Scotland.

The Scottish Liturgy

When James VI of Scotland came south to be James I of England the crowns of Scotland and England were united. But the religions of the two countries were different: Presbyterianism, through the leadership of the Calvinist John Knox, had made stronger inroads into Scotland than England and it was not at all clear that the Church of England with its bishops and Book of Common Prayer could take control of the Scottish Church. Charles I, however, wished to see a unified church and commissioned the Scottish bishops to produce a new prayer book, which appeared in 1637. This book was based on the more Catholic 1549 BCP rather than the Protestant edition of 1552 and showed the influence of William Laud. He tried to impose it on the Church of Scotland and this generated intense opposition. A 'National Covenant' swept away episcopal government the following year, and the book disappeared from view. But in 1689, after the 'glorious revolution' in which William and Mary replaced the Stuart James, a minority of Scottish churchmen refused to take the oath of loyalty to the new monarch and like the 'Non-jurors' south of the border endeavoured to uphold an episcopalian church order. They reprinted the 1637 Prayer Book, and also issued the order for Holy Communion in separate 'wee bookies' for widespread distribution. At this point there was also a revival of interest in the liturgies of the ancient Eastern Orthodox Church and these influenced some of the revisions of this order. Bishop Rattray of Blairgowrie produced one of these orders in 1764 and this became the definitive liturgy of what was now known as the Scottish Episcopal Church.

The American colonies were soon to fight and win their War of Independence from the British crown. After independence American Anglicans needed to establish their own episcopal order rather than look to the Church of England for oversight, and so the clergy and people of Connecticut elected Samuel Seabury to be their first bishop. He sailed for England and approached the Bishop of

London who previously had been responsible for all Church of England congregations overseas (the first to be established was at Jamestown in 1607). However, Seabury could not take the oath of allegiance to the British Crown as he belonged to the newly independent United States, and so the bishop declined to ordain him. Seabury approached the Scottish bishops, who were not part of the established church and so did not require an oath of allegiance to the crown. They agreed, and consecrated him in Aberdeen in 1784, an event which in a formal sense created the Episcopal Church of the United States. The important point here is that when Seabury returned to America he took with him the Scottish Liturgy and introduced it into the American Church. It soon became the basis of the liturgy used in that church and lay behind the Holy Communion rite in the American Book of Common Prayer published in 1789.

A key feature of the Scottish liturgy of 1764, which found its way into the American book, is the introduction of a 'Prayer of Invocation' within the Consecration Prayer. This occurs after the reciting of Christ's words of institution:

> And we most humbly beseech Thee, O merciful Father, to hear us, and of Thy almighty goodness vouchsafe to bless and sanctify with Thy word and Holy Spirit these Thy gifts and creatures of bread and wine, that they may become the Body and Blood of Thy most dearly beloved Son.

These words show the influence of the Liturgy of St Clement from the ancient Eastern Orthodox Church, which Bishop Rattray had published in 1744, for such a prayer of invocation is an important part of that rite. Their presence signifies a remarkable shift in what the liturgy is claiming to do. Whereas in the 1552 BCP the liturgy was essentially an act of remembrance, through the repetition of Christ's words of institution at the Last Supper (so that communion was a way of remembering what Christ had already achieved on the cross), now something else is happening, an act of God in the present, touching and changing the believer through consecrating the bread and the wine they receive. The Holy Spirit is being asked to make this happen, to turn an act of remembrance into an act of spiritual sanctification. This is highly significant: it means the action of the liturgy is replacing the reading of scripture as the declared point of contact between God and the believer. In other words, this Prayer of Invocation is giving the liturgy a much greater weight and significance within the life of the Anglican, even a primary significance. And from such a change it is possible to conclude that what the High Church party were attempting to do in seventeenth-century England, a 'Catholic moderation of Reformed Protestantism', had now in the Scottish Liturgy become something else, a 'Catholicism with a Reformed moderation'.

This kind of invocation would find its way into later editions of the Scottish Liturgy and the American BCP, as already pointed out, and eventually into the South African Anglican liturgy of 1924, before finally finding its way into the Church of England through the 1928 revision of the Book of Common Prayer (this book, though twice thrown out by Parliament, was approved for use by the bishops and became widely used in 'high church' parishes).

But what of the wider life of Anglicanism beyond its liturgies? Was this also to become more Catholic in character and practice? Many nineteenth-century voices certainly thought so. Their story takes the story of Catholic discipleship within Anglicanism to a new level of intensity and to this story we must turn.

Discussion Questions

1 In what sense can an Anglican priest *absolve* a penitent from their sins?
2 Do you agree with the sentiment of King James I when he states 'whenever any point of the Religion I profess shall be proved to be new, and not Ancient, Catholic, and Apostolic (I mean for matter of faith), I will as soon renounce it'? What are your reasons for agreeing or disagreeing?
3 When Anglicans participate in the Holy Communion service at what point or in what way do they most directly encounter the presence of Christ?

Further Reading

Revision of the Book of Common Prayer

Cuming, Geoffrey (1982), *A History of Anglican Liturgy*, 2nd edition, London: Palgrave Macmillan.

Cuming, Geoffrey (1983), *The Godly Order: Texts and Studies relating to the Book of Common Prayer*, London: Alcuin and SPCK.

Perry, W. (1922), *The Scottish Liturgy: Its Value and History*, London: A. R. Mowbray and Co. Reprinted by Bibliobazaar, 1990.

Procter, Francis and Walter Howard Frere (1949, 1951, 1965), *A New History of the Book of Common Prayer*, London: Macmillan and Co.

Rowell, Geoffrey (1990), 'Anglicanism and Confession', in Rowell and Dudley, eds, *Confession and Absolution*, London: SPCK.

The High Churchmen

Chapman, Raymond, ed. (2008), *Before the King's Majesty: Lancelot Andrewes and His Writings*, Norwich: Canterbury Press.

Hylson-Smith, Kenneth (1996), *The Churches in England from Elizabeth I to Elizabeth II: Volume I: 1558–1688*, London: SCM Press.

McAdoo, H. R. and Kenneth Stevenson (1995), *The Mystery of the Eucharist in the Anglican Tradition*, Norwich: Canterbury Press.

Spurr, John (1991), *The Restoration Church of England 1646–1689*, New Haven: Yale University Press.

Trevor-Roper, Hugh (2000), *Archbishop Laud, 1573–1645*, 3rd revised edition, London: Weidenfeld & Nicolson.

6

In the Catholic Fold

6.1 *Breaking Free from the State*: Episcopalians and Keble

Anglicanism was born as a state church. Henry VIII's Act of Supremacy in 1534 not only declared Henry to be the 'supreme head' of the Church of England, but also irrevocably tied that church to him and his successors. It was no longer to have divided loyalties, to the Roman pontiff on the one hand and the English monarch on the other. No longer would figures like Thomas Becket and Thomas More seek to uphold the claims of Rome, while monarchs like Henry II seek to strengthen their own claims over the church. The king was now to be in charge of both ecclesiastical and civil realms. In the Articles of Religion Cranmer, ever the loyal servant of Henry VIII, gave formal expression to this principle:

Article 37 – Of the Civil Magistrates

The King's Majesty has the chief power in this realm of England and other of his dominions, unto whom the chief government of all estates of this realm, whether they be ecclesiastical or civil, in all causes appertains, and is not nor ought to be subject to any foreign jurisdiction.

Where we attribute to the King's Majesty the chief government, by which titles we understand the minds of some slanderous folks to be offended, we give not to our princes the ministering either of God's word or of sacraments, . . . but only that prerogative which we see to have been given always to all godly princes in Holy Scriptures by God himself, that is, that they should rule all estates and degrees committed to their charge by God, whether they be temporal, and restrain with the civil sword the stubborn and evil-doers.

The Bishop of Rome has no jurisdiction in this realm of England.

The laws of the realm may punish Christian men with death for heinous and grievous offences.

It is lawful for Christian men at the commandment of the Magistrate to wear weapons and serve in the wars.

It is important to note the second paragraph of this statement with its careful separation of 'the ministering either of God's word or of sacraments' from the powers of the monarch. The king was not a priest or a bishop and had no authority in the pulpit or at the altar: this spiritual authority was to remain with the clergy. This demarcation of areas of responsibility reflected the two kingdoms theology of Martin Luther, in which the visible kingdom, which included the visible church, was under the monarch (often described in Protestantism as the magistrate, as in the last line of Article 37), whereas the invisible kingdom, which included the invisible and true church, was under God alone. The magistrate controlled the visible church, including the making of appointments to bishoprics and other clerical roles, and of taking control of church lands, property and funds when necessary, but had no right to preach from the pulpit or preside at the celebration of the sacraments. These were signs of the invisible kingdom and derived their authority from Christ's words in Scripture. This nuanced outlook is the essence of Magisterial Protestantism, and it is a view of the relationship between church and state that was decisively set in place by the Elizabethan Settlement, and then theologically justified by Richard Hooker (see, for example, Hooker in Chapman 2009, chap. 10).

In the seventeenth century it is possible to trace a split among those who held this view. On the one hand a more exalted view of kingship began to re-surface within the Church of England. As we have already seen, James I ascended the English throne believing that the fate of the monarch and episcopacy was linked ('No bishop, no king'), which implied a divine sanction for the monarchy. This doctrine was promoted as 'the divine right of kings' by James and then by the unfortunate Archbishop Laud. After the restoration of the monarchy in 1660 this doctrine was widely held by High Churchmen, even when James II seemed intent on replacing the Church of England with Roman Catholicism. The split itself became clear in 1688, when parliament invited William of Orange to take the throne in place of James. Some High Churchmen could not accept that their oaths of loyalty to James II could be undone by parliament in this way, and (as seen above p. 94) refused to swear allegiance to the new monarch. They were removed from their posts but not prevented from continuing to minister as priests. These 'Non-jurors' remained a small but influential group into the early years of the eighteenth century and continued to uphold an exalted view of the monarchy alongside their high view of the church and its ministers. Most bishops and clergy, however, *did* take the oath of allegiance to William, having a lower view of the status of the visible church and its governorship by the monarch. Many were guided by the kind of Protestant theology described in the first part of this Studyguide; others were 'Latitudinarian', which meant they had latitude (that is they were quite relaxed) about such dogmatic and liturgical questions. If a new king like William was going to allow the church to live in peace and continue its work of preaching the word and celebrating the sacraments, this was perfectly acceptable. The true church, the invisible church, lay out of sight and was not affected by changes in the temporal governorship.

The division between the two views affected not only the ministry of Anglican clergy but, for some, their home life and even their beds! Samuel Wesley, the father of John and Charles, withdrew from sleeping with his wife for a time over a disagreement with her about the legitimacy of William of Orange: Samuel sympathized with the Non-jurors. However, both parties agreed that the monarch was the supreme governor of the Church of England and that the church's temporal authority derived from this connection. This view has sometimes been described as Erastianism (named after the Swiss theologian Thomas Erastus), maintaining that the state has ascendency over the church in ecclesiastical as well as civil matters.

Two developments began to challenge this *modus vivendi*. The first was the establishment of Anglicanism outside the Church of England. As we have seen (p. 100), those who could not accept the overturning of episcopacy by Presbyterianism in Scotland did not remain in the Church of Scotland but, after a long struggle between the restoration of the Stuart monarchy in 1660 and revolution of 1690 (when Presbyterianism gained control of the Church of Scotland), formed themselves into the Episcopal Church in Scotland (renamed as the Scottish Episcopal Church in 1979). They remained loyal to the Stuart monarchy and suffered penal restrictions from the authorities in the eighteenth century. However, their church formed a distinct identity, not least with the introduction of the Scottish liturgy in 1764, and showed that it was possible to be an Anglican (though this term was not often used within the church) without being embroiled in an establishment with the monarchy.

A second challenge was posed by the coming into being of the American Episcopal Church during and after the American War of Independence (1777–83). During that war Anglican churches had suffered because of their association with the British crown. There were many defections to other denominations and church property was destroyed. It was important, then, for American Anglicans to find a distinct identity apart from the Church of England. This was helped when Samuel Seabury was consecrated as its first bishop in 1784 not by an English bishop but by the Scottish Episcopal bishops, as we have seen (though other American bishops were consecrated in England in 1787 and 1790). A 'General Convention' was held in 1789 which drew up and adopted a constitution and canons for the church, and the Book of Common Prayer was revised for use within it. In the Church of England these developments were regarded with suspicion and sometimes prejudice, but in America they helped to re-establish the presence of Anglicanism. Episcopalians, as they came to be known, pioneered the setting up of seminaries for the training of clergy, establishing the General Theological Seminary in New York in 1816 (English clergy at this time were not trained in seminaries but were ordained after taking degrees at Oxford or Cambridge). Again, therefore, this showed that it was possible to be Anglican without being part of an establishment with the monarchy.

A more direct challenge to the establishment of the Church of England arose out of parliamentary reform in the 1820s and 1830s. Since the Act of Union with Ireland (1800–01), which resulted in Ireland sending MPs to Westminster, the government needed the support of Irish voters. These were mostly Roman Catholics, and through their MPs they put increasing pressure on the government to lift the restrictions on Roman Catholics in England. This happened in the Test and Corporation Acts 1828, and the Catholic Emancipation Bill of 1829. English Catholics could now be MPs and could vote on any laws, including laws which governed the established church, which was the Church of England. Furthermore the Whig Reform Bill of 1832 allowed many more men to vote and so widened the franchise yet further, weakening the power of the English landed gentry who had provided the backbone of support for the Church of England. These changes were capped by a government proposal in 1833 to suppress ten Irish Anglican bishoprics and divert the money used to pay them for non-denominational education (the 'Irish Temporalities Act'). This created consternation in Anglican circles: it was perceived as non-Anglicans deciding the fate of Anglicans. The state, then, was no longer acting as the main stay of the church, as it had done in the seventeenth century, but was now taking up a very different role. Thomas Arnold, the famous headmaster of Rugby School, declared in late 1832 'the church as it now stands, no human power can save' (Chadwick 1971, p. 47).

The University of Oxford had been a centre of High Church thinking since the time of William Laud (who had helped to reform and renew the university, making significant donations to the Bodleian, the university library). In the early nineteenth century it was still necessary for new students at the university to subscribe to the Articles of Religion. There were figures like Charles Lloyd (1784–1829), the Regius Professor of Divinity, who emphasized the way in which the Book of Common Prayer contained doctrine and texts from the early and medieval church. He influenced the future leaders of the Oxford Movement and prepared the ground for their re-assessment of the relation of church and state. (On the high church background to the Oxford Movement see Nockles 1994.)

It was John Keble (1792–1866), a saintly country vicar, professor of poetry in the university, author of *The Christian Year* of 1827, and future editor of Hooker's *Works* (1838), who spoke out in protest at what was happening, galvanizing opinion in the university. In his Assize Sermon in the University Church, preached before the assize judges who were visiting the city on 14 July 1833, he argued his case in an elliptical way by first describing the possibility of a nation (that is, Britain)

> having for centuries acknowledged, as an essential part of its theory of government, that, as a Christian nation, she is also part of Christ's Church, and bound, in all her legislation and policy, by the fundamental rules of that Church . . . throwing off the restraint which in many respects such a principle would impose on them, nay, disowning the principle itself.

He then argued that this way of thinking was now embedding itself in Britain, an 'alarming' development, and it was infecting home life as well as public measures. He asked, rhetorically, whether 'APOSTASY [was] too hard a word to describe the temper of the nation?' (Bettenson and Maunder 1999, pp. 353–4). His point was that it was not!

Keble, then, branded what the government was trying to do with the Irish Temporalities Act as a 'national apostasy', for it was entrusting to those who were not part of the apostolic faith of the established church some control over the management of that faith.

It was highly surprising for a conservative cleric within the established church to criticize the government in this way. For most of the eighteenth century such figures had accepted whatever the crown in parliament decreed. Now, though, Keble was daring to imply that the church had its own authority apart from the state, an authority which allowed it to criticize the state when necessary.

6.2 *In the Apostolic Succession*: Newman and Pusey

This was a wake-up call to fellow high churchmen. One was Hurrell Froude (1803–36), a conservative, quick witted and intense person who was a brilliant scholar of the fathers of the church and a pious believer. He brought Keble and John Henry Newman together. Newman (1801–90), son of a banker, was also highly strung and intense and had been brought to faith by the Evangelical revival. As a young man he had written the popular hymn 'Lead kindly light'. He was now vicar of the university church and a great preacher who stirred the emotions of his congregation. Matthew Arnold, the poet and son of Thomas Arnold, vividly described Newman's power and appeal as a preacher at the university church:

Forty years ago he was in the very prime of life; he was close at hand to us at Oxford; he was preaching at St Mary's pulpit every Sunday; he seemed about to transform and to renew what was for us the most national and natural institution in the world, the Church of England. Who could resist the charm of that spiritual apparition, gliding in the dim afternoon light through the aisles of St Mary's, rising into the pulpit, and then, in the most entrancing of voices, breaking the silence with words and thoughts which were a religious music, – subtle, sweet, mournful? I seem to hear him still, saying: 'After the fever of life, after wearinesses and sicknesses, fightings and despondings, languor and fretfulness, struggling and succeeding; after all the changes and chances of this troubled, unhealthy state, – at length comes death, at length the white throne of God, at length the beatific vision.' (Arnold 1885, pp. 139–40)

This evocative quotation shows how Newman caught the attention of the students at the university, and what he was promising to do, but it does not describe the content of his message as a leader of the Oxford Movement. For this we must go to the *Tracts for the Times,* which Newman and Froude launched soon after Keble's sermon. Newman wrote the first, which was printed and sent to vicarages up and down the country. It was entitled 'Thoughts On The Ministerial Commission, Respectfully Addressed to the Clergy' and was a rallying call to the Church of England to rediscover its inherent authority, an authority not derived from establishment with the state (as many had thought), nor on the shifting sands of popularity (as for the non-conformists), but from another source, a deep and secure authority that would allow it to stand up to the government:

> Now then let me come at once to the subject which leads me to address you. Should the Government and Country so far forget their GOD as to cast off the Church, to deprive it of its temporal honours and substance, *on what* will you rest the claim of respect and attention which you make upon your flocks? Hitherto you have been upheld by your birth, your education, your wealth, your connexions; should these secular advantages cease, on what must CHRIST'S Ministers depend? Is not this a serious practical question?

Newman then turns to the Methodists, Baptists and other 'dissenting' congregations to see if they provide an answer:

> We know how miserable is the state of religious bodies not supported by the State. Look at the Dissenters on all sides of you, and you will see at once that their Ministers, depending simply upon the people, become the creatures of the people. Are you content that this should be your case? Alas! Can a greater evil befall Christians, than for their teachers to be guided by them, instead of guiding? How can we 'hold fast the form of sound words', and 'keep that which is committed to our trust', if our influence is to depend simply on

our popularity? Is it not our very office to *oppose* the world? Can we then allow ourselves to *court* it? To preach smooth things and prophesy deceits? To make the way of life easy to the rich and indolent, and to bribe the humbler classes by excitements and strong intoxicating doctrine? Surely it must not be so;—and the question recurs, on what are we to rest our authority, when the State deserts us?

Newman's prose is more direct and passionate than Keble's. It rises in a crescendo to a point where he finally reveals the true source of that authority:

CHRIST has not left His Church without claim of its own upon the attention of men. Surely not. Hard Master He cannot be, to bid us oppose the world, yet give us no credentials for so doing. There are some who rest their divine mission on their own unsupported assertion; others, who rest it upon their popularity; others, on their success; and others, who rest it upon their temporal distinctions. This last case has, perhaps, been too much our own; I fear we have neglected the real ground on which our authority is built, – our APOSTOLICAL DESCENT.

Then using scriptural language Newman rousingly describes what he means by this:

We have been born, not of blood, nor of the will of the flesh, nor of the will of man, but of GOD. The LORD JESUS CHRIST gave His SPIRIT to His Apostles; they in turn laid their hands on those who should succeed them; and these again on others; and so the sacred gift has been handed down to our present Bishops, who have appointed us as their assistants, and in some sense representatives. (http://www.newmanreader.org/works/times/tract1.html)

In this outlook there is little sense of the church deriving its authority from being faithful to the word of scripture. Instead the authority comes from its physical and spiritual connection with the earlier generations of the church, through the episcopacy. This was the doctrine of apostolic succession, that the local church was physically and spiritually connected to the church of previous generations, going back to the apostles, through the laying on of hands by bishops at ordinations and consecrations. It would lead to an emphasis on the distinctive authority of the clergy over and against the secular authorities, with the clergy seen as the carriers of the apostolic succession in the present, and to a growing sense of the authority of the church over and against the state.

A clear implication, which Newman did not immediately draw out, is that this apostolic descent in turn connects the Church of England with the other churches of Christendom who uphold apostolic succession. Newman is implicitly reaffirming the Catholic identity of the Church of England, but now in a way that sets it apart from the state. This is a significant development on what the High Churchmen had argued.

Newman attracted another figure to join the leadership of the movement, Edward Bouverie Pusey (1800–82). Pusey was the Professor of Hebrew in the university and a painstaking scholar. A grave and serious figure, he had moved from theological liberalism to conservatism. He wrote many of the *Tracts for the Times,* but his tracts were more treatises than manifestos. His Tract No 18 on fasting, for example, was the length of a book. But he demonstrated that the movement was as much about spiritual revival as politics: prayer, fasting and discipline as well as ecclesiastical politics were to be part of Catholic renewal. James Pereiro has recently argued that this can be summed up as being about the formation of a Catholic 'ethos' of holiness, an ethos that is revealed more and more as it is lived out over time (see Pereiro 2007).

There were ninety tracts in all, published between 1833 and 1841, and they argued for a recognition of the Church of England as a divine institution ('Christ's body and blood') with its foundation in heaven and, as mentioned, connected through history with the early church through Apostolic succession. They argued that the BCP was to be the rule of faith, and that the priesthood should be seen not merely as a civic role within the earthly city but as the representative of Christ: priests were to minister his sacraments of the heavenly city ('his very self here below'). They believed the Church of England steered a *Via Media* between Protestantism and Romanism (not just a Lutheran-type Protestant middle way between Calvinism and Catholicism). They criticized both 'Popery and Dissent', appealing to the ancient fathers of undivided Christendom: the Church of England had wonderfully survived the Reformation with its Catholic creed and ministry unimpaired, but the growth of Protestant practice had now obscured this inheritance. The Church should clear this practice away and become faithful to its true nature.

Within this agenda it was crucial for Oxford University to provide a lead, and within the university the Regius Professor of Divinity should play a leading role. But when the chair became vacant R. D. Hampden, a low churchman (or what today would be called a liberal), was nominated by the Crown. Newman and Pusey sought to block the appointment. This aroused a wave of protest, not least from Thomas Arnold at Rugby who called Newman and Pusey the Oxford 'malignants' and opposed their 'ecclesiasticism'. They were also attacked by Richard Whately, an ex-Oxford don who was now Archbishop of Dublin and had previously been one of Newman's mentors. Many Evangelicals also turned against the movement, not least Evangelical bishops such as John Bird Sumner who would later become Archbishop of Canterbury. They loathed 'popery' and saw the movement as opening the Church of England to its 'infection'.

There was prodigious editing and publishing of ancient theology by Keble, Newman and Pusey and their circle, not least the *Library of the Fathers*, published from 1836, which brought together the major theological works of the Early Church. The *Library of Anglo-Catholic Theology* began to be published from 1841, making the works of seventeenth-century Anglican High Church theologians (the 'Caroline Divines') available to a wide readership.

Newman, however, went one step further. In his famous *Tract 90* he compared the teaching of the Articles of Religion with the decrees of the Roman Catholic Council of Trent (the great Counter-Reformation Council of 1545–63 that had opposed the teaching of the Protestant Reformers and encouraged a revival of Roman Catholicism), and argued that they were *consistent*. This was clearly going much further than the High Churchmen, who were as critical of Roman Catholic teaching as Puritan teaching. This alienated many of his followers. Newman had been aware that a number of his younger supporters were increasingly attracted towards Roman Catholicism, and so was wanting to show that they could hold onto their Catholic beliefs while remaining within the Church of England. But for many others he was arguing the unarguable, and there was a wave of criticism. Henry Edward Manning (later Cardinal Manning) declared that Tract 90 was 'too clever by half'.

In hurt and dismay Newman withdrew from the university and the movement and went to live a semi-monastic life at Littlemore near Oxford. One of his supporters, William G. Ward (1812–82), a philosophical theologian and fellow of Balliol College, published *The Ideal of a Christian Church* (1844), which praised the Roman Catholic Church for its structure. He was deprived of his degree by the university authorities for heresy in 1845. He then sought to be received into the Roman Catholic Church and this was soon granted to him. He was followed by Newman a few months later: Newman had now completely lost confidence in the apostolic authority of the Church of England.

However, this was not the end of the movement. It moved into a second phase, in which many of the undergraduates who had come under Keble and Newman's spell at Oxford moved into parishes up and down the country and started to instil their theology among the people there. The intellectual movement centred on Oxford was over but the renewal movement in the parishes was only just beginning. This is usually called Tractarianism or Anglo-Catholicism and it drew inspiration not only from Oxford but from Keble's parochial work in Hampshire and from a Cambridge society dedicated to the study of ecclesiastical art.

6.3 *A Church for all*: from Hampshire to Holborn

Catholic renewal was not just about theological ideas. As S. A. Skinner has argued (Skinner 2004), the main focus of the Oxford Movement was parish renewal, for it was through the life of a church within the community that a Catholic identity and holiness would truly be formed. With the state becoming increasingly secular, and with industrialization disrupting and dislocating whole communities, parish churches were to be the engine of renewal: 'The unit of the parish was the means by which organic pre-commercial society and its concomitant social harmony might be reclaimed . . . a conscious repudiation of statist or societal solutions' (*ibid.*, p. 144).

The parish of Hursley in Hampshire, where John Keble was incumbent, became the paradigm for the early leaders of the movement. Keble was intimate with 'the problems of poverty, the difficulties of domestic economy and the ravages of disease . . . [in his writings] he comments on farm labourers breaking machines, mentions the conditions of workhouses, shows his attitude to beerhouses and their effects on the population, and passes judgment on the price of corn and the distribution of allotments' (*ibid.*, pp. 145–6). Keble was frequently ill from his visitations to the parish sick, showing his pastoral dedication. But he was not just administering a bandage to wounds. He was also proactive in practical and astute ways: at Hursley he sponsored the creation of allotments for those without land; he founded a parish savings bank in the hope of encouraging poor parishioners to save during seasonally high wages; and, if all else failed, he supported emigration schemes (*ibid.*, p. 146).

This concern for the life of the poor alongside the rich was also expressed within the church building: numerous Tractarian writers developed a concept of Christian equality under which the rich could be ordered to leave their superiority in the porch, and the poor 'properly enfranchised in lasting compensation for their trials in the secular world' (*ibid.*, p. 259). This is seen in opposition to box pews and pew rents. One Tractarian cleric wrote that

> The world has come into our churches to mark out too distinctly the RICH and the POOR, where RELIGION only in former times distinguished the holy from the unholy. Now the naves of our churches are too much secularized and defaced by *pews*, marking out the wealthy and the great; and open seats marking out the poor . . . No, this *cannot be right.*' (William Bennett in 1845, quoted in Herring 2002, p. 119)

So new Tractarian churches would have no box pews: anyone would be able to sit anywhere. An early example is St Saviour's in Leeds, which was paid for anonymously by Pusey. It was built in one of the new working class areas to the east of the city and opened in 1845 with the support of Dr W. F. Hook, an entrepreneurial vicar of Leeds (who arranged for the building of several new churches across the rapidly growing city). Hook had himself had been inspired by the Oxford Movement, and in 1839 had asked Newman and Pusey to support the building of a new church. In a letter to them he wrote 'so much is talked here about the Oxford sayings and writings, that I should like also to let my people to see what are Oxford *doings*' (Yates 1975, p. 3). In 1842, after the publication of Newman's Tract 90 and the attendant furore, Hook began to have doubts about the project. However, Pusey was not to be deflected and the church was built and dedicated by a reluctant Charles Longley, the Bishop of Ripon, who was cool about the Romanizing tendencies of the Tractarians, though he supported their return to a high doctrine of the church and its ministry. Longley blocked a number of Tractarian features of the new building but allowed Pusey to put a carved inscription above the main door: 'Ye who enter here, pray for the sinner who built it' (*ibid.*, pp. 3–4). For many years parishioners did not know who this was. The building of St Saviour's demonstrates, though, the early commitment of the Oxford Movement to serving the poor as much as the rich.

The strength of feeling behind this commitment is demonstrated by an account of the consecration of St Saviour's by Robert Gray (who would later become Bishop of Cape Town):

> I shall not easily forget the glorious services of that day . . . The earnest burst of prayer from that whole congregation was such as I never heard before . . . I have never seen anything so striking as the devotion . . . Laity of my own age and station sobbing aloud, and engaged for hours in prayer – most of the congregation spending the time before the service (a full hour at times) in reading the Psalms, or kneeling in private devotion, and Pusey's sermons most awakening. (Rowell 1983, p. 166)

The type of theology underlying this levelling agenda is illustrated by Robert Wilberforce who was archdeacon of the East Riding of Yorkshire, a son of the evangelical William Wilberforce and one of the leaders of the Oxford movement (before his reception into the Roman Catholic Church in 1854). He first described how the church 'must preach humility in the palace and self-respect in the lowly hovels of the poor. It must enforce such lessons of self-denial as may mitigate the glare of earthly splendour, while it compensates the afflicted for the necessary privations of their lot.' Addressing the clergy of the East Riding in 1846 he then provided the following theological justification for this agenda, a justification with its roots in the incarnation itself:

> the Church of Christ is the real bond of national life, the true principle of concord among men, the redresser of the fall, the assertion of a federal being and family alliance, whereby all members of Christ are made members of one another.

If only churchmen could realize 'the marvellous fact of his Incarnation, that crowning mystery, whereby GODHEAD and Manhood, whereby matter and spirit are indissolubly combined', then they might truly understand 'their birth-right' as 'members of the Christian family'. The church, then, had its own authority rooted in Christ's incarnation, an authority over every member of society quite distinct from the authority of the state. Wilberforce wanted church people to truly absorb this theology into their whole way of thinking: 'Such a habit would re-act upon their belief, as well as upon their worship; they would understand better the purposes for which they met, and the nature of that society which held them together' (Skinner 2004, pp. 259–60). Catholic renewal, then, was ultimately about bringing every member of society back into the church, the body of Christ, a society of equals distinct from the state.

This social levelling for communal solidarity was illustrated at one of the most famous Oxford Movement churches, St Alban's in Holborn. It was opened in 1862 in an area of great deprivation to the north of the City of London. Conditions in the poor districts of London were desperate, with squalor, disease and often starvation being common: one priest wrote of the 'the murky atmosphere of fog and dust' pervading the narrow courts and alleys, with half-naked children playing in the gutter 'many of them stunted, half-witted and deformed, and all wan and sickly looking' (Rowell 1983, p. 117). Alexander Mackonochie was the vicar of St Alban's from 1862 to 1882, and to the condescending wonder of many outside observers, he made it very clear that the church was for everyone and especially for the poor. Slowly but surely he encouraged them to come into the church and make it their own: 'The bonnetless and the shoeless were in sufficient numbers, and as there were no pew-rents and no appropriations, they were enabled to feel that they had as good a right to their own church as anyone else' (M. Reynolds in Hylson-Smith 1998, p. 70).

To encourage all age groups to belong to the church Mackonochie developed guilds and associations for men and boys, and for women and girls, and various other agencies ranging from a blanket-loan fund to a cricket club. The results were dramatic: 'From the time of its consecration until 1867 there was steady progress, with large and increasing congregations. The annual total number of communicants rose from about 3,000 to more than 18,000 . . .' (*ibid.*, p. 71).

What, though, was the nature of the religion that these poor parishioners would find within these new churches? St Saviour's and St Alban's were only early examples of a type of church that would soon be appearing across many of the industrial cities of Britain. What kind of discipleship was at the heart of their worship and corporate life in general and how did it find expression in ritual, music and buildings?

Discussion Questions

1 What are the theological reasons for the Church of England either strengthening or weakening its connections with the state?
2 'The LORD JESUS CHRIST gave His SPIRIT to His Apostles; they in turn laid their hands on those who should succeed them; and these again on others; and so the sacred gift has been handed down to our present Bishops' (Newman in Tract 1). How can this doctrine be supported? How can it be criticized?
3 The Oxford Movement opposed pew rents so that the poor could see that the church belonged to them as much as to the rich. What would be the equivalent kind of action in churches today?

Further Reading

Chadwick, Owen (1960), *The Mind of the Oxford Movement*, London: A & C Black.

Chandler, Michael (2003), *An Introduction to the Oxford Movement*, London: SPCK.

Herring, George (2002), *What was the Oxford Movement?*, London: Continuum.

Nockles, Peter (2003), in S. Platten, ed., *Anglicanism and the Western Christian Tradition*, Norwich: Canterbury Press, pp. 144–91.

Nockles, Peter (1994), *The Oxford Movement in Context: Anglican High Churchmanship 1760–1867*, Cambridge: Cambridge University Press.

Pickering, W. S. F. (2008), *Anglo-Catholicism: A Study in Religious Ambiguity*, second edition, Cambridge: James Clarke and Co.

Skinner, S. A. (2004), *Tractarians and the 'Condition of England': the Social and Political Thought of the Oxford Movement*, Oxford: Clarendon.

7

Catholic Religion

7.1 *Preaching Boxes into Temples*: the Camden Society

Box pews were not the only feature of church buildings that the Tractarians wanted to change. The whole layout and decoration of the church needed purging of Erastianism (which is the domination of the church by the state). Church buildings needed their focus to be the celebration of the sacraments, which meant clearing out massive three-decker pulpits, restoring a clear view from the nave where people sat to the altar at the east end, and generally refurbishing the sanctuary and chancel within which the altar stood. The font was also to be reinstated in a prominent position near the main entrance, and in medieval parish churches ancient sedilias (seats for the priest, deacon and subdeacon), aumbries (recesses in the wall for sacred vessels) and piscinas (bowls with a drain into the churchyard for washing the sacred vessels) were to be uncovered. Churches were to cease being simple meeting houses or preaching conventicles and restored to being temples or shrines where, through the sacramental rites, the holy of holies would become present once more.

It was two Cambridge undergraduates who, inspired by what they read and heard from Oxford, launched this movement. John Mason Neale (1818–66) who also became a great hymn-writer, and Benjamin Webb (1819–85) decided in 1839 to found what they called the Cambridge Camden Society. They wanted the society to forward the cause of 'Ecclesiology'. By 'Ecclesiology' they meant the principles which guided medieval church builders and in particular the Gothic style of the decorated period. This was not just for aesthetic reasons but because it embodied the expression of a Catholic sacramental theology. Hence, for them,

> [Baptismal] regeneration is symbolized by octagonal fonts; the Atonement by a cruciform plan and by gable crosses; the Communion of Saints by monuments and the lay chapel. Windows symbolize the Light of the World; a circle above a triple window typifies the crown of the King of Kings; a hood mould above all three lancets means the unity of the Godhead. A two-light window symbolizes the two Natures of Christ ... (Basil Clarke in Rowell 1983, p. 102)

Neale and Webb published tracts and pamphlets, including the unambiguous 'Twenty-three Reasons for Getting Rid of Church Pews'. They opened a list of members and quickly gained a wide membership including many bishops and patronage from the Archbishop of Canterbury. They stated how they were offended by the condition of many parish churches, which had become mere 'preaching boxes' often used without any sense of reverence. Not only were pews rented out to the wealthy but stoves for heating were often placed in inappropriate places, including the sanctuary. (Whitby Parish church today, with its box pews, iron stoves and chimney stacks presents a typical example of what the Camden Society was against). It set about establishing principles for restoring churches to their original pattern, where the altar rather than the pulpit would be the primary focus of the building and where the whole fabric would be restored and decorated, so enhancing the experience of worship.

The Society's advocacy of the medieval Gothic form was encouraged and inspired by the brilliant Augustus Pugin (1812–52), a Roman Catholic writer and architect who regarded the Gothic form as the purest architectural style for churches dedicated to Eucharistic worship. (Pugin would later assist Charles Barry in designing the new Houses of Parliament.) Neale and Webb promoted their ideas through the journal *The Ecclesiologist,* and developed a number of manuals on how to design every aspect of a neo-Gothic church. In *A Few Words to Church Builders* they gave advice on building a new church including the style suited to the size of the church, and stipulated that as an absolute minimum a church should have a chancel as well as a nave. They also advised on the style of the windows, the use of stained glass and the symbolism to be used for saints depicted within them, and the need for an octagonal font. In *A Few Words to Church Wardens* they gave advice on how to keep damp out of the church by keeping the church yard from being overgrown; also how to look after the windows, and the altar: 'It is a shame to see in many Parish churches a shabby table because it is good for nothing else'. Their comments on the current state of fonts were heartfelt: 'I need not say how painful it is, on lifting up the cover of the Font, to find it used as a box to hold rubbish, torn books, ends of tallow candles, and the like'. *A Few Words* also includes an appeal not to teach the school children in the church because 'the children get to look on the church as a common place' (Webster 2003, pp. 201, 206).

Neale set a very high standard:

> A Church is not as it should be, till *every* window is filled with stained glass, till every inch of floor is covered with encaustic tiles, till there is a Rood screen glowing with the brightest tints and with gold, nay, if we would arrive at perfection, the roof and walls must be painted and frescoed. For it may safely be asserted that ancient churches in general were so adorned. (Rowell 1983, p. 104)

The supreme example of this approach to church building is All Saints, Margaret Street, just off Oxford Street in London, designed by William Butterfield and built between 1849 and 1859. From the exterior the church is hidden behind other buildings and unassuming. But on entering the building visitors have their breath taken away by a mesmerizing richness of colour and design. This leads the eye to the sanctuary, where the altar is placed and where the holy mysteries of the mass are celebrated. The church is widely regarded as a masterpiece of its type and an inspirational example of how the principles of Catholic sacramental theology represented by the Oxford Movement could be visually expressed. The Camden Society hailed it as a church 'in which the embodiment and the success of our principles find their best illustrations' (*ibid.*, p. 104).

Rowell sums up the wider significance of the ecclesiologists: 'to their ardent belief in an archetypal symbolism of church architecture we owe the common conceptions of what a proper church building ought to be' (*ibid.*, p. 104). Some, though, were not impressed. Francis Close, the Evangelical incumbent of Cheltenham and later Dean of Carlisle, published a pamphlet entitled *The Restoration of Churches is the Restoration of Popery*. In general, however, the Cambridge Camden Society helped to energize and guide a massive programme of church building that swept the country in the middle of the century (helped by the relatively low cost of building with stone in this period). Every city and town and many villages witnessed either the construction of Victorian Gothic churches or the sensitive restoration of medieval cathedrals and churches. More churches were built in Britain in the mid-Victorian period than in any century since the middle ages, and most of them are still visible within the urban and rural landscapes of this country today.

7.2 *Ritual in Worship*: from Pimlico to Edinburgh

Catholic theology, church re-ordering and neo-Gothic architecture were not the only distinctive features of the Catholic revival within Anglicanism. The ways in which worship was conducted were also dramatically reformed. The early leaders of the Oxford Movement had been 'high and dry' when it came to the conduct of worship: while their theology was 'high' their worship was 'dry': there was no thought of ornate ritual or vestments or incense but a plain and undemonstrative style of leading worship that was little different from Protestant ways. In the second half of the nineteenth century, however, this began to change and with that change came some intense persecution of the movement.

One of the first churches to introduce innovations was St Barnabas', Pimlico, London, under William Bennett (quoted above p. 115). This church was founded out of the smart parish church of St Paul's, Knightsbridge, in 1846–47, to serve the poor of the parish. Bennett was a devoted pastor as well as being one of the leaders of the Oxford Movement. He knew that preaching theological principles from the pulpit would not be enough: there was a need for some visual representation of the theology of the Oxford Movement, and especially of the central place of the sacraments in discipleship. He looked to the ritual of the medieval Catholic church to do this. So he placed two lighted candles on the altar, and faced east for the prayer of consecration (rather than standing on the north side of the table, as stipulated in the rubrics at the start of the Lord's Supper in the BCP). Furthermore, he allowed some of the communicants to receive the bread directly into their mouths (so that they did not finger the body of Christ); nor did he hand over the chalice to the communicant during communion but, to show greater reverence for the blood of Christ, took it to their lips himself. He also began his sermons with the refrain 'In the name of the Father and of the

Son and of the Holy Ghost', and used the sign of the cross. These were medieval Catholic practices and were also found in the contemporary Roman Catholic Church, which had recently been legalized and revived with a great flourish in Britain (attracting high profile converts such as Newman and Manning, as we have seen). Here lay trouble for Bennett, for where he saw ancient Catholicism others saw 'popery'. The Bishop of London, Charles Blomfield, objected to Bennett's innovations and sought to get them stopped. The case was reported in the press and soon St Barnabas' was swamped with supporters and with angry opponents who accused Bennett of popery. They threatened to pull the church down and the police were called to keep order. Bennett was eventually forced to resign by Blomfield (Chadwick 1971, pp. 301–3).

But the controversy drew attention to the 'ritualist' cause and other parishes decided to support it. In 1857 one of the assistant clergy at St Barnabas', Charles Lowder (1820–80), moved to a mission house in the very poor East London parish of St George's-in-the-East. He moved with a fraternity of other priests calling themselves the Society of the Holy Cross, and they created a kind of religious community in the mission house (following a pattern of living together that the clergy at St Saviour's in Leeds had pioneered). They organized daily prayer, frequent preaching, a boy's choir and Bible instruction classes. They constructed an iron church in the garden of the house where they started to wear vestments for the celebration of communion (rather than normal cassock and surplice), again following medieval and current Roman practice. As in Pimlico, fierce opposition developed, mainly from people outside the parish, who stirred up crowds from within the parish to disrupt the services. In 1859 worship was disturbed for months by shouting, whistling, letting off firecrackers and vandalism to church furnishings. But Lowder was 'a brave withdrawn man with a steely will' (Chadwick 1971, p. 498). He was not to be deterred and he noted 'The very dregs of the people were taught to think about religion. Many were brought to church through the unhappy notoriety . . . and some who came to scoff remained to worship' (Rowell 1983, p. 131).

These riots were reported in the national press and the National Protestant Society and the 'Anti-Puseyite League' sponsored some of the protesters.

Nonetheless Lowder and his fellow-workers persisted in their labours, and the work progressed. Public interest and sympathy were aroused by the evident dedication of the fraternity, and in particular by the devoted service of

Lowder and his staff during the East London cholera epidemic of 1856. By the time of his death in 1880 Lowder had won the affection and respect of the East End population whom he had lovingly served for almost forty years. He had gained the honourable title of Father Lowder . . . (Hylson-Smith 1998, pp. 69–70)

Within all this, ritualism in Eucharistic worship was central, because it 'embodied as nothing else could the sense of the reality of Divine grace in a way which could be grasped by the poor and unlettered' (Rowell 1983, p. 117). Lowder 'considered that it was as much his duty as a parish priest to put before the eyes of his people the pattern of the worship in Heaven, as it was his duty to preach the Gospel' (*ibid.*, p. 133).

Alexander Mackonochie (1825–87), already mentioned above, continued this tradition of using Catholic ritual in worship, which again generated violent and persistent protest from parties outside the parish, including legal action sponsored by the Church Association. This Protestant body spent £40,000 in legal action between 1868 and 1880, and scores of priests were prosecuted. The association objected most strongly to the doctrine of the real presence of Christ in the Eucharist, and tried to ban the elevation of the bread and the wine during the Eucharistic prayer (which symbolized this doctrine), as well as excessive kneeling during the prayer of consecration, ceremonial use of incense, adding water to the wine in the chalice (another medieval practice) and altar lights. 'The Church Association hounded Mackonochie for year after year, but in the end the ritualism was not stopped, little was achieved, and Mackonochie himself was a broken man. He died on holiday, in the snow at night on a bare mountain in Scotland, guarded only by his two dogs' (Hylson-Smith 1998, p. 72). His funeral, like that of Lowder, drew vast and silent crowds who demonstrated a deep and lasting respect for this pioneer of Catholic renewal.

The persecution of these pioneers helped to raise the profile of what was now being called Anglo-Catholicism.

To illustrate the kind of impact this movement had in countless parishes across the country, and also to show how it spread beyond the Church of England, Old St Paul's Church in Edinburgh can be mentioned. This church belonged to the Scottish Episcopal Church (as opposed to the Presbyterian Church of Scotland) and in the 1880s was surrounded by the most run down and deprived district in the Old Town of Edinburgh. The church was hidden away next to some bridge arches and had an unprepossessing and uninviting exterior. But the worship within was systematically and firmly changed under the leadership of two Rectors, R. Mitchell-Innes (1886–98) and his curate A. E. Laurie, who became Rector 1898 and stayed until 1937. The first surpliced choir was created in 1885, and a subscription was started to build a new organ. The building was extended, with the chancel floor being raised above that of the nave and laid with marble, to create a sense of the high altar being raised above the level of the people. Old pine choir benches were then replaced by carved stalls, and an ornate reredos behind the high altar was completed in 1896, again to draw attention to the high altar. The Sung Eucharist gradually replaced Mattins as the main Sunday service. Coloured stoles for the priest were introduced, then full vestments (replacing the traditional cassock and surplice). Wafer bread replaced common bread, and incense was introduced, which 'caused a fuss'. Altar servers were introduced in 1905. All the changes were 'carefully explained and resistance was firmly extinguished'. Everything was done in a search for a form of worship that would glorify God with a colour and beauty that would enliven the drab lives of those who lived in the most congested slums in Scotland (Holloway 1989, pp. 35–6).

As with the other churches mentioned above, the renewal of worship was only one aspect of a wider life of Old St Paul's in the community. A number of societies were created, such as the Band of Hope, the Temperance Society, the Working Men's Society and guilds that cared for every age group. Entertainment events took place, such as soirees, tableaux vivants, limelight transparencies, gymnastic displays, concerts and an Indian Clubs display. There was also social action in an area were half the children went barefoot, where there were high rates of drunkenness and crime amid the wretched poverty of the slum. Mitchell-Innes and Laurie 'saw it as their personal mission, and that of Old St Paul's, to bring help and comfort to the hungry, the deprived and the suffering, and much of their days were taken up with an unending round of visiting poor one-room and two-room houses, up the stairs of the tall tenements' (*ibid.*, p. 33). And in 1902 Laurie acquired the lease of a nearby building to open a dispensary, directed by a qualified doctor and a trained nursing sister and helped by a number of medical students.

All this shows a distinctive combination of ritualism centred on the sacrament of the Eucharist, with a Catholic theology underpinning that worship, and with social engagement and action in the wider community beyond the congregation. Old St Paul's is a good example of the breadth and energy of Anglo-Catholicism at the turn of the century.

Some statistics can illustrate the impact of ritualism on the wider life of the church and especially on its worship. It has been estimated that between 1841 and 1871 Tractarian clergy never made up more than 5 per cent of the total number of clergy (Herring 2002, pp. 75–6). But yet by the beginning of the twentieth century, eastward facing celebration, weekly communion and candles on the altar had become the norm, with a widespread acceptance of vestments. Reservation of the sacrament and confession, however, remained contentious. A more general renewal of ritual in worship, and especially of Eucharistic worship, is indicated by the following: in 1854 a daily service was held in only 650 churches in England, whereas in 1919 Morning and Evening Prayer were read daily in 5427 churches. In 1854 there was a weekly service of Holy Communion in 128 churches (in other churches it took place on a monthly or quarterly basis), but by 1919 this figure had reached just under 12,000 churches, while the celebration of daily Communion had risen to 1215 churches, compared with just three in 1854 (Kaye-Smith in Pickering 2008, pp. 88–9).

One other indicator of the growing strength Anglo-Catholicism in the nineteenth century, to its high point at the start of the twentieth, is membership of the English Church Union, a society for those dedicated to the advancement of Catholic practice and understanding in the Church of England. When it began in 1860 it had 200 members, from 1860 to 1880 it grew to 17,700, from 1880 to 1894 it doubled its membership, and by 1901 membership was put at 39,000 (*ibid.*, p. 93). Women were allowed to join but were called 'women associates'. The Union was organized into 64 district unions, and within these into 377 local branches (*ibid.*). Pickering comments that by any reckoning the growth of the English Church Union must be seen as a great achievement for Anglo-Catholicism, even though some members would call themselves Tractarian rather than Anglo-Catholic, retaining a loyalty to the High Church tradition over any desire to move closer to Roman Catholicism.

Two hymns illustrate the kind of atmosphere and spirituality of ritualism. The first, 'Let all mortal flesh keep silence', was based on words from an ancient liturgy of the Greek Orthodox Church and put into verse form by the Revd Gerard Moultrie in 1869. It is a hymn full of awe and mystery, but its second verse makes a direct link between the descent of Christ described in verse 1 and the elements of bread and wine in the Eucharist. It therefore gives us an evocative statement of the doctrine of the real presence of Christ in the Eucharist, a statement that fits perfectly with the ritual of St Barnabas', Pimlico and Old St Paul's, Edinburgh:

The first verse begins by introducing the one who comes among his people:

Let all mortal flesh keep silence,
and with fear and trembling stand;
ponder nothing earthly minded,
for with blessing in his hand
Christ our God to earth descendeth,
our full homage to demand.

The second verse then indicates where precisely this is to be found:

King of kings, yet born of Mary,
as of old on earth he stood,
Lord of lords in human vesture,
in the Body and the Blood
he will give to all the faithful
his own self for heavenly food.

Francis Stanfield (1835–1914) expressed this theology in a more pietistic form in his hymn 'Sweet Sacrament divine'. In this hymn the host within the home of the Eucharistic bread and wine is personalized to such an extent that it is seen as accomplishing the work of salvation. The first and last verses provide good examples of this:

Sweet Sacrament divine,
hid in thine earthly home;
lo! Round thy lowly shrine,
with suppliant hearts we come;
Jesus, to thee our voice we raise
In songs of love and heartfelt praise
sweet Sacrament divine.

Sweet Sacrament divine,
earth's light and jubilee,

in thy far depths doth shine
the Godhead's majesty;
sweet light, so shine on us, we pray
that earthly joys may fade away:
sweet Sacrament divine.

7.3 *Personal Discipline*: Confession and the Religious Life

Catholic Anglicans were to have sacramental worship at the heart of their discipleship, for this was where their unity with Christ was given physical and spiritual expression. This worship was to be in a Christian fellowship that did not derive its legitimacy from establishment with the state but had its own inherent authority, coming through the apostolic succession from Christ himself. It was a fellowship for all people and not just the wealthy, which meant it was specially welcoming to the poor and marginalized in society. It was a worship that would take place in buildings ordered and decorated for this purpose, with a focus upon font and altar rather than lectern and pulpit (though these still had a part to play). The worship was to be ordered with a form of ritual that would draw attention to the real presence of Christ within the sacrament. This would, in turn, transform church buildings from being meeting halls to being temples, where Christ, the holy of holies, would be present at the altar.

But what of personal discipline and devotion? The Catholic revival was not just concerned with what went on in church on Sundays. It was also concerned with the rest of the week, as it were, and how the disciples lived out their lives as Catholic Christians. There were a number of aspects of medieval devotion recalled by the revival, including observing Lent, going on retreat and keeping a rule of life (a regular pattern of prayer and giving). Three examples of this disciplined and devotional approach to the Christian life can be highlighted: the saying of confession before a priest, the revival of the religious or monastic life, and in the twentieth century the rise of mystical approaches to prayer.

Confession

John Keble was the first to see the need for a revival of the sacrament of confession. With a new emphasis on the Eucharist coming from the Oxford Movement, and more frequent celebrations, he believed that worshippers should be given the opportunity to prepare properly for it. He pointed to the way the Order for the Anointing of the Sick in the BCP contained the traditional words of confession and he argued that these words should be made available for regular use by everyone. Keble himself was used as a confessor by a number of friends and acquaintances and in his letters he gives sympathetic and charitable counselling to others (Rowell 1983, p. 37). He believed the practice of confession would allow a parish priest to know and guide his people, so that they could be led gently to speak of the deep matters of the faith and of their own spiritual needs. Keble, then, saw counselling or spiritual direction as part of confession, but he did not wish to give 'minute and incessant direction' (*ibid.*). He saw the confessor, himself included, as unable and unworthy to give expert guidance. In 1846 Pusey asked him to be his confessor, but he shrank from this: 'as to directing you I know I shall be utterly bewildered, were it only from ignorance and inexperience. You must really think beforehand what is most likely to do you good.' Nevertheless he heard Pusey's confession and he still thought it a good discipline for everyone to adopt. He thought the advice of the confessor should be 'a few grains of old English common sense, or rather of Christian prudence and charity, applied to the realities of English life: a grace to be specially prayed for as well as cultivated . . .' In slightly sentimental Victorian vein, he looked forward to the sight of 'a noble-hearted English peasant on his knees in humble confession, making an unreserved offering of himself, and never dreaming that what he is about is at all out of the common' (*ibid.*). Pusey was more emphatic: 'I am more and more convinced that nothing except an extensive system of confession can remedy our evils' (*ibid.*, p. 92).

In the second stage of the movement when ritualism began to spread out into parishes across the British Isles the encouragement of confession followed in its wake. In a 'Mission to London' in 1869, involving leaders such as Lowder, Mackonochie and Bennett and stretching across 120 different churches, confession played an important part in some of them. At St Alban's, Holborn, the practice of the clergy hearing confessions by special appointment was abandoned in favour of the clergy being in church at fixed times so that parishioners could make a regular habit of attending confession 'without fuss or mystification' (*ibid.*, p. 135). But not everyone was impressed. The Evangelical journal *Record* viewed with alarm the place given to confession in the Mission, commenting that 'the attempt seems to be one which grafts the earnestness of revival preaching on the sacerdotal errors of Romanism, and associates the call to repentance with the deadly poison of the Confessional' (*ibid.*, pp. 134–5). Others also condemned it, including Lord Shaftesbury and, more surprisingly, Bishop Samuel Wilberforce who on other points was a supporter of the Oxford Movement. He thought the practice was substituting 'confession to a man for the opening of the heart to God' (*ibid.*, p. 136). But in general terms in the late nineteenth century both Evangelical and Catholic traditions were developing and encouraging clergy to offer counselling to their people and the rise of confession fitted comfortably within this. The provision of help and guidance of individual parishioners was becoming more and more important within Anglicanism (Anthony Russell in *ibid.*, p. 137), and confession became established within this wider trend.

By the turn of the century, then, confession had become well established in many Anglo-Catholic parishes, though it was hardly ever obligatory. It is very difficult to estimate how many people went to confession but for some it became the litmus test of commitment. One priest from a poor parish wrote the following in his parish magazine:

> Then as to the number of confessions made. To my mind this is by far the truest test of progress of spiritual work. And this is certainly increasingly becoming better proportioned to the Communions made – even more amongst men and lads, as I have before more than once noted. (Pickering 2008, pp. 80–1)

Finally it is worth noting that in the twentieth century the practice of confession also grew amongst middle-of-the-road Anglicans. Also it was no longer condemned by Evangelicals. The latter half of the twentieth century eventually saw, however, a general decline in the use of confession across all denominations, not least within Roman Catholicism (*ibid.*, pp. 83–4).

The Religious Life

But what of those men and women who wished to express a complete personal discipline and devotion within this tradition? What could they do or where could they go beyond attending their local church? One answer was first mooted by Pusey in 1839: that committed women might join a 'sisters of charity', who would 'begin by regular employment as nurses, in hospitals and lunatic asylums, in which last Christian nursing is so sadly missed'(Rowell 1983, p. 93). In this Pusey was influenced by French seventeenth-century religious communities, such as the sisters of St Vincent de Paul, who combined a monastic lifestyle with service to the poor. Dr Hook, the Vicar of Leeds, was supportive of the idea and had a sister who was drawn to such a life, but he warned that such a development might arouse suspicion from those who opposed anything resembling a Catholic religious order. Pusey, though, was not to be deflected. In 1841 he enabled Marian Rebecca Hughes to become the first woman to make a religious profession in the modern Church of England. She made her profession in Oxford before Pusey and then attended a communion service celebrated by Newman at the university church. It would take a few years before a community was formed around her, but in 1849 she became the first Superior of the Convent of the Holy and Undivided Trinity at Oxford. Meanwhile in 1845 Pusey had founded another female religious community at Park Village, Regent's Park in London. These sisters were to visit the poor or the sick in their own homes, visit hospitals, workhouses, or prisons, instruct destitute children, and assist in the burial of the dead. By 1850 they had established a daily pattern of saying the monastic services (the offices) interspersed with their work commitments. One novice reported the pattern in the following way:

The sisters rose at five . . . The service called Lauds was at six a.m., said in the Oratory . . . at a quarter to seven the Sisters assembled in the same room and Prime was said . . . Breakfast followed, which was taken in silence; indeed silence was observed all day, except at the hours appointed for recreation. After the meal we said Terce and then went to hear Morning Prayers read in the church . . . The Sisters who taught in the poor school went to their duties . . . The school lasted till twelve, when we went home and said Sext. We had dinner at twenty minutes to one, still in silence. The food was plain, good, and sufficient. After dinner we talked together in the Common Room. At three we said None ... The school was dismissed for the day at half-past four. At five there were three quarters of an hour for spiritual reading, then Vespers. Supper followed at six o'clock, and after it a few moments' ... relaxation. We then prepared for church: ... those who could not go after the fatigues of the day read the service at home. On our return from church at eight o'clock Compline was said, and the Sisters remained in the Oratory after its conclusion for private devotion till twenty minutes past nine, when Mattins was said. (*Ibid.*, p. 94)

But the community was not able to find the stability it needed at Park Village because it was under the direction of a local parish priest who had a 'cramping effect'. It needed autonomy, and so in 1856 it moved away, joining another community of sisters at Devonport in the Diocese of Exeter, where Bishop Philpotts (the same Philpotts caught up in the Gorham case: see Chapter 3.3) was a keen supporter. They became the Society of the Holy Trinity. Their superior, Lydia Sellon, recognized the importance of contemplative prayer within the life of the community and arranged for some sisters to have this as their primary vocation. Pusey regarded Miss Sellon as 'the restorer after three centuries of the Religious Life in the English Church'. Rowell comments that 'there can be little doubt that what lay behind this was both Miss Sellon's organising genius and the trust that grew between her and Pusey through difficult years' (*ibid.*, p. 95).

From the mid-century onwards a number of other female communities were founded, the most famous being the Wantage Sisters, founded in 1848, and the Community of St Margaret, founded at East Grinstead in 1855 by Neale. These were also 'active' or 'mixed' communities, combining the monastic life with a life of service. The East Grinstead sisters were unusual because they served the rural poor rather than the urban poor. A community of deaconesses was founded by Elizabeth Ferard in 1861, and in 1907 the first enclosed or contemplative order for women was founded, the 'Sisters of the Love of God' at Fairacres in Oxford. At about the same time another community, the Sisters of the Community of the Holy Comforter, also decided to become contemplatives and eventually moved to Malling Abbey in Kent. In the twentieth century Franciscan sisters created a contemplative community at Freeland in Oxfordshire.

For men the development of religious communities was slower. When Newman left Oxford and moved to Littlemore in 1841 he lived a community life with some companions, but there were no vows. Some of the Anglo-Catholic slum priests lived in a similar way in their vicarages but again vows were not taken. But in the last part of the nineteenth century and early twentieth century a number of male communities were established, three of which can be mentioned here. Richard Benson, who was vicar of Cowley then a village about two miles from Oxford, was the pioneer in 1865. He founded a community named the Society of St John the Evangelist and the brethren quickly became known as the Cowley Fathers (even though some were not ordained). It was established to provide a life of prayer under monastic vows and also to undertake missionary and educational work. Its commitment to mission meant that its brethren travelled the length and breadth of the country as missioners, including leading a ten day mission at Old St Paul's in Edinburgh in 1893. The Society grew quickly and established separate congregations in the US, with houses at Cambridge and Boston, Massachusetts, and in Canada with a house at Bracebridge, Ontario.

Another male religious community was founded in 1892 by Charles Gore who was then the principal of Pusey House in Oxford and, after Pusey's death in 1882, the widely acknowledged leader of the movement. Gore was something of a prophetic visionary. He gathered a small group of men together and they named the new venture the Community of the Resurrection. The following year when he became vicar of Radley in Oxfordshire the community moved to the vicarage there, and then in 1898 to Mirfield in West Yorkshire where it could be in closer contact with the industrial population of the north of England. Gore's vision was for a community that was adapted to the changed circumstances of the modern age. The pattern of community life was more open and flexible than in other communities, though when Walter Frere was Superior from 1902 he steered it towards a more conventional monastic pattern (Gore himself found he was unable to live with the brethren and in 1894 moved to Westminster to become a canon at the Abbey).

The Community of the Resurrection, in keeping with the academic interests of its founder, combined the monastic life with educational and scholarly work. A theological college for working class ordinands was opened in the old stables of the house at Mirfield, and quickly established itself as a major source of Anglo-Catholic clergy for the Church of England. Brethren also travelled to South Africa and what is now Zimbabwe (then Rhodesia) and opened secondary schools and a theological college, which have educated and trained future leaders of post-independent Zimbabwe and South Africa, both in the state and church (later alumni including the astonishing Archbishop Desmond Tutu, the scourge of apartheid and Nobel Peace Prize laureate). One of the most famous of the brethren was Trevor Huddleston who, when Rector of Sophiatown in post-war Johannesburg, became a prophetic agent of resistance against the apartheid regime and author of the bestselling *Naught for Your Comfort*, which in the 1950s alerted the public in Britain and further afield to what was happening in South Africa (see further Wilkinson 1992).

A very different community has been the Society of St Francis. This was founded in the 1930s by several groups who had been inspired to live by the ideals of St Francis of Assisi. One of the these groups had been living at Hilfield in Dorset from 1921, led first by Brother Giles and then Brother Douglas and who worked to help unemployed and homeless men who tramped the roads in Dorset. The brothers provided a home for these destitute men and campaigned to change the laws which forced them to walk the roads of Britain in search of work. Another community ran a parish and boys' home in London. Another was formed in India in 1922 to foster a multi-racial community and had an English house at St Ives run by Father Algy Robertson, one of their number whose ill-health had forced him to return to Britain. During the 1930s it became apparent that they would all gain strength if they united. This was especially encouraged by their wider network of supporters, called the Third Order of St Francis (as opposed to the brothers who would become the First Order). Douglas and Algy led this merger of communities and the first life vows of the Society of St Francis were taken in 1937. In 1964 a female Franciscan community, the Community of St Francis, also came under the wing of the Society. Today there are around 70 brothers in the European Province, with more in Australia and New Zealand and 80 in the Melanesian Brotherhood in the Pacific region. There are around 30 sisters as well (see further Dunstan 1997).

Meanwhile the Third Order, of lay and ordained men and women living in their own homes and committed to keeping a simple rule of life, has continued to grow and flourish to the point where there are now around 1800 members in its European province and more in North America, Australia, New Zealand and elsewhere. While many of these Third Order Franciscans would not see themselves as modern representatives of the Oxford Movement and Anglo-Catholicism (Evangelicalism has always been an important influence in Anglican Franciscanism), their commitment to a rule of life and to a community, albeit dispersed, shows how the ideals that Pusey revived in the 1840s have now spread far beyond monks and nuns. Here is a way in which the discipline and devotion of the medieval Catholic church has been revived and adapted for the conditions of the modern world, in a way which makes that inheritance available for every Anglican.

Discussion Questions

1 Font and altar, or lectern and pulpit: which should be the focus of churches today?
2 Lowder 'considered that it was as much his duty as a parish priest to put before the eyes of his people the pattern of the worship in Heaven, as it was his duty to preach the Gospel' (Rowell 1983, p. 133). How would you defend Lowder? How would you criticize him?
3 How much truth is there in Bishop Samuel Wilberforce's claim that confession to a human being is a substitute 'for the opening of the heart to God'?

Further Reading

Chadwick, Owen (1971), *The Victorian Church*, Volume 1, 3rd edition, London: Adam and Charles Black, republished by SCM in 1970.

Dunstan, Peta (1997), *This Poor Sort: History of the European Province of the Society of Saint Francis*, London: Darton, Longman and Todd.

Hill, Rosemary (2008), *God's Architect: Pugin and the Building of Romantic Britain*, Harmondsworth: Penguin.

Pickering, W. S. F. (2008), *Anglo-Catholicism: A Study in Religious Ambiguity*, 2nd edition, Cambridge: James Clarke and Co.

Rowell, Geoffrey (1983), *The Vision Glorious: Themes and Personalities of the Catholic Revival in Anglicanism*, Oxford: Oxford University Press.

Rowell, Geoffrey (1990), 'Anglicanism and Confession', in Rowell and Dudley eds, *Confession and Absolution*, London: SPCK.

Webster, Christopher (2003), *Temples . . . Worthy of His Presence: The Early Publications of the Cambridge Camden Society*, Spire Books.

Wilkinson, Alan (1992), *The Community of the Resurrection: A Centenary History*, London: SCM Press.

Yates, Nigel (2000), *Anglican Ritualism in Victorian Britain 1830–1910*, Oxford: Clarendon Press.

Part 3

Ways of Discipleship from the Enlightenment

8

Reason as Judge

William Blake's pen and watercolour print of Sir Isaac Newton from 1795 gives a sharp insight into our next theme. Newton the mathematical genius (whom we will examine below) was a hero for many caught up in the eighteenth-century Enlightenment in Britain and across Europe. Blake presents Newton as a kind of Greek god, with compass and diagrams in hand, measuring and recording the cosmos. Blake was suggesting, ironically perhaps, that human reason harnessed within scientific enquiry was now able to map and make sense of the whole mysterious reality around us: that humankind can gain the measure of all things. Blake's imaginative drawing shows it was an awe inspiring but dangerous aspiration.

The Enlightenment's elevation of human reason over other authorities such as church tradition and sacred scripture is the subject of this chapter. We examine this elevation especially within Anglicanism, and here a pre-Enlightenment figure is crucial, a theologian who drew on Catholic theology and especially the work of Aquinas as well as the insights of the Reformation and helped establish a distinctively Anglican synthesis. Richard Hooker (1554–1600) was a figure who had relatively little influence in his own lifetime and cannot be described as one of the leaders of the English Reformation but who, gradually and incrementally, through the posthumous publishing and reading of his voluminous works, gained a definitive influence over Anglican self-understanding. His integration of scripture, tradition and the reason of natural law (in a definition drawn from Aquinas) prepared the ground for the moral theology of the Caroline Divines (see Chap. 5) and laid the foundation for Anglicanism's own Enlightenment. He showed that reason, guided by natural law based in the eternal nature of God, has a key role within the choices and dilemmas of daily living. It is because of this elevation of reason that he needs to appear at the head of this third part of this Studyguide.

8.1 *Reason over Tradition*: Richard Hooker's Foundation

Hooker came to prominence when he was a preacher at the Temple courts in London. He later became Rector of Boscombe, where he wrote his major work *The Laws of Ecclesiastical Polity*. In this sub-section we will approach his work by asking a specific question about discipleship, one which can take us to the heart of his work (but which will not allow us to gain a complete overview of his vast and complex system, for which there is no space in these pages). The question is this: what happens when new dilemmas face the follower of Christ and neither scripture nor church tradition is clear what he or she should do?

Hooker gave the following answer: through the use of human 'reason'.

Richard Hooker's life

1554   Born in Exeter.

1558   Elizabeth becomes Queen.

1559   The Act of Settlement, restoring the Protestantism of Edward VI.

1568   Hooker enters Corpus Christi College, Oxford, becoming a Fellow in 1579.

1585   Hooker appointed Master of the Temple, London (that is, a chaplain to the law courts).

1588   English war with Catholic Spain leads to defeat of the Spanish Armada.

1588   Marriage to Joan Churchman.

1591   Appointed to the parish of Boscombe near Salisbury.

1593   *Of the Laws of Ecclesiastical Polity*, Books 1–4 published.

1595   Rector of Bishopsbourne.

1597   *Of the Laws of Ecclesiastical Polity*, Book 5 published.

1600	Hooker dies of complications following a chill (2 Nov).
1648	*Of the Laws of Ecclesiastical Polity*, Books 6 & 8 published.
1662	*Of the Laws of Ecclesiastical Polity*, Book 7 published.

Hooker's theology emerges out of his controversy with the Puritans, and especially with his colleague Walter Travers at the Temple, with whom he sparred when he preached. Hooker would preach in the mornings and Travers preached in the afternoons. It was said that Hooker preached 'Canterbury' and Travers preached 'Geneva'! In particular, Travers claimed that there was only one authority which should guide the Christian life, that of scripture. Any aspect of church life that was not validated by scripture, such as the wearing of vestments, should therefore be abolished.

Hooker's approach, on the other hand, was based on the idea (originally from Aristotle and also employed by Aquinas) of there being a natural law or pattern of characteristic behaviour directing things to their perfection, which Hooker believed to be set down by God and which could be uncovered and defined by human reason. These laws are 'investigable by reason, without the help of revelation' (*Laws* I.ii.6, viii.9). An example would be the law of inheritance: any society needs a clear and orderly way of passing property between generations and while different societies will do this in different ways the general characteristic of having such a law is common to all.

Hooker uses this notion of natural law to defeat the Puritans' claim that scripture is the only authority within the Christian life. For Hooker it is one authority among others, although as a Reformed Protestant he gives it the 'first place both of credit and obedience'. But reason (with its access to natural law) comes next, and after that comes 'the voice of the Church' (that is Tradition):

> What scripture doth plainly deliver, to that first place both of credit and obedience is due; the next whereunto any man can necessarily conclude by force of reason; after these the voice of the Church succeedeth. That which the Church by her ecclesiastical authority shall probably think and define to be true or good, must in congruity of reason overrule all other inferior judgments whatsoever. (Laws V.8.2)

Therefore when scripture is not clear about a certain issue or question it is reason that takes charge and, through returning to the principles of natural law, provides an answer. But when natural law is indifferent to the issue or question, then the tradition of the church comes into play and determines what should happen. So there are three authorities in the Christian life: scripture, which is primary; then the reason of natural law, which is secondary; and then the tradition of the church, which is tertiary, though this tradition still takes precedence over all other kinds of authority, as he mentions above.

So, for example, on ministerial order, the Puritans argued that the New Testament does *not* say there should be a threefold order of bishops, priests and deacons. Instead Calvin argued that scripture shows ministry should be comprised of pastors, doctors (that is, teachers), elders and deacons. He believed that only those things *prescribed* by Scripture should be in the church: everything else was to be removed. Hooker, on the other hand, argued that only those things *prohibited* by Scripture should be removed from the life of the church. There was much in the current life of the church that Scripture was indifferent to (this is the principle of 'adiaphora', adopted from Lutheranism and still employed in ecclesiological debate today: see, for example, the Windsor Report on current disagreements over sexuality (Anglican Communion 2004, paras 87–96). These things could remain if they were congruent with natural law and were part of the longstanding tradition of the church. Scripture, he then pointed out, does not prohibit the threefold ministry: it is something *indifferent* to its authors. Furthermore, this ministry has been found to work effectively over the centuries and is therefore congruent with natural law. Furthermore it has been upheld by church tradition and so has a claim on our continued loyalty. The threefold order is therefore 'reasonable and defensible'. It could be changed in different times if circumstances require it: if there is 'just and reasonable cause to alter them' (*Laws* V.lxv.2).

In the *Laws* generally reason is defended as not only presupposed for an accurate understanding of scripture but as competent to determine a broad range of issues not explicitly covered in scripture. 'Indeed, Hooker held that the Church could reasonably prescribe contrary to a biblical precept, if the purpose of the precept in its historical context could be understood to be irrelevant in current circumstances' (A. S. McGrade in Sykes and Booty 1988, p. 106).

Hooker's theological ethics, then, show how it is possible to be a good Protestant who both subscribes to the primacy of scripture and recognizes that inherited patterns of church life can also be practised (provided they are not prohibited by scripture and are congruent with natural law). This way of thinking provided, for example, a justification for the continuation of the establishment of the Church of England under the crown in Elizabeth's reign: such an arrangement was not prohibited by scripture, it was congruent with the natural law (in that to avoid anarchy people generally need governing by a ruler i.e. a monarch), and it had a place in church tradition. Hooker also showed that it was possible for the Church of England to sometimes appear to be quite Catholic in its outward appearance (as when it recognizes the real presence of Christ in the Eucharist, especially in comparison with the churches of Geneva and Zurich) and yet still be thoroughly Protestant in its theological priorities. The use of the notion of natural law was certainly controversial, and was rejected by the Puritans, but was not illogical from Hooker's point of view. Within the terms that he worked, his *Laws* were a brilliant and thoroughgoing justification of the peculiar church order that Elizabeth had put in place.

8.2 *Reason in Nature and Politics*: Newton and Locke

Hooker elevated reason above church tradition as an authority within the Christian life, but kept it subservient to scripture. The Age of Enlightenment, or as it is sometimes called the Age of Reason, with its origins in the scientific breakthroughs of the seventeenth century and its full philosophical and cultural expression occurring within the eighteenth century, would go one step further and elevate reason *above* scripture as well as tradition. In this section the stories of two paradigmatic Anglican figures are told, stories which show the emergence of a novel form of Christian belief and discipleship within Anglican history.

Sir Isaac Newton (1642–1727), a committed lay member of the Church of England as well as a mathematician and natural philosopher, stands at the headwaters of this age with his supreme application of human reason to the laws of the universe. He was from Lincolnshire and, after an unremarkable career at school, went up to study law at Trinity College, Cambridge. He was not well off and in order to pay his fees he was forced to be a servant for the wealthier students. He quickly discovered mathematics and read all the books he could find on the subject. When the university was forced to close because of an outbreak of plague Newton returned to Lincolnshire and here, apparently purely for his own entertainment, made most of his groundbreaking mathematical discoveries. It was also here, according to legend, that he saw an apple fall off a tree and wondered what made objects fall to the ground. He then returned to Cambridge but, because he was very shy and unable to take criticism, he did not publish his ideas, though some of them began to spread through word of mouth.

In stunningly original ways he pursued research into gravitation and realized that the force which pulled an apple to the ground might be the same one that kept the moon revolving around the earth. He found he could explain motions of celestial objects by the mathematical rules he had deduced during his stay in Lincolnshire, including the rules of centrifugal force, which flings an orbiting body away from the thing it is orbiting. He calculated that an orbiting body is kept in place by a combination of this centrifugal force and the force of gravity, which attracts it to the thing it is orbiting. He also went on to deduce the 'inverse square law' of gravity, which states that the gravitational force between two objects varies by the reverse of the square of their distance (Hill 2004, p. 58).

Other astronomers were thinking along similar lines (including Sir Christopher Wren, the future architect of St Paul's Cathedral) but were puzzled as to why the planets move around the sun in ellipses rather than circles. One of them, Sir Edmund Halley, had invited Newton to dinner and during the meal asked Newton 'if he knew what path a planet would trace if it were governed by the inverse square law alone'. Newton immediately replied that it would indeed be an ellipse. Astonished, Halley asked him how he knew. 'Why,' replied the mathematician, 'I have calculated it' (*ibid.*, p. 59). His calculations, though, could not immediately be found in his chaotic rooms at his college, so he had to re-write them. When Halley saw them he knew that they must be published. So in 1687 he provided the finances to publish the first volume of Newton's *Mathematical Principles of Natural Philosophy*, or the *Principia*, as it came to be known. 'It is generally recognized as the greatest scientific work ever published, in part because Newton successfully explained a whole variety of phenomena, from the motion of cannon balls to the tides of the sea, in terms of a few simple mathematical and physical laws – primarily the laws of gravity' (*ibid.*).

Within the context of this chapter what is also important about the *Principia* is the way it also expressed Newton's religious convictions: belief in God is part and parcel of the admirable order of the universe. He acknowledges Divine transcendence, omnipotence and perfection. God is the Supreme Being, with complete authority over the material universe as well as over human souls, which owe him absolute submission. In a later letter he described how 'when I wrote my treatise about our system, I had an eye upon such principles as might work with considering men for the belief of a Deity; and nothing can rejoice me more than to find it useful for that purpose' (letter to Bentley, 1692, quoted in Hill 2004, p. 62). Reason is being used to support religion, but notice that it is reason and not religion that is judge.

Newton was also keen to uphold the Church of England. He was no supporter of the Catholic policies of James II and when he became a member of parliament he voted to offer the crown to the Protestant William of Orange over James in 1688. However, his application of reason to religion led him into some unorthodox waters. He undertook an extensive study of the Bible and concluded that the doctrine of the Trinity could not be found within its pages, and therefore that Christ was not God but simply the most exalted of God's creatures. This was not unlike the views of the Arians of the Third and Fourth centuries and would have landed Newton in huge controversy if it had become widely known. He was also drawn to a millenarian outlook (the belief that this age is soon to end and will be followed by a thousand years of blessedness before the end of the world), and his thoughts on this were published after his death in the 1733 book *Observations on the Prophecies of Daniel and the Apocalypse of St John*. He was also, strangely, fascinated by alchemy (the attempt to turn base metals into gold). Unsurprisingly he did not make any progress in his investigations.

Another major figure, again a lay person, also illustrates the combination of unfettered reason with devout though unorthodox Anglican faith. John Locke (1632–1704), who is often described as 'the father of the Enlightenment', was a philosopher who also became an influential statesman. He was born ten years before Newton but his major works were published after Newton's *Principia* and were written in the wake of that book's breathtaking enhancement of the authority of human reason.

Locke came from Somerset, the son of a Puritan clerk, and his family only just had the means to send him to Christ Church, Oxford. Entering the university meant subscribing to the Articles of Religion and becoming an Anglican. While at Oxford he was influenced by the work of the French philosopher Descartes whose emphasis on reason made a lasting impression. Locke then trained as a medical doctor and was employed by Lord Ashley, the first Earl of Shaftesbury, who was an important figure in the court of Charles II. At one point Locke successfully oversaw an operation on Shaftesbury's liver, which was extremely risky at the time, demonstrating his skill as a surgeon. At another point Shaftesbury was implicated in a plot against James II and had to flee to the Netherlands. Locke had to follow and remained there until the 'Glorious Revolution' of 1688 when William of Orange took the throne at the invitation of parliament. Locke returned to public life and became an adviser to the court while also working at the Board of Trade. But he spent most of his time writing and became a vocal defender of free enquiry and toleration. In his *Letters concerning Toleration* (1689) he pleaded for religious liberty for 'all' (excepting atheists and Roman Catholics whom he considered a danger to the state). His ideal was a national church with an all-embracing creed that gave wide scope for individual opinion, on the grounds that human understanding was too limited for one man (such as a pope or a king) to impose his beliefs on another. These views were very influential in America and France, not least in the run up to the American War of Independence (1775–82) and the French Revolution of 1789.

Locke's greatest philosophical work was his *Essay on Human Understanding* (1690). This demonstrated the way that free enquiry, guided by logical thinking and unencumbered by the suffocating traditions of the past, can lead the enquirer to some radical conclusions. His basic argument was to uphold empiricism, the view that secure knowledge is gained through the human senses, against Platonism, with its belief in the transcendental reality of ideas. The human mind is a blank sheet and all our ideas come from experience, that is from sensation or reflection. Pure reality cannot be grasped by the mind, and so there is no sure basis for believing in the metaphysical reality of ideas. Plato's notion of there being something called 'substance' is 'an uncertain supposition of we know not what'!

However, interestingly, Locke was not an atheist or an agnostic. He believed that the existence of the soul was probable, and he believed the existence of God can be discovered with certainty by reason. He argued that God gives his law as a rule of conduct to humankind. In *The Reasonableness of Christianity* (1695) he argued that the only secure basis of Christianity is its reasonableness, though he also accepted that the miracles recorded in scripture are proofs of its divine origin. Reason, however, was given the last word in whether or not an event was supernatural. It also had the last word in the interpretation of scripture. Locke saw the essence of Christianity as the acknowledgment of Christ as the Messiah, who was sent into the world chiefly to spread the true knowledge of God and of our duties as human beings. In a radical way he saw all other doctrines as secondary and incapable of conclusive proof.

It is not surprising that when it was published the book caused great controversy. It showed how unfettered human reason could lead Protestant Anglicans to some surprising conclusions. High Churchmen saw it as an attack on Orthodox Christian belief, though compared to the ideas of radical Enlightenment thinkers on the Continent it was a notable defence. However, Locke did not want to undermine the authority of scripture and in his last years he produced *A Paraphrase and Notes on the Epistles of St Paul* (published 1705–7) and *A Discourse on Miracles* (1706). These upheld the authority of scripture and did not attempt the kind of historical and critical study of the text of scripture that was about to begin in Germany. It would not be until the middle of the nineteenth century that Anglican biblical scholarship would feel 'unencumbered by the suffocating traditions of the past' and start to dissect and analyse the scriptures in a scientific way (see Chapter 9.3).

To sum up, then,

> Locke believed that human reason should be the final arbiter of what we believe, in politics, ethics and religion alike; and he believed that the values of tolerance and individual liberty, of education and freedom, would provide the proper environment for the edifying exercise of religion. This philosophy was the philosophy of the Enlightenment in a nutshell. (Hill 2004, p. 36)

It can be added that Locke brought to birth a new kind of Christian discipleship, with reason at its heart, a discipleship that would come to prominence during the eighteenth century and (in amended way) in the nineteenth century within European culture and not least within Anglicanism.

8.3 *Reason in Religion and Ethics*: Butler and his Successors

Joseph Addison (1672–1719), a journalist and politician, gave popular expression to the view that human reason can unlock the secrets of existence. In his great hymn of 1712, drawing on imagery from Psalm 19, he attests that God's universe is a wonderfully ordered creation, governed by reason and so open to investigation by human intelligence. The first and second verse begin the hymn by describing the order and beauty of what we observe in the skies above us, by day and then by night:

> The spacious firmament on high,
> with all the blue ethereal sky,
> and spangled heavens, a shining frame,
> their great Original proclaim.
> The unwearied sun from day to day
> does his Creator's power display;
> and publishes to every land
> the work of an almighty hand.
>
> Soon as the evening shades prevail,
> the moon takes up the wondrous tale,
> and nightly to the listening earth
> repeats the story of her birth:
> whilst all the stars that round her burn,
> and all the planets in their turn,
> confirm the tidings, as they roll
> and spread the truth from pole to pole.

Such order and beauty clearly show evidence of a creator's hand. But it is the third verse that is most telling, because this is where the order and beauty is explicitly identified with 'reason', a capacity that human beings also possess:

> What though in solemn silence all
> move round the dark terrestrial ball?
> What though no real voice nor sound
> amid their radiant orbs be found?
> In reason's ear they all rejoice,
> and utter forth a glorious voice;
> for ever singing as they shine,
> 'The hand that made us is divine.'

So it is reason that can unlock the secrets of the universe and where it has come from and so reason must be given a primary position in the business of human living.

Two philosophers and one spiritual writer also played a major part in helping to reinforce the notion that the Christian religion, and within that the faith of the Church of England, are securely based on the dictates of reason. All were Anglican clerics who wrote their books within busy ecclesiastical careers. All produced work of great literary power.

Joseph Butler (1692–1752) was the son of Presbyterian parents and from an early age demonstrated remarkable powers of reasoning. Like Locke he won a place at Oxford, entering Oriel College, which meant becoming a member of the Church of England. He was ordained two years later and became preacher to the Chapel of the Rolls, one of the London law courts, where his reputation was made by the brilliance of his sermons before judges and lawyers. He later moved to other posts, eventually becoming rector of Stanhope in County Durham in 1726. Here he lived in seclusion, carried out pastoral duties and wrote *The Analogy of Religion*, which was published in 1736. In 1738 he became bishop of Bristol, where he came into conflict with John Wesley and George Whitefield. He interviewed Wesley on three occasions and finally told Wesley that he had no business preaching in his diocese (which legally he was entitled to do). Wesley, though, had built up a close rapport with the poor of the city and ignored Butler. George Whitefield, who was a colleague of Wesley's at this stage, was also famously criticized by Butler: 'Sir, the pretending to extraordinary revelations and gift of the Holy Spirit is a horrid thing – yes it is a horrid thing' (Turner 2002, p. 34). It would be hard to find a clearer example of the widening gulf between Evangelical and Enlightenment views of discipleship even though Butler and Wesley, as Turner points out, shared much theology (*ibid.*, p. 35).

There is an apocryphal story that Butler was offered the archbishopric of Canterbury but declined it because he believed it was 'too late to try to support a falling Church'. He did, though, accept the see of Durham in 1750. When he died two years later he was widely regarded as having lived a life of exemplary moral and intellectual integrity. He has been described as 'honest enough to admit the existence of doubts, and brave enough not to be paralysed by their existence' (Leslie Stephen in Livingston 2006, p. 46).

He published two major works, the first *Fifteen Sermons* in 1726 (from his time at Rolls Chapel) (examined below) and the second *The Analogy of Religion* of 1736. This book shows that he was one of the greatest exponents of natural theology in post-Reformation England.

In the *Analogy* Butler argues that Christianity is not unreasonable and that religion in general is reasonable. He does this through arguing that nature can be seen as an analogy for religion. In other words there are certain features of nature which we accept as uncontroversial even though they are beliefs rather than empirical facts, such as the belief that 'there is an intelligent Author of Nature, and *natural* Governor of the world' (Butler 1856, p. 76). Butler argues that it is the same with revealed religion. Making his case on pragmatic grounds, stating that 'to us, probability is the very guide of life' he argues that with both there is the same kind of approach to truth:

> It will undeniably show ... that the system of Religion, both natural and revealed, considered only as a system, and prior to the proof of it, is not a subject of ridicule, unless that of Nature be so too. And it will afford an answer to almost all objections against the system both of natural and revealed Religion ... (*ibid.*, p. 78)

Butler concludes his introduction by firmly nailing his colours to the mast of reasonable probability: 'the chief objections which are levelled against [revealed religion], are no other than what may be alleged with like justness against the latter, where they are in fact found to be inconclusive; and that this argument from analogy is in general unanswerable, and undoubtedly of weight on the side of religion ...' (p. 79).

Butler's argument would become vulnerable to David Hume's critique of natural theology (examined in the next chapter), but here it is important to note its influence especially in the nineteenth century, when it was widely studied by candidates for ordination. John Henry Newman, for example, acknowledged his great debt to the teaching of the *Analogy* on probability and what he called the 'sacramentalism' of nature. It seemed to encapsulate the reasonableness of the age.

One of Butler's most famous successors was Archdeacon William Paley (1743–1805), a blunt Yorkshireman who liked to tell ribald jokes and who also wrote one of the most powerful defences of the teleological argument or proof for the existence of God ('teleology' concerns 'ends', in this case the ends or purpose of nature). Paley argued that a scientific examination of the world showed that it had a purpose and therefore there must be a creator behind it. This he did in his *Natural Theology* of 1802. He began the book imaginatively by asking us to suppose that we were accompanying him on a walk across a heath and he pitched his foot against a stone. If we then asked him how he supposed that the stone came to be there he might

> possibly answer, that, for anything I knew to the contrary, it had lain there for-ever: nor would it perhaps be very easy to show the absurdity of this answer. But suppose I had found a watch upon the ground, and it should be inquired how the watch happened to be in that place; I should hardly think of the answer I had before given, that for anything I knew, the watch might have always been there. [I would have to answer that] There must have existed, at some time, and at some place or other, an artificer or artificers, who formed [the watch] for the purpose which we find it actually to answer; who compre-hended its construction, and designed its use.

In the same way, Paley argued, the ordered mechanism of nature, seen in the way an eye is clearly designed to see, and a fish to swim, and the blood vessels to allow circulation, show that they have been designed to perform these functions.

> Every indication of contrivance, every manifestation of design, which existed in the watch, exists in the works of nature; with the difference, on the side of nature, of being greater or more, and that in a degree which exceeds all com-putation. (Paley 1802, p. 1)

Science, in other words, was increasingly revealing the existence of a cosmic watchmaker, that is, of God.

Paley's book became a bestseller in the early nineteenth century and satisfied many religious people that science and reason could provide a solid foundation for faith. It provided further support for the key role given to human reason in Christian discipleship in this era.

Ethics

But what difference did the Enlightenment make to the practice of Christian discipleship? From within Anglicanism, William Law (1686–1761) provided one answer and he became one of the most widely read spiritual writers of the period. He was born in Kings Cliffe in Northamptonshire and educated at Cambridge. When the Hanoverian George I ascended the throne in 1714, Law felt unable to take the oath of allegiance and became a Non-juror (see above p. 94). He became a private tutor to the Gibbons at Putney (tutoring the father of the great historian) and during this period published his most famous book, *A Serious Call to a Devout and Holy Life* (1728). He later returned to Kings Cliffe where he was joined by a Mrs Hutcheson and Miss Hester Gibbon and all three, together, helped organize schools and alms houses. He led a life of great simplicity and devotion until his death.

Law had been shocked by the lifestyles of many people professing to be Christians, declaring that

> One cannot imagine anything more absurd than wise, sublime and heavenly prayers, tagged onto foolish worthless life where neither work nor leisure, time nor money, are under the direction of those same wise and heavenly prayers. (Law 1728, I)

In *A Serious Call* Law sets out to correct this. It has a vigorous style combined with a simplicity of teaching. It is full of entertaining vignettes of fictional characters whom Law uses to illustrate the points he is making. He believes that Christianity, at heart, is all about living correctly. He argues the case for a moderate temperance, humility and self-denial, and for living a devout life that has the overall purpose of glorifying God. Typically for his age he places reason at the centre of this discipleship. On almost the final page of the book we find this unequivocal statement:

> Reason is our universal law, that obliges us in all places, and at all times; and no actions have any honour, but so far as they are instances of our obedience to reason. And it is as base and cowardly, to be bold and daring against the principle of reason and justice, as to be bold and daring in lying and perjury. (Law 1728, Chap. XXIV)

The book became a best seller, and has had a greater impact than any other post-Reformation devotional book apart from *The Pilgrim's Progress.* It had a major impact on John Wesley, Samuel Johnson, Henry Venn the vicar of Huddersfield and John Keble, among others. In the spirit of Law's work Johnson memorably declared, 'We may take Fancy as a companion, but must follow reason as our guide.' All these figures, however, would come to look beyond reason for other well-springs for their faith and practice.

Law's book describes the Christian life in general terms. But when difficult moral decisions are to be made, what ethical approach should be used? For an answer that appeared at the same time as Law's book, and one that became increasingly influential within Anglicanism in the nineteenth and twentieth centuries, it is again necessary to look at Joseph Butler. In his *Fifteen Sermons* of 1726, preached before the legal establishment at the Rolls Chapel and later printed with a lengthy preface (and reprinted in a combined volume with the *Analogy*), he described an approach to ethics which moved beyond the kind of casuistry found in Jeremy Taylor's writings (see above p. 99), as well as an older medieval Catholic tradition, which in the face of difficult moral choices was based on applying general abstract principles and working out what they stipulate. Butler proposed something different, an approach that would begin with empirical study of the situation in which the moral choice was occurring:

> There are two ways in which the subject of morals may be treated. One begins from inquiring into the abstract relations of things: the other from a matter of fact, namely, what the particular nature of man is, its several parts, their economy or constitution; from whence it proceeds to determine what course of life it is, which is correspondent to this whole nature. (Butler 1856, pp. 371–2)

In such an investigation, then, we will not be committed to any *a priori* theory of human nature but will begin with human nature and its predicament as we find it. The immediate situation as it appears to us is to be the starting point of moral reasoning, and from there we will work out what course of action will best move things forward. Butler, then, is presenting an inductive as opposed to a deductive approach, in that he starts with the situation on the ground and then draws out of that appropriate ethical guidance, rather than deducing ethical guidance from first principles. It has been described as a form of empirical consequentialism (Badham 2009, p. 44). Butler declares that this approach to ethics 'is more easily applicable to the several particular relations and circumstances in life' and he describes how his sermons 'proceed chiefly in this latter method' (Butler 1856, p. 372). His whole approach has been summed up by Donald Mackinnon as 'the appeal to fact, to what we know of ourselves and . . . a readiness always to sacrifice the nicety of theoretical construction to the actuality of human behaviour' (Badham 2009, p. 44).

Butler's pragmatic approach to ethics gained widespread influence within Anglicanism especially in the twentieth century. Paul Badham, for example, describes how it underpinned many of the official Church of England reports into moral and social issues in the 1960s and 70s, such as those on divorce, abortion and homosexuality. The reports began with a presentation of what was happening in society at large around these issues and then proceeded to make recommendations about the practices of church and society, rather than beginning with biblical or theological principles (*ibid.*, p. 45). They provided support to the governments of the day as they liberalized the law around these issues.

Butler's empirical consequentialism can also be seen as an antecedent of Joseph Fletcher's controversial 'situation ethics' of the 1960s, which also bases moral decisions on the situation as it happens to be found by the moral agent. Fletcher, coming from the American Episcopal Church, published his book, *Situation Ethics: The New Morality,* in 1966. He wanted to get away from 'legalism', which he described as any system with rigid absolute rules, without falling into the trap of antinomianism (complete moral lawlessness). He found a vague middle way in the command to love your neighbour as yourself, which he described as the only absolute command. He argued that while laws and moral traditions might guide us, we cannot know for certain in advance what love will require of us in a particular situation. He looked to the teaching of Jesus and argued that throughout the Gospels we see Jesus always putting the command of love over all other laws; and that Jesus always related his teaching to the situation of the individual. Hence the one question to be asked in all contexts is simply 'what is the most loving thing to do in this situation?' If one truly loves one's fellow human being as oneself then, as Jesus said, this is to fulfil the law: 'love's decisions are made situationally, not prescriptively'.

Butler should not be linked with situation ethics, for in other parts of his writings he spoke of general moral principles that drew on the natural law tradition, yet he and Fletcher share a commitment to empirical consequentialism as the starting point of moral judgement. Fletcher provides a modern example of an Anglican who, in Mackinnon's words, begins with what we know of ourselves and has 'a readiness always to sacrifice the nicety of theoretical construction to the actuality of human behaviour'. Fletcher's approach does not stand up to close scrutiny by moral philosophy yet his book became very popular in the late 1960s and 1970s and it continues to be influential in some quarters, both within and beyond Anglicanism.

A more recent example of empirical consequentialism is provided by Paul Badham in his discussion of the vexed issue of whether it is right to allow voluntary euthanasia: 'Applying the law of love to a person suffering unbearably in the final stages of a terminal illness and asking for assistance to die it would seem apparent that in that situation the most loving thing to do is to accede to that request' (Badham 2009, p. 47).

* * *

All of the figures in this chapter show human reason being given a heightened role in guiding and directing the Christian life. They gradually reveal the influence of the Age of Reason or the Enlightenment, on Anglican thinking. However, human reason has its limits, and the second generation of Enlightenment philosophers mapped out what these limits are. In the next chapter we will see how Anglican thinkers and leaders responded to this bracing critique and how they presented a more nuanced expression of Christian discipleship appropriate for the modern age.

Discussion Questions

1 Hooker used the notion of natural law to defeat the Puritans' claim that scripture is the only authority within the Christian life. Is Hooker's argument still valid?
2 Locke stated that 'the only secure basis of Christianity is its reasonableness'. Is this right?
3 Should the Anglican facing difficult moral choices begin with general first principles and then seek to apply them, or begin with empirical study of the actual situation and base decisions on the consequences of the actual options?

Further Reading

Hooker

Chapman, Raymond, ed. (2009), *Law and Revelation: Richard Hooker and His Writings*, Norwich: Canterbury Press.

Lake, Peter (2003), 'The Anglican Moment'? Richard Hooker and the Ideological Watershed of the 1590s', in Stephen Platten, ed., *Anglicanism and the Western Christian Tradition*, Norwich: Canterbury Press.

McAdoo, Henry (1992), 'Richard Hooker', in Geoffrey Rowell, ed., *The English Religious Tradition and the Genius of Anglicanism*, Ikon 1992.

Percy, Martyn (1999), *Introducing Richard Hooker and the Laws of Ecclesiastical Polity*, London: Darton, Longman and Todd.

Enlightenment Anglicans

Butler, Bishop (1729), *Fifteen Sermons,* in *The Analogy of Religion . . .* (1856), London: Henry G. Bohn.

Hill, Jonathan (2004), *Faith in the Age of Reason*, Oxford: Lion Hudson plc.

Law, William (1728), *A Serious Call to a Devout and Holy Life.*

Livingston, James C. (2006), *Modern Christian Thought: The Enlightenment and Nineteenth Century*, 2nd edition, Minneapolis: Fortress Press.

Paley, William (1802), in the edition of 2006, *Natural Theology*, ed. Matthew Eddy and David Knight, Oxford: Oxford University Press.

9

Broad Religion

9.1 *Reason with Faith*: Coleridge's Philosophy

While reason is sovereign over scripture and tradition within Enlightenment Anglicanism, there is a further strand of thinking which presents a less clear cut and richer view of what this 'reason' might be. It comes from the great Romantic poet and theologian Coleridge, who in his writing reacted against a narrow rationalism within eighteenth-century philosophy (such as in Bentham's utilitarianism) and theology (such as in Paley's natural theology). Coleridge is a difficult and unsystematic writer but an undeniably creative one, and he is increasingly recognized as having laid the foundations of an enduring understanding of Christianity that could not be undermined by scientific discoveries or the critical historical study of scripture (something which could not always be said of the Protestant and Catholic traditions examined above).

To understand Coleridge's religious thought we must first place it in its philosophical context. Two philosophers, one deconstructive of Christianity, and the other bracingly reconstructive, must be recalled. Coleridge builds on their work.

David Hume (1711–76) may seem a surprising figure to include here. He, after all, was no Anglican but a Scottish atheist, who produced a number of brilliant and startling works of philosophy, from his *Treatise of Human Nature* (1739) and his *Enquiry Concerning Human Understanding* of 1748 (with its famous dismissal of the logical possibility of miracles), to his *Dialogues Concerning Natural Religion*, published posthumously in 1779. Hume used a clear and common-sense approach to logic to show that there was no actual reason to believe in the existence of God. Most devastating of his arguments were those which dismissed the possibility of natural religion, that is, the use of the natural world's qualities to argue for the existence of God. A traditional argument for the existence of God (from Aquinas and the scholastic philosophers of the Middle Ages) was that nothing can exist without a cause: so a football rolling across a football pitch must have been kicked. They argued that this must also apply to the universe: its very existence demands that it must have a cause outside of itself. 'But Hume points out that the general rule to which this argument appeals is based on experience: everything we see within the universe is caused, and we therefore suppose that this is a general rule for objects within the universe at large. But why should this be true of the universe itself? We have only seen one universe, so we don't know what is normal for universes' (Hill 2004, p. 170). In other words, there might just as easily be no cause at all! And even if the universe does have a cause, why should it be a good god?

Hume also undermines a related argument, the argument from design, which is an attempt to prove the existence of God through looking at the design of nature and deducing that there must be a designer behind it all (as Paley does with his watch and watchmaker argument presented above). Hume points out that even if *some* objects appear to have a purpose, this does not tell us anything about the universe as whole. Paley's analogy of a watch is no more reasonable than the analogy of a plant; and we know that plants are not created by anyone, but grow from seeds. 'Perhaps this universe grew from a seed left by an earlier one' (*ibid.*, p. 170).

Hume's case as a whole was that the existence of God and therefore Christianity's truth as a whole could *not* be demonstrated rationally. It could all be nothing more than a set of superstitious beliefs shored up with dubious arguments!

Immanuel Kant (1724–1804) moved beyond Hume with brilliance as well as German thoroughness. He was a Lutheran from a Pietist background who spent all his life in Königsberg (today Kaliningrad). He followed a strict routine, so much so that others could set their watches by the moment Kant went past on his afternoon walk. But his peace of mind was shaken when he came across Hume's writings. He declared that Hume had 'roused him out of his dogmatic slumbers'. After reading the Scotsman he accepted the claims of the British empiricist tradition (which included Locke as well as Hume), which argued that our knowledge is derived from sense experience. But he integrated this with the German idealist tradition, which argued that our ideas are innate and part of the mental equipment within our minds, and it is they that shape and form our sensory knowledge. But his empiricism meant that he denied we can gain secure knowledge of what is beyond our sensory experience, of what is beyond sight or touch or hearing, etc. So to try to extend our knowledge beyond our immediate human experience into the realms of heaven or immortality or the spiritual world would be to 'be like a fish trying to guess what life on land would be like' (Hill 2004, p. 180).

In his masterpiece of 1781, *The Critique of Pure Reason*, Kant therefore mapped the limits of what human reason can and cannot achieve. This meant that reason cannot be used to prove the existence of God and the validity of Christianity but nor, crucially, could it be used to *disprove* those things: they are beyond the scope of what reason can do. In this respect Kant neutralized Hume's attack on religion and re-opened the possibility of it being reasonable to be a Christian. No longer could it be said that Christian belief was irrational, but nor could Christians claim that it was *necessary* to believe in God: everyone was now free to make up their own minds.

Kant himself believed in the existence of God, but this was on other grounds, and in particular because the existence of conscience within human beings requires the existence of one who is the source of that conscience. For Kant, God's existence is a presupposition of the moral life: it was a 'postulate of practical reason'.

Samuel Taylor Coleridge (1772–1834) was a poet, philosopher, literary critic, and theologian who more than any other individual 'was responsible for the rebirth of a vital English theology out of the cold and spare remains of late eighteenth-century orthodoxy and rationalism' (Livingston 2006, p. 86). This happened through his encounters with two great figures and through the synthesis of their ideas which he produced in his own writings. The first was the poet and fellow Anglican William Wordsworth whom he met in 1795 and whose poetry made a profound impression. They became great friends and jointly published the *Lyrical Ballads* in 1798. Wordsworth's poetry made Coleridge re-think his philosophical ideas and especially turned him away from the empiricist philosophy of Locke and Hume, a philosophy which stipulated that knowledge was only gained through sense impressions. What struck him in Wordsworth's poetry was 'the union of deep feeling with profound thought: the fine balance of truth in observing, with the imaginative faculty in modifying the objects observed'. An extract from Wordworth's 'Lines composed a few miles above Tintern Abbey', written and published in 1798, illustrate very well what caught Coleridge's attention:

> And I have felt
> A presence that disturbs me with the joy
> Of elevated thoughts; a sense sublime
> Of something far more deeply interfused
> Whose dwelling is the light of setting suns,
> And the round ocean and the living air,
> And the blue sky, and in the mind of man:
> A motion and a spirit, that impels
> All thinking things, all objects of all thought,
> And rolls through all things. (lines 93–102)

Wordsworth is describing not merely what his senses have perceived (the object) but something more, something that has come from within his own mind (the subject), and the unity of these two things is powerfully described by phrases from the poem. For Coleridge great poetry like this 'is not a contrivance but a genuine creation. Such creation requires Imagination, for a poem is not an assemblage but a new whole, a spiritual unity. Artistic creation, then, is the fusion of mind and materials, or subject and object, into a spiritual unity through the faculty of Imagination (Livingston 2006, p. 87).

So he began to see the mind as active and not merely as a passive receptacle of sense impressions. It was his encounter with another figure, the philosopher Kant, who allowed him to philosophically clarify the role of the mind in perception. Coleridge and Wordsworth had travelled together to Germany and while Wordsworth explored the countryside Coleridge studied the German language, attended philosophical lectures, and purchased a large number of German philosophical works which he brought back with him to England. It was through the study of these that he found that Kant confirmed his belief in the Imaginative faculty. 'What Kant corroborated in Coleridge's mind was the belief that "the highest truths are those which lie beyond the limits of experience". Kant had affirmed that all our metaphysical truths are postulates of our practical reason – that is, of our *experience as moral beings*, not of our empirical or sensory knowledge. Like Kant, Coleridge believed that such metaphysical postulates as God, freedom, moral conscience, and immortality are derived from our moral convictions. 'My metaphysics', he says, 'are merely the referring of the mind to its own consciousness for truths indispensable to its own happiness' (Coleridge, *ibid.*, p. 87).

All this did not mean, then, that Coleridge was against the use of reason in the Christian life. Far from it – he believed the imaginative faculty was also the faculty of true reason. This was more than a mere 'understanding', the faculty of receiving sense impressions and taking them at face value. As Basil Willey famously put it,

> Understanding is the faculty by which we generalize and arrange the phenomena of perception. Reason is 'the knowledge of the laws of the whole considered as one'; Understanding is the 'science of phenomena'. Reason seeks ultimate ends; Understanding studies means. Reason is 'the source and substance of truths above sense'. Understanding is the faculty which judges 'according to sense'. Reason is the eye of the spirit, the faculty whereby reality is spiritually discerned. (Willey 1980, p. 29)

Coleridge did not deny that this understanding had a place and role in the ordinary business of living, but when it came to what was most important – the things of God and freedom and moral conscience – it was 'Reason' that was sovereign.

Coleridge, then, was still working out of the Enlightenment tradition and still believed in the key role of reason within discernment and within Christian faith and life in general, but it was an altogether wider and richer concept of reason than in the earlier philosophers and theologians we have examined. It has been described as a 'polar logic' in which 'subjectivity and objectivity are brought together' (Platten 2008, p. 325). It is 'an intuitive apprehension by which the total personality – senses, will, and emotions – acts as a whole' (Livingston 2006, p. 88). It expressed what his whole life had been searching for:

> the seminal principle, the original impulse, which was in him from childhood, was a sense of the whole as a living unity, a sense of God in all and all in God, a faith in a divine spiritual activity as the ground of all existence. (Willey 1980, p. 4)

This means Christianity cannot be proved by looking for evidence or winning arguments in a debate or somehow proving the existence of God, as in the work of Paley. A deductive form of logic will not work:

I more than fear the prevailing taste for books of natural theology, physio-theology, demonstrations of God from Nature, evidences of Christianity, and the like. *Evidences of Christianity!* I am weary of the word. Make a man feel the want of it; rouse him, if you can, to the self-knowledge of his need of it; and you may safely trust it to its own evidence remembering only the express declaration of Christ himself: *No man cometh to me, unless the Father leadeth him.* (Livingston 2006, p.89)

For Coleridge, then, the truth of the faith is discerned through this intuitive apprehension by the whole person. Discipleship cannot be about subscribing to a set of doctrines but embracing a way of life and a living process. Rational arguments on their own will not make a case for following Christ: the person must 'Try it!' The proof is found in the practice. So Coleridge brings faith to the centre of the stage for living the Christian life, suggesting it is the key to finding true reason and understanding: reason and faith become one. To follow Christ, then, was the most rational thing anyone could do, but to see this requires the intuitive apprehension of the venture of faith:

Faith subsists in the synthesis of the reason and the individual will. By virtue of the latter therefore it must be an energy, and inasmuch as it relates to the whole moral man, it must be exerted in each and all of his constituents or incidents, faculties and tendencies . . . it must be a total, not a partial; a continuous, not a desultory or occasional energy. And by virtue of the former, that is, reason, faith must be a light, a form of knowing, a beholding of truth. In the incomparable words of the Evangelist, therefore – *faith must be a light originating in the Logos, or the substantial reason, which is coeternal and one with the Holy Will, and which light is at the same time the life of men.* Now as life is here the sum or collective of all moral and spiritual acts . . . so is faith the source and sum, the energy and principle of the fidelity of man to God, by the subordination of his human will, in all provinces of his nature to his reason, as the sum of spiritual truth, representing and manifesting the will Divine. (Coleridge *Essay on Faith,* V 565, quoted in Livingston, p. 90)

This is an original integration of faith and reason. It shows the English Romantic poetic tradition fused with German Romantic and Idealistic philosophy, producing a foundation for Christian faith and, and within that, of discipleship, which is not susceptible to being disproved by science or the critical study of scripture but which authenticates itself. This is through the venture of faith, through which, in Wordsworth's words, we come to feel 'a presence . . . of something far more deeply interfused . . . a motion and a spirit, that impels all thinking things, all objects of all thought, and rolls through all things . . .'

9.2 *An Inclusive Church*: Maurice's Ecumenism

What kind of Christian life follows from this philosophical foundation? Coleridge influenced a wide range of people including a group of students at Cambridge University. One of those, a law student called Frederick Denison Maurice (1805–72), was a leading light of a debating society in which 'Coleridge himself was an invisible but omnipresent figure' (Morris 2005, p. 34). After achieving a first class degree Maurice, from a Unitarian background, felt unable to take his degree because he could not subscribe to the 39 Articles, which was a requirement of the university at that time. He was, though, on a spiritual pilgrimage and a few years later, partly as a result of Coleridge's influence, decided after all to join the Church of England and be ordained. He soon became one of its leading theologians and was a key figure in establishing a form of Anglicanism that built on Coleridge's philosophical foundations, reconciling faithfulness to scripture with Catholic tradition in a rational synthesis. He lies at the heart of the third strand of Anglicanism being studied in this book, the strand broadly associated with the Enlightenment. He provides an extended answer to the opening question above.

Maurice was born near Lowestoft. His father was a Unitarian minister and a keen supporter of the anti-slavery league. He took his son to meetings of the society and instilled a social radicalism in him from an early age. But his mother and sisters were keen Calvinists and supporters of the Evangelical Revival and there was division in the family, which hurt the sensitive Maurice. His lifelong commitment to ecumenical inclusion may well have sprung from this experience. When at Cambridge Maurice began writing for journals including the *Westminster Review* and after leaving the university he pursued a career as a journalist and was appointed editor of the *Metropolitan Quarterly Review* and then the prestigious journal *The Athenaeum*. But one of his sisters contracted a fatal illness and Maurice set aside some of his work in order to help nurse her.

This experience made him see the shallowness of his faith and he began to study theology in depth. It was at this point that he was led to seek membership of the Church of England and was admitted in 1831. He also, as mentioned, decided to seek ordination and studied theology at Exeter College, Oxford. He was ordained in 1834 and after a curacy near Leamington was appointed chaplain to Guy's Hospital, London. In this period he was influenced by the Oxford Movement but disagreed with Pusey over baptismal regeneration: he did not think that administration of the sacraments on its own conferred salvation. During this period he worked on his first major work, *The Kingdom of Christ*, which was published in 1838. This was an extended response to Pusey and the Oxford Movement but was presented as 'Hints to a Quaker concerning the Principles, Constitution and Ordinances of the Catholic Church'. It was misunderstood and attacked by many even though it was presenting a fundamentally orthodox point of view. However, it established Maurice's academic credentials and he was appointed Professor of English Literature and History at the newly established King's College, London, becoming Professor of Theology in the same college in 1846. He also became chaplain to Lincoln's Inn law courts where his preaching drew large congregations.

Maurice took up a distinctive position within the debates of the time, criticizing the partisanship of Evangelicals and Tractarians and calling for an abandonment of parties. He found himself in the middle of controversy when he supported Christian Socialism in 1848 (as we shall see in the next section), and was heavily criticized for some of his theological views in his *Theological Essays* of 1853. In this volume he questioned the reality of the *endlessness* of punishment in hell: he believed the word 'eternal' in the New Testament had nothing to do with time. This was unacceptable to many and after a great row he was forced to resign from King's, which was a severe blow.

Maurice continued to preach and to support Christian Socialism, not least through founding the Worker's Education College in 1854. This provided evening classes for working people, and he recruited a talented range of people to do the teaching, including John Ruskin the art historian and Octavia Hill the housing reformer (see below Chapter 10.2). He had already helped to establish Queen's College, Harley Street, a teacher training school for women, showing his commitment to education for women as well as men. Maurice was passionate about education in general believing it to be the place of social transformation. This commitment was taken up by many others including Frederick Temple, a future Archbishop of Canterbury, and, in the twentieth century, by Temple's son William who, uniquely, followed his father to also become Archbishop (see below Chapter 10.3). In many ways, as suggested by the introduction, the promotion and sponsorship of education for all could be seen as the defining practical expression of Enlightenment Anglicanism.

Maurice published over five million words during his life but his books are no longer in print. They are written in a dense and yet extended style, which makes them hard to read. Yet they contain key insights which have been influential in the recent development of Anglicanism. This is especially true of *The Kingdom of Christ* and its inclusive vision. In a lengthy dedication letter to Coleridge (written later in his life to Coleridge's son the Revd Derwent Coleridge), Maurice describes the way Coleridge influenced his thinking, not least through showing how 'the highest truths are those which lie beyond the limits of Experience' and how he was the first to apply this principle to theology (p. xxv), with the implication that truth is above any one person's perception of it and 'most of all above myself and my own petty notions and apprehensions [and] that is worthy to be sought after and loved above all things, and that He who is Truth, is ready, if we will obey Him, to guide us into it' (p. xxix). Maurice, then, believed that human apprehension of religious truth is proximate and partial. Jeremy Morris helpfully summarizes his view: 'Whenever someone claims to know the whole truth – to represent exclusively the true spirit of the gospel – we are entitled to be skeptical. There is always much to be learned from others who profess to follow Christ and yet seem different from us' (Morris 2007, p. 8).

This is why in *The Kingdom of Christ* Maurice conducts a probing analysis of each denomination and party within English Christianity. He believed that each had key insights into the truth of Christianity even though each had then mistakenly developed these insights into self-contained systems:

Our consciences, I believe, have told us from time to time that there is something in each of them which we ought not to reject. Let us not reject it. But we may find, that there is a divine harmony, of which the living principle in each of these systems forms one note, of which the systems themselves are a disturbance and a violation. (Maurice 1891, vol. 2, p. 401)

In the case of Quakerism, for example, he drew attention to its doctrine of the 'inner light', and in the case of Lutheranism and Reformed Christianity, to justification by faith alone, the supreme authority of Scripture, and the doctrine of divine election; and in Unitarianism, to its yearning after unity. While the history of Christendom was a descent into rigid theological systems and sects, nevertheless the Catholicity of the Church could still be found: 'God, Maurice was saying, continued to be present with and in his Church in all its desperate divisions. And so Maurice's providential reading of the Church's history directed him towards a theological rehabilitation of the idea of Christian unity' (Morris 2007, p. 10).

As an expression of this Christian unity Maurice identified six 'signs' of Catholicity which he believed every Trinitarian denomination already possessed. These were baptism, Eucharist, scripture, creeds, the apostolic ministry, and liturgical tradition. Maurice believed each could be traced back to the Gospel itself. They could be recognized by each denomination in each other and so help the search for greater unity. This was indeed the method taken up by the churches in the twentieth-century ecumenical movement, not least through the widespread adoption of the Chicago-Lambeth Quadrilateral (see Chapter 11) which Anglicans have used to find common ground and degrees of unity with other churches (though Maurice's 'liturgical tradition' does not appear in its list of signs).

In the final section of *The Kingdom of Christ* Maurice turned his attention directly to the Church of England. He applied the same kind of approach to the internal divisions within the church. In each of the main parties – Evangelical, Liberal and Catholic – he again found both positive principles and mistaken development. By implication, Anglicanism was greater than the sum of its parts. It needed each of the parties yet it needed to rise above their conflict: 'This was the root of the argument for the "comprehensiveness" of the Church of England with which Maurice's name has become indelibly associated. He marked out a vision of church unity that applied as forcefully to his own Church as it did to relations to separated churches' (Morris 2007, p. 11).

There are weaknesses in Maurice's argument, not least his sketchy presentation of Christian history. His case depended on what had actually happened in the historical development of different traditions, and he does not always supply the evidence for his case. His presentation of Roman Catholicism was much more negative and unsympathetic to that denomination than to others and this shows some bias. And he advanced a dubious argument about the national character of the English race and why the Church of England suited its character. Yet despite these weaknesses *The Kingdom of Christ* remains a great book of lasting significance for Anglicanism because, as Morris argues, it initiated the modern ecumenical method of looking for the 'positive principles' in separated churches through joint historical study of origins and development. And its argument for 'comprehensiveness', for all its evident weaknesses, became a vital tool for Anglicans as they sought to understand how it was possible for a church so apparently divided in principle and practice to remain one. Morris explains why this is so:

> By attaching significance in particular to the possession of the 'signs' of Catholic Church, Maurice could affirm the Catholicity of the Church of England, at the same time as acknowledging regretfully its internal conflicts over the interpretation of doctrine. (*Ibid.*, p. 12)

For Maurice, then, Anglicanism was a broad and inclusive church. It was constituted by Catholic tradition as well as the application of a faith-based reason, though the latter took precedence over the former ensuring that no party or system over-reached itself. To be an Anglican disciple, then, was to belong to a church fundamentally open to the insights of other traditions as it sought the kingdom within and beyond them all.

9.3 *What, then, of Scripture?* Jowett and Colenso

We have seen Coleridge elevate the place of reason within the Christian life, a reason rooted in imagination and faith. In *The Kingdom of Christ* Maurice connected this outlook with respect for the historical tradition of the Church, and he traced an underlying unity behind its outward fragmentation. But what about the other great authority with Anglicanism, namely scripture? What place did these Enlightenment forms of Anglicanism make for the Bible in the Christian life?

The status of scripture became an urgent issue in the nineteenth century as critical and scientific methods of study were increasingly applied to the Bible. In Germany Samuel Reimarus (1649–1768) had led the way in critically analyzing biblical history: with wit and clarity he exposed the inconsistencies in different biblical narratives. For example, he calculated that if Exodus was correct there would have been three million Israelites who passed through the Red Sea. If the column had been ten people deep it would have needed to be 180 miles long, taking at least nine days to cross. He also examined the resurrection narratives, noting the inconsistencies between them and concluding that the resurrection could not have been an event in history. Reimarus also raised the question of the difference between the historical message and life of Jesus and the church's memory and portrayal of him in the New Testament, an issue subsequently summarized as the difference between the Jesus of history and the Christ of faith.

Reimarus did not publish his most controversial views during his life time but they appeared anonymously in a volume published by G. E. Lessing in Germany after his death. They spread through the German academic world and launched the modern critical study of the Bible. Into this heated environment stepped Coleridge when he travelled through Germany with Wordsworth in 1798. Coleridge saw that the work of Reimarus and his followers was not necessarily a devastating blow to Christianity. Coleridge knew how anti-Christian sceptics like Tom Paine were having a field day demonstrating the contradictions and incongruities in the biblical texts. He also saw how many Christians were trying to defend themselves through holding tightly to a doctrine of biblical inerrancy, that the word of Scripture was literally truthful whatever others may say. Coleridge called this 'bibliolatry' and pointed out that it was playing into the hands of sceptics like Paine who could declare that Christian adherence to scripture was irrational and therefore indefensible. Coleridge, influenced by Lessing, laid the foundations of a different and rational way of viewing scripture. In his post-humously published *Confessions of an Enquiring Spirit* (1840) he argued, first, that the Bible should be read like 'any other work'. It is a collection of books, stories, poems and songs and can be studied in the same way that the works of Shakespeare can be studied and found inspirational. Some of Shakespeare's works are less than inspirational (Coleridge cites *Titus Andronicus*): in the same way some parts of the Bible, such as the curses within the Psalms, are less authoritative than others. For Coleridge, to say that 'the Bible contains the religion revealed by God' is not the same as saying 'Whatever is contained in the Bible is religion, and was revealed by God': one can hold to the former while rejecting the latter. The Bible contains all that is necessary for faith and for practice; it is the 'the appointed conservatory, an indispensable criterion, and a continual source and support of true belief' (Livingston 2006, p. 92). How, then, should it be read? Coleridge argues that the Bible needs to be read 'in faith', with the outlook and expectation of the Christian religion as handed down through the Christian tradition including beliefs and doctrines of the creeds, the ongoing life and ministry of the church, the experience of prayer and the 'communion of saints':

> Friend, it is my conviction that in all ordinary cases the knowledge and belief of the Christian religion should precede the study of the Hebrew Canon. Indeed, with regard to both Testaments, I consider oral and catechismal instruction as the preparative provided by Christ himself in the establishment of the visible Church.

It is through having a desire to love and learn about Christ that the scriptures will take on a special character as sacred writings that reveal God. Then

> In them you will find all the revealed truths which have been set forth and offered to you . . . in addition to these, examples of obedience and disobedience . . . the lives and actions of men eminent under each dispensation, their sentiments, maxims, hymns, prayers – their affections, emotions, conflicts; in all of which you will recognise the influence of the Holy Spirit, with a conviction increasing with the growth of your own faith and spiritual experience. (*Ibid.*, p. 92)

There is a connection here with Coleridge's views on the importance of reason being rooted in faith: the experience of living and, for discipleship, the experience of seeking and following the Lord, is the key that opens the secrets of God's being and presence in the world and especially in the scriptures. Faith will find faith, not in the bare words of scripture on the printed page, but in the experience lying behind the writing of those words.

Coleridge's *Confessions* did not receive a wide readership – his style was inaccessible to many and the book was not widely promoted. However, it did influence a number of his followers, not least Maurice, and by the mid nineteenth century had guided the thinking of a wide range of academics. One group centred on Oxford began to popularize them in a volume of essays of 1860, though initially with explosive results.

Benjamin Jowett (1817–93) was a formidable classical scholar and translator of Plato and Aristotle. He was also ordained and rose to become Master of Balliol College, Oxford. He was reputed to be knowledgeable about many academic subjects and there is there is a famous clerihew which has him saying 'I am the Master of this college; what I don't know isn't knowledge!' As a young academic he travelled in Germany, meeting Schelling on one occasion and purchasing and becoming absorbed in the study of Hegel's works. In an 1845 letter he wrote that 'it is impossible to be satisfied with any other system after you have begun with this' (Abbott and Campbell 1897, p. 92). He was especially taken with Hegel's recognition of the historical evolution of the human mind (*ibid.*, p. 130, for more on Hegel see Chapter 10.1). Jowett would apply this philosophical notion to the study and interpretation of scripture, with controversial results. This occurred in his famous essay for *Essays and Reviews,* 'The Interpretation of Scripture'. The 1860 book, a collection of seven essays by Oxford scholars and churchmen, was a landmark because for the first time it showed acceptance of the historical-critical study of the Bible in English-speaking church circles. Jowett was regarded as the leading voice in the book. Like Coleridge, he was aware that critical and scientific methods of study were making great progress but that the churches were not presenting the Bible or the Christian faith in a way that took on board these advances: 'In a few years there will be no religion in Oxford among intellectual young men, unless religion is shown to be consistent with criticism' (*ibid.*, p. 345). Others had recognized the problems facing Christian belief from critical study of the Bible, but had feared the consequences of upsetting the apple cart if they were openly acknowledged. Jowett felt that silence was worse and was morally reprehensible. Like Reimarus he pointed to the clear discrepancies between different parts of the Bible, for example between the books of Kings and Chronicles. He also pointed out how the doctrines of the Creeds were read back into scripture without evidence that they were there in the first place. For example, there was little evidence that the New Testament writers believed in the doctrine of the Trinity. Instead, following Coleridge, he believed the Bible should be studied 'like any other book' (Jowett 1907, p. 53), with the intention of finding the original meaning. This 'can only be done in the same careful and impartial way that we ascertain the meaning of Sophocles or of Plato . . . No other science of Hermeneutics is possible but an inductive one, that is to say, one based on the language and thoughts and narratives of the sacred writers' (*ibid.*).

The results of such inquiry will show that the Bible contains a variety of beliefs and practices of a widely different nature – 'a mixture of the monstrous and the sublime, the true and the false'. But Jowett could make sense of this by drawing on Hegel's idea of progressive revelation through history, allowing him to argue for 'a general conception of growth or development in Scripture, beginning with the truth of the Unity of God in the earliest books and ending with the perfection of Christ'. This conception saves the interpreter 'from the necessity of maintaining that the Old Testament is one and same everywhere …' (*ibid.*, p. 63), while also giving a sense of '"the increasing purpose which through the ages ran"' (*ibid.*), and a 'continuous growth of revelation which he [or she] traces in the Old and New Testament'. The influence of Hegel is also apparent in the way Jowett illustrated his notion: the history of God's people reflected in the scriptures is like the progress a child makes as it grows into adulthood: a child behaves in certain ways and responds to certain kinds of promise and discipline. But when the child becomes an adult he or she understands the world in a different way: 'looking back on the entire past, which he reads anew, perceiving that the events of life had a purpose or result which was not seen all the time' (*ibid.*, pp. 64–5; see also Hinchliff 1987, p. 81). The Bible reflects this providential growth, with later stages of the biblical tradition expressing a more mature outlook, which qualifies and even changes the outlook of the earlier stages. And, for Jowett (as for Coleridge before him) Christ's life was above all the final inspiration, the hermeneutical key through which the rest should be read and understood. Progressive revelation reaches its climax in him: as he wrote in a letter, 'the life and death of Christ is the soul, the imitation of Christ – the inspiration of Christ – the sacrifice of self – the being in the world and not of it, the union with God and the will of God such as Christ had' (Abbott and Campbell 1897, vol. 2, p. 273, quoted in Livingston 2006, p. 248).

Jowett's contribution to the volume provides an important example of the application of reason to religion in dialogue, the one posing questions to the other and leading the enquirer forward in their journey into spiritual truth. His openness to the insights of critical reason reflects the values of the Enlightenment, and his belief in the unfolding nature of biblical inspiration reflects the influence of one of its key thinkers, Hegel.

In the short term the book ran into a storm of anger and protest in the wider church, with bishops, church convocations and finally the Archbishop of Canterbury condemning it. Legal action was taken against two of the essay-ists (action that was later thrown out by the Privy Council), and a petition of protest against the volume was signed by 11,000 clergy! Jowett was deeply hurt and peremptorily withdrew from any further theological writing, concentrating instead on the translation of Plato.

Others, however, were prepared to take up the cause, the most famous of whom was Bishop John Colenso of Natal. Colenso (1814–83) was from Corn-wall and had studied and taught mathematics at Cambridge before his first appointment to a tiny parish in Norfolk. He was influenced by F. D. Maurice and adopted an open and critical view of scripture. He combined pastoral duties with biblical study. Remarkably he was then invited to become Bishop of Natal and when he arrived in South Africa he began to work for improvement in the conditions of the black population. He published the first edition of his massive *The Pentateuch and the Book of Joshua Critically Examined* in 1862 and would publish subsequent editions up to 1879. This book challenged the idea that Moses was the author of the Pentateuch and questioned the historical accuracy of the books. It argued its case with painstaking detail, for example calculating the amount of fodder the people of Israel's herds would have needed in the wil-derness and the impossibility of finding such quantities. He also calculated the amount of manure the animals would have produced!

There was again a huge storm of protest in Britain as well as South Africa and Robert Gray the Anglo-Catholic Bishop of Cape Town (see above p. 116), with the support of Charles Longley the Archbishop of Canterbury, tried to depose Colenso as bishop. Colenso gained legal support from the Privy Council in Britain, however, and remained in post, while Gray solemnly excommunicated him and appointed a new bishop over the same territory. Colenso remained as bishop alongside the new bishop until his death in 1882 (and remained highly respected in his own diocese), continuing to publish his scholarship and stand-ing by it in a way that Jowett had not done.

This whole episode provides a flashpoint, not unlike the Gorham case, in the ongoing tension between the three traditions of Anglicanism examined in this Studyguide. It illustrates the depth of the diversity within Anglicanism. In passing it is important to note that the controversy over *Essays and Reviews* and Colenso led Longley to call the first Lambeth Conference in 1867. Many bishops felt the need to meet and decide on a common approach to the crisis, and Longley as Archbishop acceded to their request and created a conference that has continued to be called every ten years or so. (For more on the Lambeth Conference see Chapter 11.)

In the longer term, historians now recognize that *Essays and Reviews*, and Colenso, helped to allow a more open attitude towards differences of religious conviction within the church and beyond:

> Though their work appeared largely negative, the authors of *Essays and Reviews* made an invaluable contribution to the progress of Christian thought in an age of scientific revolution. They played the commanding role in the renewal of scholarly freedom in the Church at a time when that freedom had suffered an eclipse. If their work was too destructive, it can be argued that such weapons were required to shatter the false foundations on which the faith had been lately constructed. (Livingston 2006, p. 250)

The next generation of biblical scholars, represented by J. B. Lightfoot, B. F. Westcott and F. J. A. Hort, would be less dismissive of parts of the New Testament and make a case, on critical grounds, for the historical reliability of portions of its narrative, generating much less hostility and firmly establishing the place of this kind of study within the church, where it has remained ever since. But this would not have been possible without *Essays and Reviews* and Colenso.

Discussion Questions

1 Coleridge believed the imaginative faculty was also the faculty of true reason. How could this claim be defended? What does it imply about discipleship?
2 Writing about the different Christian denominations, F. D. Maurice commented: 'Our consciences, I believe, have told us from time to time that there is something in each of them which we ought not to reject. Let us not reject it.' Has this been true in your experience?
3 Do you agree with Jowett that progressive revelation in scripture reaches its climax in Christ and that his life is the hermeneutical key through which the rest of the Bible should be read and understood?

Further Reading

Hill, Jonathan (2004), *Faith in the Age of Reason*, Oxford: Lion Hudson.

Hinchliff, Peter (1987), *Benjamin Jowett and the Christian Religion*, Oxford: Oxford University Press.

Jowett, Benjamin (1907), 'The Interpretation of Scripture' (first published in *Essays and Reviews*, 1860), in *Scripture and Truth*, with an introduction by Lewis Campbell, London: Henry Frowde, reprinted by Bibliolife.

Livingston, James C. (2006), *Modern Christian Thought: The Enlightenment and Nineteenth Century*, 2nd edition, Minneapolis: Fortress Press.

Morris, Jeremy (2005), *F. D. Maurice and the Crisis of Christian Authority*, Oxford: Oxford University Press.

Morris, Jeremy (2007), *To Build Christ's Kingdom: F. D. Maurice and His Writings*, Norwich: Canterbury Press.

Willey, Basil (1980), 'Benjamin Jowett: On the Interpretation of Scripture' in *More Nineteenth Century Studies* (first published 1956), Cambridge: Cambridge University Press.

Willey, Basil (1980), 'Samuel Taylor Coleridge', in *Nineteenth Century Studies: Coleridge to Matthew Arnold* (first published 1949), Cambridge: Cambridge University Press.

10

A Social Mission

10.1 *The Purpose of History*: from Hegel to T. H. Green

The Enlightenment was born out of scientific and technological progress. The results of this progress were so impressive, not least in medicine, that European cultural life embraced the notion that reality as a whole is not static but is somehow on a forward trajectory, leading humanity towards a better and better state of affairs. Church life and theology, including Anglican thought and practice, was caught up in this new paradigm. This chapter examines how it came to dramatic expression through social and educational reform and progress. Indeed for Enlightenment Anglicanism in the nineteenth and early twentieth centuries, mission itself became identified with these broad social aims.

A key figure behind all this was yet another German philosopher, already mentioned as an influence on Benjamin Jowett, namely George Wilhelm Friedrich Hegel (1770–1831). He was a Lutheran who began his philosophical career at Jena, where he wrote his pioneering masterpiece *The Phenomenology of Mind* (1806). He then moved to Nuremberg, working as a headmaster of a high school, until his reputation as a philosopher became established and he was appointed Professor of Philosophy at Heidelberg in 1816 and then, in 1818, to a similar post in Berlin. He remained in Berlin until his death, becoming the dominant philosopher of his generation. His writings included *Science of Logic* (1816), *The Philosophy of Right* (1819), a treatise on social and political matters, and the *Encyclopedia of the Philosophical Sciences* (between 1817 and 1830), a vast compendium of knowledge presented within the categories of his system.

Hegel believed that behind the changing world in which we live lay a rational spirit or mind, which he called *Geist*. This led him to state that 'whatever is rational is real and whatever is real is rational'. He believed that all things *tend* to the complete and perfect design of this 'mind' by a logical process. He went beyond Kant because he saw this process as working itself out through human history: 'in contrast to Kant, who thought he could say on purely philosophical grounds what human nature is and always must be, Hegel accepted Schiller's suggestion that the very foundations of the human condition could change from one historical era to another. This notion of change, of development through-out history, is fundamental to Hegel's view of the world' (Singer 1983, p. 9). Friedrich Engels, looking back on Hegel's significance within European thought (not least for himself and for Karl Marx), confirms this assessment:

> What distinguished Hegel's mode of thinking from that of all other philoso-phers was the exceptional historical sense underlying it. However abstract and idealist the form employed, the development of his ideas runs always parallel to the development of world history, and the latter is indeed supposed to be only the proof of the former. (*Ibid.*, p. 9)

But in what way do all things tend to the complete and perfect design of mind/spirit through history? Hegel postulated the existence of a unifying process that he called the 'dialectic'. In this process an original tendency, or 'thesis', gives rise to its opposite tendency, an 'antithesis'. Both are then resolved into a higher unity, a 'synthesis'. This takes place, step by step, through the unfolding process of world history. So, for example, he interpreted recent events, and the especially the rise of Napoleon, in these terms: the *ancien regime*, the old monarchies of the Bourbons and Habsburgs, was the thesis; the French Revolution, with its start-ling upturning of this order, was the antithesis; out of this violent juxtaposition emerged a unifying regime that brought together the best of both, the rule of Napoleon, which was the synthesis and, for Hegel, a great step forward for the life of Europe including for his own Prussia.

Hegel believed that this dialectic could be traced throughout human history, and at each stage the rational principle of *Geist* was progressively realized. He believed that his own era was one of great progress and promise, based on the increasing dominance of reason over human affairs:

> Never since the sun has stood in the firmament and the planets revolved around it had it been perceived that man's existence centres in his head, i.e.

in thought, inspired by which he builds up the world of reality . . . not until now had man advanced to the recognition of the principle that thought ought to govern spiritual reality. This was accordingly a glorious mental dawn. All thinking beings shared in the jubilation of this epoch. (*Lectures in the Philosophy of History,* in Singer 1983, p. 21)

So reason has a key role to play in life and, by implication, in Christian discipleship. Its role is not to prove the existence of some transcendent eternal divine order: Hume had undermined that pretence. Nor is it to resign itself to the opposite, of upholding atheism and a Godless and religionless world: Kant had ruled that out of court. Its work is to 'build up reality': to create the ways of thinking and the consciousness that will make this a better world, a world where matter and spirit are united in the consciousness of freedom. Reason is the interpretative key that unlocks these mysteries of life and also gradually reveals itself through this process. For example, through the critical study of history and especially of Christian history, human reason will uncover the ways that *Geist* or spirit/mind has been at work leading people into truth. This will show what needs to happen in the present and the future so that through the progress of Christian civilization, the world may be lead towards the perfect divine consciousness. The aim of such intellectual and practical endeavour, then, was (to adapt Karl Marx's phrase) not just to interpret the world but to change it.

It is this turn from heaven *above* to the world *around*, and specifically to the world in its historical development from past to future, that was articulated in its most sophisticated form by Hegel. He and the wider German school of philosophy that he represents in turn influenced and inspired a range of other philosophers and theologians in the nineteenth and twentieth centuries in the West as a whole and helped to shape the mature expression of Enlightenment Christianity. A few Anglican examples can now be mentioned.

One of the first was Thomas Arnold (1795–1842) who stands at the headwaters of a revised view of church and society. He was headmaster of Rugby School and became a professor of modern history at Oxford at the end of his life. He belonged to a wider group which also included Richard Whately (see above p. 113), Julius Hare and Connop Thirlwell (see Forbes, 1952).

Arnold believed in the essential unity of the secular and religious, of Church and state, and was later seen as one of the founders of the Broad Church movement, a late-Victorian movement which opposed the idea of boundaries between church and society and within the church. He was opposed to the 'ecclesiasticism' of the High Churchmen and the Oxford Movement. Under the influence of the German school (Herder more than Hegel), Arnold saw spiritual reality as bound up and expressed within the broad development of human civilization in general. He believed each period of civilization was also a period or epoch of universal history. Duncan Forbes usefully summarizes Arnold's thinking:

> For Arnold, the history of Greece, the history of Rome, and the history of modern Europe constitute three such periods of civilization, three steps forward on the path of man's intellectual and moral development ... Roman law, Greek intellect, Christian ethics, he conceives as perfect in themselves. There is progress only if these fall into good racial ground. Morally, therefore, though 'our life is in a manner a continuation of Greece, Rome and Israel', yet it 'exhibits a fuller development of the human race, a richer combination of the most remarkable elements', because the perfection achieved by Greece, Rome and Israel in their various fields of endeavour mingled with the virtues of the German nations, and the result was a step forward. (*Ibid.*, pp. 67–8)

This sweeping vision (with some possibly racist overtones) lay behind Arnold's educational work. Its belief in progress inspired others to take up the work of reform, apply the critical powers of reason to the different dimensions of life in society and the state, and so to help shape a better world.

A more direct example of Hegelian influence upon Anglicanism was through Benjamin Jowett, whose debt to Hegel has been mentioned above (pp. 170–1). A further example was through the philosophical school of British Idealism, which was fostered within England by the philosophers T. H. Green, F. H. Bradley and Bernard Bosanquet (among others), and in Scotland by Edward Caird. Apart from Green these figures were not Anglicans, but they influenced a generation of Anglican leaders in the way they translated and adapted Hegel's framework for the British context, providing a philosophical scheme that was open to and sometimes required the insights of religion. The first of these, Thomas Hill Green (1836–82) was educated at Rugby School (though after Arnold's time) and then at Balliol College, Oxford, under Jowett. He became a tutor at the college and then a professor of moral philosophy in the university. He made a great impression on his contemporaries through his unaffected sincerity. He also supported projects for educational and social reform in the slum districts of Oxford, spending time with the poor alongside his lecturing, illustrating the way that in the latter half of the nineteenth century a Hegelian philosophical framework could easily feed social mission (through Green was not an uncritical student of Hegel).

Green's political views are illustrated by his speech of 1881 'Liberal Legislation and Freedom of Contract'. In this speech he was critical of J. S. Mill's view of liberty as the simple absence of coercion or compulsion upon an individual. For Mill, liberty is experienced when no one interferes or forces you to do anything. Green rejected this definition: 'When we speak of freedom as something to be so highly prized, we mean a positive power or capacity of doing or enjoying, and that, too, something we do or enjoy in common with others.' So it is more than an absence: it is a positive capacity to be able to choose and then hold to a purpose despite other impulses. This in turn depends on other people providing the training and support to do this:

> We mean by it a power which each man exercises through the help or security given to him by his fellow men and which he in turn helps to secure for them . . . the mere removal of compulsion, the mere enabling of a man to do as he likes, is in itself no contribution to true freedom. (Green 1881, pp. 370–1)

The social group, then, of which the individual is a member, makes an intrinsic contribution to his or her liberty. For example, the freedom to read books is dependent on the reader being taught to read in the first place. Without the help and direction of a teacher and an educational system the individual would not have the power to read widely and deeply. Freedom, then, is a positive power, a power that is exercised through the help of others and is in this way socially based.

This implies that we are responsible for each other's freedom. When, for example, members of the population are unable to read or prevented from reading through sickness or other forms of deprivation there is a duty on those who are fit and well to play their part in bringing about such collective freedom. They are to contribute their time, energy and resources so that the less fortunate may have the health and encouragement to enjoy this aspect of freedom: it is a corporate responsibility that depends on the whole medical, educational and social situation in which people live. It was this train of thinking that led Green from the lecture hall into the slums, and would inspire many others to follow him. Historical development has a purpose, the realization of freedom, but the achievement of that purpose rests with men and women assisting each other to bring it about.

Green died prematurely, at the age of 46, and his leadership of the British Idealist school of philosophy was taken up by the Scottish philosopher Edward Caird, who succeeded Jowett as master of Balliol. Caird like Jowett wanted the undergraduates of his college to become public servants, in government, church and law, and by the turn of the century old members of the college had indeed come to dominate the British civil service and legal system. Jowett and Caird saw the role of public servants as one of working for the increasing realization of the perfect society, a society that was slowly emerging. Caird called on the undergraduates to fulfil the duties 'of the station in which we stand', so that this present world may have 'its worth deepened . . . item by item, with all the elements that constitute it multiplied a hundred-fold in value, raised to a higher spiritual power'. Caird warned his listeners, though, that this ideal world would only be realized 'with persecutions' (Caird 1908, pp. 70–1). One of those undergraduates was William Temple (see below section 10.3), and he was caught up in this challenging and progressive optimism. He believed, like his peers, that he would have a significant role to play in the unfolding life of the nation. In his case, at least, this sentiment proved to be true.

10.2 *Reforming Society*: Christian Socialism and Octavia Hill

How was this broad intention reflected in practical action? Some examples of social and educational initiatives from the nineteenth and twentieth centuries need to be described. This section is not about single issue campaigns, such as William Wilberforce's campaign to end slavery or Lord Shaftesbury's campaign to reform working conditions within factories. Nor is it about those who wanted to restore a pre-industrial social order in which every citizen had a place in an organic whole (as with the early leaders of the Oxford Movement). Its subjects are those who wished to address the state of society as a whole, subjecting its structures to a critique based not only on scripture but on the kind of political philosophy that came out of the Enlightenment, in which the ideals of liberty, equality and co-operation loomed large. These figures were concerned to change society rather than conserve it, to usher in a better world rather than to try to preserve one that was passing away, and this through the progressive realization of a more just and equal social order.

Christian Socialism

The first example pre-dates British Idealism but held much in common with it, not least a commitment to establishing Enlightenment political ideals within a spiritual framework. It arose out of the Chartist Movement, which in 1848 reached the peak of its power in Britain. This was a working class movement seeking political reform, especially universal male suffrage, annual parliaments, voting by ballot, payment of MPs, equal electoral districts and abolition of the property qualification for MPs. In other words it wanted to open up the political process to all classes and especially the new working class based in the growing industrial conurbations. It culminated in a mass demonstration at Kennington Common in London in 1848, on 10 April.

Christian Socialism was founded by three prominent church people who witnessed this and wanted to respond positively. Charles Kingsley (1819–75), Vicar of Eversley in Hampshire and an author, was one, F. D. Maurice, at this stage a professor of Divinity at Kings College, London, was another, and John Ludlow (1821–1911), a barrister and an observer of the recent revolution in France in February 1848, was the third. He had seen how the Parisians had ejected the monarchy and established the Second Republic inspired by socialist ideals, especially the ideal of equality. Ludlow had come back from France declaring to his friends that 'the new Socialism must be Christianized'.

They published a penny journal, *Politics for the People,* from 6 May 1848, to consider political questions from a viewpoint sympathetic to the poor. In their writing they were keen to recognize God's sovereign rule over humankind. Charles Kingsley wrote 'Letters to Chartists' under the pen-name Parson Lot, and the journal ran to 17 issues. Then in 1850 they launched *Tracts on Christian Socialism,* which included 'Cheap Clothes and Nasty' by Kingsley, an indictment of the tailoring sweatshops in the East End of London. Maurice, Ludlow and Kingsley also founded a 'Society of Promoters' to set up co-operative workshops in London for tailoring, printing and other crafts, in order to provide fair wages and decent working conditions for those trapped in the sweatshops. Maurice was also passionate about education, as we have seen, and started evening classes for workers, which gradually developed into the Working Men's College in Great Ormond Street in 1854.

There was something new and important in all of this: Christianity was being presented as not primarily concerned about personal salvation (as with Evangelicals at this time), or as primarily concerned about becoming connected with the historic Catholic tradition of the church (as with followers of the Oxford Movement), but as fundamentally concerned with the condition of society as a whole, inclusive of non-Christians as well as Christians. The condition of the working population, who made up the vast majority of people, was of paramount importance, and the churches should do all they could through practical measures to improve it.

The Christian Socialists did not make a significant impact at the time. Very few workers joined the movement. The tailoring co-operatives closed quite quickly and the adult education movement did not immediately spread across the country. Nor was there an immediate impact on attitudes in church circles. This was the era of self-help individualism and if you were poor most believed it was 'the result of vice'. However, Maurice, Ludlow and Kingsley's movement launched an idea in Christian thinking, the idea that social conditions as a whole needed changing, and this idea began to catch the imagination of those on the edge of the movement.

It is important to note, however, that Maurice himself, confusingly, believed the aim of Christian Socialism was to uncover an already existing divine order in society, rather than construct something new. He believed his vocation

is not to build, but to dig, to show that economics and politics . . . must have a ground beneath themselves, that society is not be made anew by arrangements of ours, but is to be regenerated by finding the law and ground of its order and harmony, the only secret of its existence in God. (F. Maurice 1884, vol. 2, p. 136)

He also stated 'the Church exists to maintain the order of the nation and the order of the family' (Vidler 1948, p. 184). However, in practical terms his work, like that of the other Christian Socialists, promoted change rather than conservation in British society.

Octavia Hill

Among those inspired by the early Christian Socialists was Octavia Hill (1838–1912), like Maurice the child of a Unitarian household who became committed from an early age to working for the poor. Her mother enlisted her to teach from the age of 14 in a guild for poor women in London. Hill was upset by the wretched conditions in which the women lived and the way they were beyond caring about them. She resolved to do what she could to improve them. She met Maurice in 1852 and they supported each other's work. He recruited her to teach in the Working Men's College from 1856. Her encounter with him also had a deep impact on her religious outlook and she saw that it was possible to be both an Anglican and a radical reformer. She was baptized and confirmed in the Church of England in 1857. She also made contact with John Ruskin who had been teaching at the college, and when Ruskin's father died and left him an inheritance Ruskin decided to invest part of it in a housing scheme that she wanted to establish.

Hill had very clear plans, which revolved around improving the housing and charging nominal but compulsory rents. She ensured that each family would have two rooms instead of one, with regular cleaning, ventilation, clearance of the drains, repairs, and redecoration. Bad tenants and those who habitually did not pay their rents were turned out, despite her deep misgivings. The key to her system was the weekly visit by her assistants to collect rent. This allowed the ladies who performed this job to check on every detail of the premises and to broaden their contact with the tenants, especially the children. They became what we would call social workers and were always available if there were personal problems to be resolved.

Gillian Darley explains that 'in common with Josephine Butler and Florence Nightingale she believed that the model of the family and the ideal of the home should underlie all charitable work. Like Mary Carpenter, who argued against institutions and in favour of "cottage homes", Hill was a passionate advocate of small-scale solutions' (Darley 2004). She was concerned, then, not just about the state of the dwellings themselves but the whole lives of her tenants. She would try and find employment for them, and would organize outings to the countryside for the children. She created a tenants' meeting room, and the space around the terrace was cleaned up to be a playground. As soon as one set of dwellings was transformed, she moved on; John Ruskin bought the freehold of other buildings and the same process began again. Any surplus over above the five per cent return that Ruskin wanted was put at the tenants' disposal: they could choose whether the money went towards a playground, sewing or singing classes, or another project.

The scheme began to grow, with more sponsors putting money forward to buy properties and more artisans being housed. She ensured that her replicable approach was widely known through a stream of published articles and her own annual reports, which were privately printed and distributed. There was interest from other cities around the country and then from overseas. She tirelessly addressed meetings and interested groups to spread the word: 'her speaking voice, naturally musical, was one of her greatest assets' (*ibid.*).

Hill's holistic approach recognized the importance of parks and commons for the quality of life of the poor as well as the rich, and she campaigned to preserve green space in London. She saved Parliament Hill, adjoining Hampstead Heath, from being developed (it was incorporated into Hampstead Heath), and in the Lake District she became a key supporter of the Revd Hardwicke Rawnsley's campaign to set up the National Trust and allow the fells and lake sides to be open to the public.

After a temporary collapse in her health, partly brought on by an extraordinary attack by Ruskin who by this stage was becoming mentally unbalanced, in the 1880s she took on a consultancy role to church appointed landlords in east and south London. She also took on the management of church housing in Deptford, Southwark and then in Walworth, south London, and gave advice on the rebuilding of an estate. She wanted to ensure that new housing was built on a domestic scale, and she believed the tenants should be involved in the design of the dwellings.

In the mid 1880s she was a key witness on a royal commission on housing and helped to influence municipal policy up and down the country, though she was opposed to the state providing welfare. Darley sums up her broad achievement in the following terms:

> She was visionary in her attempt to bring self-respect to those who had long since lost it, and inspired in the choices and manner of campaigning to improve the lives of the impoverished . . . Her work and example lived on in a younger generation of professional housing managers and, ironically enough, in decent quality social housing largely provided in the inter-war years by

local authorities. It is also at the root of the late twentieth-century change of emphasis towards smaller-scale, more personal housing management and tenant participation. (*Ibid.*)

The Christian Social Union

A more overtly Anglican example of social reform comes from a group of scholars and church leaders who sought to combine Maurice's Christian Socialism with Green's political philosophy. They were led by Charles Gore (1855–1932) who had been an undergraduate at Balliol and was influenced by biblical criticism but who also in some respects embraced Anglo-Catholicism, being made principal of the newly established Pusey House in Oxford, a library and centre for the movement founded in memory of Pusey. Gore was a gaunt and outspoken figure, with a short temper and the air of a prophet. (In 1892 he would later go on to found the Community of the Resurrection: see above p. 133). The year 1889 was a momentous one for Gore, because firstly he edited a volume of essays, *Lux Mundi,* 'a series of studies in the religion of the incarnation' which aimed to 'put the Catholic faith into its right relation to modern intellectual and moral problems'. (Gore in his own essay on the scripture followed Jowett in applying critical methods to the Bible in order to become clear about when and how its different books were written. In what became a famous footnote he pointed out that Jesus had mistakenly attributed a psalm to King David's authorship when in fact it was clear that David could not have been the author of that and many of other psalms, for their language and style showed they were composed long after the time of David. Gore pointed out that Jesus 'never exhibits the omniscience of bare Godhead in the realm of natural knowledge'; that is, that during his life Jesus had limited knowledge like the rest of us. This and the volume as a whole created another huge controversy and H. P. Liddon, the current leader of the Anglo-Catholics, disowned Gore.) Secondly in 1889 Gore founded the Christian Social Union. This he did with two other prominent leaders, the New Testament scholar and future Bishop of Durham Brook Foss Westcott (1825–1901) and the charismatic preacher and future Dean of St Paul's, Henry Scott Holland (1847–1918). The CSU had three aims:

1 To claim for the Christian Law the ultimate authority to rule social practice.

2 To study in common how to apply the moral truths and principles of Christianity to the social and economic difficulties of the present time.

3 To present Christ in practical life as the living Master and King, the enemy of wrong and selfishness, the power of righteousness and love.
(Worrall 2004, p. 59)

The CSU did not use political propaganda or outspoken denunciations but, instead, sponsored research and education to bring about social reform. It also drew attention to employers who paid poor wages for long hours and put workers in dangerous situations, for example over lead poisoning. It drew up lists of companies whose products should not be bought because of the way they treated their employees. By 1900 it had fifty branches with 4,000 members of whom nearly 1,500 were clergymen. Gore and Holland consistently campaigned in its name on behalf of the poor, lending weight to demands for a 'minimum wage' and for improvements in living conditions for workers in general. 'Gore particularly called both the Church and Nation to penitence for the neglect which had allowed such wretchedness to exist alongside such ostentation in the richest nation in the world. The Lambeth Conference of 1908 was dominated by the concerns of the Union' (*ibid.*, p. 60).

But for some the CSU was not radical enough, especially as it did not explicitly support the workers' own party, the Independent Labour Party (which after the election of its own members to parliament in 1906 became the Labour Party). Following a conference in Morecambe in 1906 the Church Socialist League was formed. This was definitely committed to Socialism in a way that Maurice and even Gore had not been. 'Apart from this definite socialism some of the attraction of the League appears to have been a revolt against the social, intellectual and southern tone of the Union' (*ibid.*, p. 61). Six members of Gore's Community of the Resurrection joined the league and became keen supporters of the Labour Party. The Labour leader Keir Hardie visited Mirfield and spoke to mass meetings of workers in the outdoor amphitheatre in the Community's grounds. The Church Socialist League shows how some Anglicans now believed that society should be reformed not just through voluntary organizing but through committed involvement in the political process. (The Community also committed itself to training working class men for the ordained ministry by opening a theological college in the old stables on its site, a college which trains ordinands to this day.)

10.3 *Practical Social Ethics*: William Temple

The different threads of social reformism we have traced through nineteenth-century Anglicanism arguably reach their apotheosis in the larger-than-life figure of William Temple (1881–1944). He was a philosopher, theologian, educationalist, campaigner, bishop and finally archbishop (of York and then Canterbury), and he shows how the figures and movements mentioned above, seemingly insignificant as they were at the time, came to make a major impact on British society in the mid-twentieth century. It can also be argued that his life brings to mature expression many of the distinctive features of the Enlightenment Anglicanism we have been studying in this third section of the book.

Temple's upbringing and education illustrates all this. He was the son of Frederick Temple who was a colleague and friend of Jowett's at Balliol and had spent the early part of his career in education, becoming first principal of Kneller Hall in 1849 (a teacher training college to supply teachers for the teaching of the poor) and then headmaster of Rugby School, during which time he campaigned energetically for educational reform. He was also a contributor to Jowett's *Essays and Reviews.* His son William was born late in his life, after he had become Bishop of Exeter, and grew up as his father moved to be Bishop of London and then Archbishop of Canterbury. William himself also attended Rugby School (where Thomas Arnold had implanted his broad churchmanship) and Balliol, where he came under the influence of Edward Caird and the British Idealist school of philosophy. Gore was an older mentor and friend, though William never embraced Anglo-Catholicism in the way that Gore did. He was also a very different character: jovial and ever cheerful (sometimes annoyingly so) in contrast to Gore's frequent irascibility. As a philosopher, reason was dominant in Temple's thinking, though both scripture and tradition became almost equally important in his later career, and he developed a deep knowledge and affection for the fourth gospel, which led eventually to the publication of the two volumes of his *Readings in St John Gospel,* (1939–40) (which were best sellers when they were published and have remained in print almost continuously ever since).

Temple's own career also illustrates the way he drew together the different strands of Enlightenment Anglicanism, with his first job being that of a philosophy lecturer at Oxford, combined with active involvement first in the Christian Social Union and then in the Workers Educational Association (bringing together workers and university teachers in co-operative education), leading to his election as its president from 1908 to 1924. He was ordained and then like his father became a headmaster of a major private school, Repton. But he did not really take to being a headmaster and moved on to be successively rector of St James' Piccadilly, Canon of Westminster, Bishop of Manchester, Archbishop of York and finally Archbishop of Canterbury during the Second World War from 1942 until his premature death in 1944. These ministerial roles were combined with ongoing philosophical and theological study, leading to the publication of a large number of books. The most important of these were three works of philosophical theology: *Mens Creatrix* (Creative Mind) of 1917, *Christus Veritas* (Christ the Truth) of 1924 and *Nature, Man and God* of 1934 (based on his Gifford lectures in Scotland).

Also, crucially, Temple maintained active leadership of the Christian Social-ist movement for the transformation of society, though he did not describe himself as a Christian Socialist. This is seen in his chairmanship of the Confer-ence on Politics, Economics and Citizenship (COPEC) in Birmingham in 1924, a gathering of 1400 ecumenical delegates that formulated general principles for the reform of society (though the principles ended up being too general to have much impact). His concern for change in society was also expressed in his Scott Holland lectures of 1928, *Christianity and the State,* where he coined the phrase 'the welfare state' as a goal for British society (Temple 1929, p. 170; see Grimley 2004, p. 1). His concern was also expressed in his addresses to the Oxford University mission of 1931 (printed as *Christian Faith and Life*) which changed the way many undergraduates in the university saw Christianity, from being an irrelevance to being a dynamic force for change. It was also seen in his chairmanship of a commission on unemployment (which had remained at very high levels throughout the 1930s). The commission's report *Men without Work,* published in 1938, on the social consequences of long term unemployment in Blackburn, Durham, Leicester, Liverpool and the Rhondda, was highly regarded in government and academic circles and led to the opening of 1,500 occupational centres for the unemployed across the country. It also occurred in the publishing of his Penguin paperback *Christianity and Social Order* in 1942, offering a set of proposals based on theological principles for post-war reconstruction in Britain (more on which below). The book went on to sell 139,000 copies, which showed that Temple was being read and heeded beyond the churches. This was followed by a series of mass meetings to generate support for these proposals, called 'The

Church Looks Forward' campaign. This campaign and Temple's book are credited with swinging a significant section of the population behind the Beveridge Report and its proposals for a welfare state, which the Labour Government of 1945–51 were then able to implement. Finally Temple gave crucial backing to Butler's Education Act of 1944, which ensured that every child in the country received the same quality of schooling. Previously the denominations had not been able to agree on a unified system, which had prevented progress, but now Temple's backing for the bill, combined with his high standing as an ecumenist among the free churches, meant that parliament passed the bill.

All of this was important in the post-war years (see Grimley 2004), but is there an ongoing legacy? Did Temple's approach to social and economic issues make a lasting contribution to Anglicanism and the wider church? A strong case can be made that his method of moving backwards and forwards from theological principles to the practicalities of change at ground level did indeed do so. This was the case especially in *Christianity and Social Order* of 1942. He drew up 'Christian social principles', which were a succinct distillation of his understanding of God's will for the future development of society, and then brought these into dialogue with a range of social questions, producing a set of practical proposals.

The first principle he described as freedom, or the principle of respect for personality in all people. He explained that 'if each man and woman is a child of God, whom God loves and for whom Christ died, then there is in each a worth absolutely independent of all usefulness to society. The person is primary, not the society; the State exists for the citizen, not the citizen for the State.' This meant that society must be so organized so that people can freely express their own personalities through deliberate choice. And that, in turn, meant that there must be 'the best possible training' so that people would know how to make deliberate choices: 'it is the responsible exercise of deliberate choice which most fully expresses personality and best deserves the great name of freedom' (Temple 1950, p. 59).

Temple did not follow J. S. Mill, then, in believing that freedom was the simple absence of coercion. He followed T. H. Green in believing that freedom was a positive quality given by others: it depended on society and, in particular for Temple, on the state fulfilling a positive role, especially through education, in equipping the person for a purposeful and creative life in which they would play their part in moving things forward. He was emphatic, though, that the state had only a conditional authority and jurisdiction to do certain things: it could never be an ultimate object of political loyalty.

The second Christian social principle was an expression of the social dimension of this freedom: 'No man is fitted for an isolated life; every one has needs which he cannot supply for himself; but he needs not only what his neighbours contribute to the equipment of his life but their actual selves as the complement of his own. Man is naturally and incurably social' (*ibid.*, p. 62). This social fellowship is expressed through family life, school, college, trade union, professional association, city, county, nation, church. All these groupings need to be nurtured by the state, which should give them the freedom they need to guide their own activities (provided the freedom of other associations is not injured). They are crucial because 'Liberty is actual in the various cultural and commercial and local associations that men form. In each of these a man can feel that he counts for something and that others depend on him as he on them' (*ibid.*, p. 64).

The third Christian social principle was also an extrapolation from what had already been said: 'The combination of Freedom and Fellowship as principles of social life issues in the obligation of Service' (*ibid.*, p. 68). Temple was thinking here of both individuals and groups, that they were to seek not their own welfare first but the general welfare of all people. He described how we should use our wider loyalties to check the narrower: 'we can and should check these keener loyalties [to family, locality, business, trade union . . .] by recognising the prior claim of the wider [humankind, nation]. So a man rightly does his best for the welfare of his own family, but must never serve his family in ways that injure the nation. A man rightly does his best for his country, but must never serve his country in ways that injure mankind' (*ibid.*, p. 70). This principle was the vaguest and most overtly Christian of the three, but it was consistent with the other two and showed their moral bearing.

The three principles, of freedom, fellowship and service, were then applied to contemporary British society, and he found the state completely failing to fulfil its responsibilities. In *Christianity and Social Order* he noted that the Second World War had removed some of the unemployment but there was still much that was wrong: 'the problems were urgent enough before the war; the war has vastly increased their urgency'. In a clearly written and cogent chapter entitled 'The Task Before Us' he deduced some broad but far reaching recommendations from the social principles. In words that recall Octavia Hill, he urged Christians to call upon the Government to make sure that every family 'should be housed with decency and dignity, so that it may grow up as a member of that basic community in a happy fellowship unspoilt by underfeeding or over-crowding, by dirty and drab surroundings or by mechanical monotony of environment'. He also called for education for all 'till years of maturity', and that every citizen should have an income to maintain a home and bring up children, and that every worker should have a voice in the conduct of their business or industry, and be given two days rest in seven 'and, if an employee, an annual holiday with pay'. There should be 'assured liberty in the forms of freedom of worship, of speech, of assembly, and of association for special purposes' (*ibid.*, p. 99).

In an appendix, 'A Suggested Programme', Temple took one further step. The historian R. H. Tawney and the economist J. M. Keynes read the manuscript of the whole book and, according to the preface, made many suggestions. Temple also knew Sir William Beveridge who was about to publish his key report *Social Insurance and Allied Services*, the foundation of the post-war legislation that established the welfare state under the Labour government. Temple was clearly influenced by Beveridge and included in the appendix some of the practical recommendations that Beveridge had been discussing. This recalls Joseph Butler's empiricism: beginning with the particular situation in which people are placed and the actual options open to them (see Chapter 8.3). Temple's policy recommendations were therefore rooted in expert analysis of the situation on the ground but also followed naturally from the principles and broad recommendations he had just described. They show him making a powerful connection between theology and the empirical reality. They included the following:

- Decent housing should be built near where workers worked.
- Family allowances should be paid to mothers for each child after the first two.
- Wages should be sufficient for a family of four.
- Milk and one good meal a day should be provided at school.
- Education should be the primary occupation of everyone up to the age of 18.
- The state should eradicate unemployment through public works, as and when it arises.
- Labour should be represented on the directorates through the Unions.
- Every citizen should have two days rest in seven, and an annual holiday with pay.

These points are examples of 'middle axioms', which are practical objectives that show how abstract theory impinges on actual problems and issues. Temple used the term 'middle axiom' in his introduction to the Malvern Report of 1941, where he defined them as 'maxims for conduct which mediate between the fundamental principles and the tangle of particular problems'. (Temple 1941, p. vii) It was a term that had been used at the COPEC conference, and was brought to international attention by W. A. Visser 't Hooft and J. H. Oldham in a preparatory book for the 1937 ecumenical Oxford conference on 'Church, Community and State'. It became widely used in British church circles after the war. It was later advocated by Ronald H. Preston as a method for Christian social ethics (see, for example, his 'Middle Axioms in Christian Social Ethics' in Preston 1981), and it can be argued, it has been used in more recent reports such as the Archbishop of Canterbury's *Faith in the City* of 1985 and the Children's Society's *A Good Childhood* of 2009. Temple did not use the term in his own books but, in *Christianity and Social Order*, provided an influential example (especially in the above points) of the method it represented. He showed how it was possible to make useful connections between Christian theology and practical social and economic problems, through the drawing up of intermediate objectives in consultation with those most informed about the empirical reality of the issues, and which different parties could then implement in their own fields (see further Suggate 1987, and Elford and Markham 2000).

As an example of Christian ethical method, then, Temple's social principles and 'middle axioms' are of lasting significance. Many of the specific proposals he advocated for British society were achieved in the years following his death, but the way in which he formulated and promoted the principles, his practical social ethics, shows something more, an enduring legacy of Enlightenment Anglicanism for discipleship in a new century.

Discussion Questions

1 Does it make any sense today to see human history as a process with a purpose and a goal?
2 Should the state or other organizations provide housing for the needy free of charge, or should every household be expected to pay rent? On what theological grounds do you base your answer?
3 In the 'middle axiom' approach to practical social ethics, faith communities develop guiding principles informed by their basic orientation, and then interact with the specialists in touch with the empirical reality on the ground in order to arrive at certain policy recommendations. These are general enough to receive widespread support while specific enough to make an impact on those in government and elsewhere (who must work out the detail of how to put them into practice). What are the strengths and weaknesses of this kind of approach?

Further Reading

Grimley, Matthew (2004), *Citizenship, Community and the Church of England: Liberal Anglican Theories of the State between the Wars*, Oxford: Clarendon Press.

Hinchliff, Peter (1992), *God and History: Aspects of British Theology 1875–1914*, Oxford: Oxford University Press.

Iremonger, F. A. (1948), *William Temple, Archbishop of Canterbury: His Life and Letters*, Oxford: Oxford University Press.

Livingston, James C. (2006), *Modern Christian Thought: The Enlightenment and the Nineteenth Century*, 2nd edition, Minneapolis: Fortress Press.

Morris, Jeremy (2007), *To Build Christ's Kingdom: F. D. Maurice and his writings*, Norwich: Canterbury Press.

Singer, Peter (1983), *Hegel*, Oxford: Oxford University Press.

Spencer, Stephen (2001), *William Temple: A Calling to Prophecy*, London: SPCK.

Suggate, Alan (1987), *William Temple and Christian Social Ethics Today*, Edinburgh: T and T Clark.

Temple, William (1976), *Christianity and Social Order*, London: Shepeard-Walwyn.

Wilkinson, Alan (1998), *Christian Socialism: Scott Holland to Tony Blair*, London: SCM.

Part 4

Anglicanism as a Whole

11

One Way or Many?

Anglicanism, as Robert Runcie (a recent Archbishop of Canterbury) used to point out, is the second largest global communion in the world. By this he meant that while other churches such as the Roman Catholic, Orthodox and Lutheran, have a greater number of adherents, none, apart from the first of these, is so widely spread around the world. Today there are around 78 million Christians within the Anglican Communion who are members of 44 independent churches. These are made up of 34 provinces, four united churches and six other churches spread across the globe (Anglican Communion Office 2008).

The global breadth and diversity of Anglicanism makes it all but impossible to describe its current state comprehensively. One observer who has recently published an overview of world Anglicanism has written how 'the sheer magnitude of the material encompassed by world Anglicanism renders it completely impossible to be aware of, let alone cover, everything' (Kaye 2008, p. vii).

The approach adopted by this Studyguide has therefore been to look behind this contemporary institutional panorama and uncover the underlying historic approaches to discipleship. It has not presented a history of Anglican institutions (see Jacob 1997, Ward 2006 and Kaye 2008 for recent examples of this), nor a mapping of Anglican doctrine and belief (see Avis 2002 and again Kaye 2008 for guidance on this), though both institutions and beliefs have been mentioned at many points. It has traced the origins and some more recent expressions of the defining features of what it has meant to live the Christian life within Anglicanism.

But a final pressing question insists on being addressed. The Studyguide has unveiled not one but three fundamental approaches to discipleship, and the question arises out of this diversity. The first approach can be described as an Evangelical Protestantism, inspired by the Reformation, which gives the words of scripture pride of place in determining the faith. The influential Anglican Evangelical writer J. I. Packer, for example, describes 'six evangelical fundamentals' with the first being 'the supremacy of Holy Scripture because of its unique inspiration' (quoted in Stott 1999, pp. 26–7). John Stott himself writes,

> The primary question in every religion relates to the topic of authority: by what authority do we believe what we believe? And the primary answer which evangelical Christians (whether Anglican, Lutheran, Presbyterian, Baptist or other) give to this question is that supreme authority resides neither in the church, nor in the individual, but in Christ and the biblical witness to him. (Stott 1999, p. 43)

Within Anglicanism the continuing global influence of this approach is illustrated by the Church of Nigeria, for example. A Nigerian priest recently described how the Church of Nigeria 'is rooted in its Evangelical heritage. The founding of the Nigerian Church is traceable to the eighteenth-century revival in the Church of England ... In Nigeria, the Bible is always the final arbiter in all matters of theology and ethics' (Fagbemi 2005). (There remains the question raised in Chapter 3.2, though, of whether 'experience' is beginning to supplant scripture as the primary authority within discipleship for some Anglican evangelicals.)

A second Anglican approach to the Christian life is found across the border in Ghana, and in many other parts of the Anglican world. This is a Catholicism which looks to the Catholic Church as a whole, and especially to the undivided church of the first five centuries, for determining the faith. John Macquarrie has been one of the most eminent recent exponents of this viewpoint within Anglican theology. He began life as a Presbyterian within the Church of Scotland but became an Anglican because he wanted to be part of such 'tradition', as we have seen it called:

> Anglicanism has never considered itself to be a sect or denomination originating in the sixteenth century. It continues without a break the *Ecclesia Anglicana* founded by St. Augustine thirteen centuries and more ago, though nowadays that branch of the Church has spread far beyond the borders of England. It is often claimed that Anglicanism has no special doctrines of its own and simply follows the universal teaching of the Church. When one considers the nature of the English Reformation, one sees that there is strong

support for the claim. In England there was no single dominant figure, such as Luther or Calvin, who might impress upon the Church his own theological idiosyncrasies. The conscious aim of the English Reformation was to return, so far as possible, to the Catholic Christianity of the undivided Church of the first five centuries. (Sykes and Booty 1988, pp. 424–5)

Recent scholarship, as we saw in Part 1, has emphasized the discontinuity of the English Reformation with what went before it. Nevertheless there are still many within Anglicanism who see continuities between contemporary Anglicanism and the ancient Western Catholic tradition as more important than Reformation discontinuities.

A third approach comes out of the Enlightenment, as we have just seen, with its elevation of reason above scripture and tradition as the final arbiter of Christian faith and practice. The influence of this approach is again found in many parts of the Anglican world today, most famously in the Episcopal Church of the United States (PECUSA), which has generally been the first to revise aspects of Anglican belief and practice to accord with post-Enlightenment Western culture, a culture in which equality and liberty are valued above all else. The ordination of women to the priesthood and then to the episcopate would be one notable example, and the consecration of the first openly gay bishop in the Anglican Communion would be another. The question remains open for some as to whether PECUSA has abandoned scripture or tradition rather than try to hold them together with the reason of Enlightenment culture.

The presence of these three approaches within Anglicanism forces a question upon us, the question alluded to above. It is this: is Anglicanism in fact three distinct ecclesial traditions rather than one? Is there any sense in continuing to speak of one entity called Anglicanism: should we not talk of different Anglicanisms?

There are a number of different arguments that have been used to support the unity of Anglicanism, some stronger than others. Let us examine each in turn.

11.1 *Over the Many*: Institutions and Instruments

It has been claimed that Anglicanism is a system of belief and practice. This claim is implicit in the Oxford English Dictionary's definition of Anglicanism as 'the system of doctrine and practice of those Christians who are in communion with the see of Canterbury'. It is a bold claim that Anglicanism is a 'system' and, if anything, this Studyguide has revealed not one system but three systems, each with their own way of ordering the relative authority of scripture, tradition and reason. At a number of 'flash points' in Anglican history we have seen these three systems are incommensurable on key questions of practice and belief, undermining the possibility of a systematic unity.

A more restricted and widely used definition is that Anglicanism is 'a system of doctrine and practice that is *distinguishable* from Roman Catholic, Orthodox and Protestant outlooks and expressed in certain key formularies, such as the Declaration of Assent of the C of E' (Cross 1997). To unpack what this means we can examine a recent version of the 'The Declaration of Assent' from the 1975 Church of England. This expresses the distinguishability of Anglicanism in the following way:

> The Church of England is part of the One, Holy, Catholic and Apostolic Church worshipping the one true God, Father, Son and Holy Spirit. It professes the faith uniquely revealed in the Holy Scriptures and set forth in the catholic creeds, which faith the Church is called upon to proclaim afresh in each generation. Led by the Holy Spirit, it has borne witness to Christian truth in its historic formularies, the Thirty-nine Articles of Religion, the Book of Common Prayer and the Ordering of Bishops, Priests and Deacons.

This is a brilliantly concise yet elegant summary of the way authority within Anglicanism comes from the three sources of scripture, tradition and reason (see Podmore 2005, Chapter 4, for an account of how this version of the declaration was produced). Those being ordained as deacons and priests must 'affirm' their 'loyalty to this inheritance of faith as your inspiration and guidance'. Yet the declaration does not resolve the key issue of whether scripture or tradition or reason is to take precedence when there are disagreements over contentious issues such as ordaining women or openly gay men to the episcopate. In the declaration scripture is mentioned first, but what is to prevent Catholics from saying that the Catholic creeds provide the lens through which to view and interpret scripture, or Anglicans rooted in the Enlightenment from saying that the phrase 'proclaiming afresh' means a whole scale reinterpretation of what has been handed down. The Declaration of Assent sets out the ingredients of Anglican identity but it does not stipulate how they are to be mixed together. So it cannot, unfortunately, support the notion that Anglicanism is a 'system' of doctrine and practice.

An institutional unity?

Does, instead, the unity of Anglicanism reside in its institutions? The Anglican Communion is a collection of independent provinces and churches that have authority over their own doctrine and church order as well as their daily affairs. Each has its own canon law, which is the body of rules or laws imposed by each church on its clergy and laity in matters of faith, morals and discipline (the canon law of the Church of England was put into its current form in 1604 and revised in 1969; for canon law across the Anglican Communion see Doe 1998). There is no papacy or Vatican curia with a 'magisterium' of juridical and executive authority over the whole body. Nevertheless there are at least four institutions or 'instruments' which might claim to bring unity to the whole: the Archbishop of Canterbury, with whom all the provinces and churches are in communion and who provides a 'unique focus of Anglican unity' (Anglican Communion Office 2008). He calls the Lambeth Conference, and Primates Meeting, and is President of the Anglican Consultative Council (see below). He is widely regarded as the *primus inter pares* (first among equals) among the bishops and more than anyone else can represent Anglicanism to other churches and the wider world. Rowan Williams is the 104th Archbishop in a succession that goes back to Augustine of Canterbury, who arrived in Kent, from Rome, in AD 597. Nevertheless his authority depends on the voluntary consent of other bishops and provinces.

The second institution is the Lambeth Conference, called every ten years or so. We have already seen how Archbishop Longley called the first Lambeth Conference in 1867 in response to the crisis over *Essays and Reviews* and Bishop

Colenso. It met at the Archbishop's main residence, Lambeth Palace in London, which gave it its name. The Archbishop of York, supported by the bishops of Durham, Carlisle and Ripon, refused to attend because he feared the conference would weaken the link between church and state in Britain (Jacob 1997, p. 163), though 76 other bishops did attend and issued an 'Address to the Faithful'. This is a reminder that the conference has often met in the shadow of crisis and division, the most recent being the conflict between provinces over the consecration of Gene Robinson, an openly gay man. At the 2008 conference there were over 800 bishops, as well as their spouses, though as in 1867 a number of other bishops deliberately stayed away for theological or political reasons. Many reports of the conference describe the way Archbishop Rowan and the organization of the conference brought the bishops together in a deep unity of prayer and fellowship. Nevertheless the conference has never claimed to be a synod. At the first Lambeth Conference in 1867 Longley made it clear that the gathering was a conference and not a synod, and that its resolutions would be purely declaratory: they would have only the influence of recommendations (Evans and Wright 1991, p. 328). This has remained the position to this day: the resolutions of Lambeth Conferences only have effect if enacted by synods in each constituent church of the Communion.

The third institution is the meeting of the Primates (the presiding bishops from the different provinces and churches). They have met since 1979, under the chairmanship of the Archbishop of Canterbury, for 'consultation, prayer and reflection on theological, social and international matters' (Anglican Communion Office 2008). These meetings now take place every year, and can meet anywhere in the world. There have been calls to increase the authority of this meeting, and its role in overseeing the Anglican Communion Covenant (see below) may achieve this.

The fourth institution is the Anglican Consultative Council (ACC), which is a body that represents clergy and laity as well as bishops. This was created by the 1968 Lambeth Conference and was given the task of co-ordinating international ecumenical and mission work. Each province and church gave its consent to the setting up of the council and sends delegates. It has met regularly since, and in different parts of the world. But it has made little impact on Anglican life, largely because, again, it has no legal or executive powers in the member churches.

The lack of legal and executive power, then, is a theme running through all these institutions. They are what they claim to be and no more, people and *spaces* in which valuable consultation and exploration can take place, without power to enforce any resolutions. The Archbishop of Canterbury can only visit other parts of the Anglican Communion when he is invited to do so; the Lambeth Conference resolutions have authority over individual Anglicans only when the local synod or council accepts that they do so; the Primates meeting and the Anglican Consultative Council can only direct different churches when those churches choose to submit to their authority. All of which means that these four institutions cannot, in fact, hold the Anglican Communion together. Their role is a different though important and valuable one: to encourage and help the provinces and churches to work together for that unity. Their authority is a moral one, based on the respect that they already have from members. Where there is no such respect, there is little they can do facilitate unity. So, to come to the main point, their existence does not definitively prove that Anglicanism is not three distinct ecclesial traditions rather than one.

It is important to add that there is currently a fifth instrument under discussion by provinces and churches, 'The Anglican Communion Covenant'. This is a statement which they are invited to adopt to express a shared commitment not to make any changes to their own life and beliefs which will create offence and division with other provinces and churches. It was an idea first proposed by the Windsor Report of 2004, written by a specially convened group of church leaders and theologians in response to deep divisions in the Anglican Communion over the ordination of Gene Robinson and a proposal by a diocese in Canada to allow the blessing of gay relationships in church. The final version of the covenant was published in November 2009 and has now been sent out to the provinces and churches for consideration for adoption. The key clauses are in the third and fourth sections. In the third section those adopting the covenant declare that 'Acknowledging our interdependent life, each Church, reliant on the Holy Spirit, commits itself

> (3.2.5) to act with diligence, care and caution in respect of any action which may provoke controversy, which by its intensity, substance or extent could threaten the unity of the Communion and the effectiveness or credibility of its mission.
> (3.2.6) in situations of conflict, to participate in mediated conversations, which involve face to face meetings, agreed parameters and a willingness to see such processes through. (Anglican Communion 2009)

In the fourth section the Covenant document then proposes a set procedure of consultation and meetings to reach agreement between different churches or, in cases where one church refuses to retract or reconsider what it is proposing, for a body called the Standing Committee of the Anglican Communion (responsible to the ACC and the Primates meeting) to take action. This action is described in the following way:

> (4.2.5) The Standing Committee may request a Church to defer a controversial action [for example to allow the blessing of gay partnerships in church]. If a Church declines to defer such action, the Standing Committee may recommend to any Instrument of Communion [the four institutions described above] relational consequences which may specify a provisional limitation of participation in, or suspension from, that Instrument until the completion of the process set out below.

This process is, then, one of specifying the extent and 'relational consequences' of the controversial action and its 'practical consequences' (4.2.7). In other words, the offending Church might no longer be invited to the meetings of the institutions. But the document adds, 'Each Church or each Instrument shall determine whether or not to accept such recommendations' (*ibid.*). So, again, the only final authority is a moral one, based on whatever degree of respect the Covenant and Standing Committee already has. There is nothing within its legalistic prose which can compel any signed-up partner to do what others want it to do. However, it should be added that the process of creating and adopting the Covenant around the Anglican Communion may well help the growth of such authority, so supporting its role in strengthening unity.

A local structural unity?

If centralized institutions do not hold the unity of Anglicanism, what about the structure of the church at local level? In England and Wales this is the parochial system, dating back at least to the tenth century, recorded in the Doomsday Book of 1086, and in continuous existence ever since. One fairly recent report suggested that it might hold the key to the nature of the church. The report was based on the most extensive survey of rural Christianity in this country ever carried out and it commented that

It is easy to debate the nature of Anglicanism in terms of a three-fold order of ministry set amidst Prayer Book, the place of Reason in interpreting scripture, and Church Tradition. A better way of characterizing the Church, however, might be in its parish organization and ethos. The Parochial System constitutes the Church of England. It is the parish not the diocese, the priest not the bishop, which forms the centre of gravity of Anglicanism. (*Church and Religion in Rural England,* 1991, quoted in General synod 1998, p. 21)

Ronald Blythe has evocatively described why this might be so and why the parish is so significant in many people's lives:

Parish scenery pulls us this way and that, it is in control of us. Even the twist and turns of a city parish's streets have their special private direction for the born parishioner. In the country, where one can often see an entire parish from boundary to boundary, one can also often see one's entire life. It is comforting – and painful. For those who have remained in the same place a parish is not an address, it is somewhere you don't need one. But if one moves away after only a few formative years there is no severing the umbilical link that feeds one with its particular parochialism. (*Ibid.* p. 22)

Within this powerful setting the priest, as the local holy man, takes 'charge of the local holy ground' (*ibid.*). And all of this is true of countless parishes across the country and explains why the parish could by the unifying element within Anglicanism.

It is an attractive argument, indicating a deeply grounded unity to Anglicanism independent of whatever goes on at national or international level. But it is also a very English-centric view of Anglicanism, implying that the parochial system of the Church of England represents Anglicanism as a whole. It could easily be argued, however, that the Church of England expresses the exception rather than the rule, as most provinces of the Anglican Communion do not operate with a parochial system in which every acre of land in the country is assigned to one parish church and its priest, or another, with clear boundaries marking out the line where one ends and another begins. Most Anglican churches outside England (and increasingly many within England), function as gathered communities, drawing their congregations from a wide area which bears little relationship with parochial boundaries. The character of the worship and community life tends to be the major factor in drawing people into itself, rather than the geographical location of the church within the community it serves. But, it should be added that this is more the case for churches in urban areas than for those in rural areas. Where distances are large, a greater proportion of the people will go to the church that is nearest to where they live. Overall, though, the words quoted above cannot be taken as a description of Anglicanism but only as a description of one segment (albeit an important one) of the parishes of the Church of England.

11.2 *Within the Many*: The Quadrilateral

We must turn away from outward institutional life, whether at national, international or local level, to find the unity of Anglicanism. Does the faith and practice of the church show more promise? F. D. Maurice, as we have seen (Chapter 9.2), argued that all the historic Christian denominations share certain key signs or marks which can allow them to value and respect each other. He applied the same argument to the parties and traditions of the Church of England. This argument was taken up by an American Episcopal priest, William Reed Huntington, who in his 1870 book *The Church Idea: An Essay Toward Unity* proposed not six but four such elements which were common to Anglican, Roman Catholic and Orthodox churches and could form the basis of 'Home Reunion' with them. Then in 1886 the bishops of the American Episcopal Church, at their meeting in Chicago, passed a resolution which adopted Huntington's four fundamental marks as a basis of ecumenical dialogue. Other bishops around the communion were impressed by this and the Lambeth Conference of 1888 also adopted the same four marks. In Resolution 11 the Lambeth bishops resolved that

> in the opinion of this Conference, the following Articles supply a basis on which approach may be by God's blessing made towards Home Reunion:
>
> (a) The Holy Scriptures of the Old and New Testaments, as 'containing all things necessary to salvation' [Article VI], and as being the rule and ultimate standard of faith.
> (b) The Apostles' Creed, as the Baptismal Symbol; and the Nicene Creed, as the sufficient statement of the Christian faith.

(c) The two Sacraments ordained by Christ Himself – Baptism and the Supper of the Lord – ministered with unfailing use of Christ's words of Institution, and of the elements ordained by Him.

(d) The Historic Episcopate, locally adapted in the methods of its administration to the varying needs of the nations and peoples called of God into the Unity of His Church.

(Anglican Communion 1888)

This statement has come to be known as the Chicago-Lambeth Quadrilateral and it is significant in a number of respects. As Adrian Chatfield has pointed out, this was the first time Anglicans had attempted a self-definition that was not English in origin, recognized a common Anglican identity, gave some definition to that identity, and did not mention Englishness as a defining characteristic (Chatfield 2007, p. 29). It clearly demonstrated how Anglicanism now transcended the belief and practice of its founding church. The statement has been quoted in official documents many times since, most recently in the Covenant (see 1.1.3 – 1.1.6, in Anglican Communion 2009). It has been especially helpful in ecumenical discussions in the twentieth century where other churches have recognized and affirmed the four marks within their own life, thus establishing common ground as a basis for moving together. In ecumenical conversations with Lutherans and Methodists and Roman Catholics, for example, it has brought to the foreground those things that Anglicans share with the Western tradition as a whole, and this has allowed the growth of mutual understanding and appreciation of other differences.

In the Quadrilateral, then, there is the start of a secure answer to our leading question: Anglicans are united by these four fundamental marks of Christian faith and practice. The Quadrilateral describes a common watermark, as it were, that runs through the three traditions described in this Studyguide. But, on the other hand, it is quite a minimalist answer to our question. It ignores other elements of the faith which many Anglicans would find equally if not more important, such as the personal experience of justification and sanctification, or the ministry of the priesthood, or the use of reason in interpreting the faith. It also ignores the colour and character of Anglican life at local level, varied yet often of an unmistakable type around the world. It describes only what Anglicanism shares with other mainline churches, a lowest common denominator across the Western tradition. Is there not something more, something distinctive to this church that further unites its different traditions? This is a challenging question because the divisions between these competing traditions run so deep. Yet another Lambeth Conference suggested that there was something more.

11.3 *Between the Many*: Checking and Redressing

The bishops who met at the Lambeth Conference of 1948 adopted a longer statement on the nature of Anglican authority. It was a surprising statement because it talked about the *dispersed* nature of Anglican authority. How could this uphold the unity of Anglicanism? It began by describing the non-coercive character of Anglican authority:

> The positive nature of the authority which binds the Anglican Communion together is . . . moral and spiritual, resting on the truth of the Gospel, and on a charity which is patient and willing to defer to the common mind.

> Authority, as inherited by the Anglican Communion from the undivided Church of the early centuries of the Christian era, is single in that it is derived from a single divine source, and reflects within itself the richness and historicity of the Divine Revelation, the authority of the eternal Father, the incarnate Son, and the life-giving Spirit. It is distributed among Scripture, Tradition, Creeds, the Ministry of the Word and Sacraments, the witness of saints, and the *consensus fidelium*, which is the continuing experience of the Holy Spirit through his faithful people in the Church.

> It is thus a dispersed rather than a centralized authority having many elements which combine, interact with, and check each other; these elements together contributing a process of mutual support, mutual checking, and redressing of errors or exaggerations in the many-sided fullness of the authority which Christ has committed to his Church. Where this authority of Christ is to be found mediated not in one mode but in several we recognize in this multiplicity God's loving provision against the temptations to tyranny and the dangers of unchecked power. (Lambeth 1948, p. 84)

This is an eloquent statement with an attractive view of authority coming from a number of sources but sharing a deeper unity based on Christ himself. It has come to be regarded in some quarters as a classical statement of the nature of Anglicanism (see Avis 2000, p. 58). Stephen Sykes calls it 'the most satisfactory public statement of the Anglican view of authority' (Sykes 1978, p. 88). For some, though, it is problematic. Edward Norman, a church historian and critic of Anglicanism, presented the following critique of the statement at the time of the 1998 Lambeth Conference:

> Here is a puzzling mixture. The manner in which doctrine is known to be authentic is dispersed in a fashion which embraces all the variants, individual and collective, which have presented themselves. There is no clue in the Report [from which the statement comes] as to how it is possible to recognize legitimate interpretations from corruptions. What is envisaged is a spiritual free-for-all in which authority is derived from diversity and truth emerges through 'elasticity'. This is rather a frank conclusion. As an account of the ingredients available for a serious discussion of the nature of authority the Report is adequate in its way, at least to the extent that it recognizes the problems. But it offers no prospect of an ordered passage beyond the preliminaries, so that the unitary body of Christ might act in unity. (Norman 1998)

Norman's point is that if authority is dispersed in this way there is no clear cut way to bring unity at moments of division and crisis. It is not adequate to the needs of a fractious church. In recent years the divisions over sexuality, which have shown anything but a common mind or *consensus fidelium* among the faithful, would seem to bear this out.

However, his critique does not acknowledge the way the statement puts emphasis on the role of *time* within ongoing discernment in reaching authoritative decisions. The statement is asking us to step back from the immediate fray of conflict and to take a longer term view, to see that over time the different authorities check each other, redressing exaggerations or errors, producing a common mind on controversial questions. The long term *end* of controversy, in other words, provides the key to how Anglican authority is actually expressed and how Anglican unity is formed. It is through a period of interaction that the church as a whole makes up its mind, under the influence of the Holy Spirit, and forges a working unity.

The Parish Communion Movement

This may all seem quite idealistic but a recent example of unity growing at local level can be cited in support. In the Victorian and Edwardian eras the main act of worship on a Sunday morning in most Anglican churches was Morning Prayer or Mattins, often supplemented with the Litany and the first part of the Holy Communion service ('Antecommunion'). The full celebration of Holy Communion would only take place once a quarter, and usually at 8 a.m. rather than mid-morning. Ordinary Anglicans, then, had little exposure to communion, and even in Anglo-Catholic parishes, where it was regarded very highly, celebrations would still take place early in the morning because of the rule that it was necessary to fast before receiving. Then in the 1920s, arising out of the increasing popularity of Anglo-Catholicism, many voices began to call for weekly communion in all parishes. These included Charles Gore, who was influenced by his study of worship in the New Testament, also the liturgical scholar A. G. Herbert, who published his influential books *Liturgy and Society* in 1932 and *Parish Communion* in 1936, and Henry de Candole, curate and then vicar at St John's Newcastle-upon-Tyne (1926–31). He instigated the '9.15' service, which brought together the said 8 a.m. Holy Communion with a 10 a.m. 'Children's Eucharist'. In this way, almost for the first time, the Church of England had a service of communion at which hymns were sung, a sermon was preached, and communion was administered to the confirmed in the congregation. 'The sundered features of worship were being brought together, and families could worship together at such a service, and, perhaps join in a "parish breakfast" afterwards' (Buchanan 1980, pp. 130–1).

The parish communion concept began to gain popularity in the 1930s and it drew support from the Roman Catholic liturgical movement taking place on the continent, which was seeking to make the mass not just a priestly event but a meaningful and up-building act of the whole congregation. At this stage Evangelicals steered clear of the movement, but in the 1940s and 1950s, when Mattins was no longer found to be adequate, the simple appeal of 'The Lord's service for the Lord's people on the Lord's day' made a big impact on many 'low' parishes. This was encouraged by the Associated Parishes organization in the American Episcopal Church, and the Parish and People organization in the Church of England. So churches began to pull their communion tables out from the east wall, in order that the clergy could stand *behind* the table, and face the people across it, as Methodists and Presbyterians had long done. In some churches the altar was brought forward to the chancel step, or onto a platform extending into the nave, so that the sense of the whole parish gathered around the table was obvious. Finally, at the Keele congress in 1967 the leadership of the Evangelical movement gave its whole hearted support to the weekly celebration of the Sacrament 'as the central corporate Service of the Church' (Crowe 1967, p. 35). In the period from the 1960s to the 1980s a majority of parishes moved to having a weekly celebration of Holy Communion as the main act of worship.

All of this is important because it shows how, over time, contentious and divisive developments within Anglicanism, such as the Anglo-Catholic promotion of Holy Communion in the nineteenth century, with all the fears of 'popery' that that engendered in other parts of the church, have been gradually assimilated and incorporated into mainstream Anglican life. The Parish Communion movement shows the incorporation of the Catholic advocacy of the mass into central and Protestant strands of twentieth-century Anglicanism, though with important revision and development of that advocacy along the way. The movement helped to overcome the wars of churchmanship by liturgically uniting those from different backgrounds; it clarified the relationship of clergy and laity so that each could see that they depended on the other; and it offered and illustrated an integrated theology of discipleship, liturgy and the church. It provides a vivid example of the influence of the *consensus fidelium* through 'the continuing experience of the Holy Spirit through his faithful people in the Church', or in differnt but consonant language, of the presence of the *missio Dei* bringing unity out of division.

The Parish Communion movement also, paradoxically, allowed fulfilment of the Book of Common Prayer's original directions for the ritual of the service, for in the opening rubrics it is directed that the table 'shall stand in the body of the Church, or in the Chancel [i.e. not in the sanctuary] . . . And the Priest standing at the north side of the Table . . . the people kneeling'; and later in the service, before the Prayer of Consecration, another rubric directs the priest to stand at the table in such a way that he may be able to break the bread 'before the people'. With the priest standing at the north side, this could only happen if the people were gathered around the table. So the movement, despite its Catholic roots, allowed a fulfilment of some of the Protestant intentions within Cranmer's sixteenth-century reforms!

Other examples of this inherent tendency towards unity could be Protestant innovations becoming part of Anglo-Catholicism, such as the Evangelical Revival's commitment to mission being embraced by the Ritualist slum priests of the late nineteenth century. This is seen in the way the first male religious order founded by followers of the Oxford Movement, the Cowley Fathers, described itself as a society of 'mission priests'. Similarly, key elements of Enlightenment Anglicanism, such as Locke's emphasis on the reasonableness of Christianity, were embraced by Charles Simeon and other Evangelical preachers in the early nineteenth century (Bebbington 1989). And Charles Gore and the *Lux Mundi* school incorporated the biblical criticism of the Enlightenment school into its Anglo-Catholic theology in the late nineteenth century (see the volume of essays *Lux Mundi* of 1889).

All of these examples provide interesting illustrations of how Anglican unity can come from a number of dispersed sources (whether local church life, scholarship, reflection on scripture, wider cultural or church movements or common sense), and that *over time* what springs from those sources is weaved and meshed together, one element checking and redressing another.

But this is not necessarily an easy or a tidy process (and for this reason may not satisfy Norman). This is a point made by Michael Ramsey, the 100th Archbishop of Canterbury, who early in his career in 1936 published *The Gospel and the Catholic Church,* a ground breaking book based on biblical scholarship as well as church history which endeavoured to overcome the damaging polarization of Protestant and Catholic traditions within nineteenth-century Anglicanism. Drawing inspiration from F. D. Maurice, he argued that Anglicanism was the product both of ancient Catholic tradition and the Protestant theology of the Reformation, especially of Luther's theology of the cross. But he did not argue for a facile unity which papered over the cracks of division between traditions. He presented a much more engaging portrait of a church with a deep degree of diversity and yet with ultimate unity. Towards the end of the book, in a passage that has been quoted often, he described how this unity was not to be found in the present but was being formed in the future, a teleological unity, arising out of the messiness and division of the present. He suggested that it is possible to recognize both the reality of division and the ultimate unity of Anglican ways of discipleship. He wrote that the vindication of Anglicanism

lies in its pointing through its own history to something of which it is a fragment. Its credentials are its incompleteness, with the tension and the travail in its soul. It is clumsy and untidy, it baffles neatness and logic. For it is sent not to commend itself as 'the best type of Christianity', but by its very brokenness to point to the universal Church wherein all have died. (Ramsey 1990, p. 220)

The teleological unity, then, is within a wider unity of Christendom. The identity and authority of Anglicanism lies in its ecumenical future, a future forged out of its tense diversity in the present.

Paul Avis has elaborated the dynamic nature of Ramsey's view of Anglicanism:

In the Anglican vocation, according to Ramsey, the paramount authority of the gospel (the Reformation's contribution), the given reality of the Church catholic (which comes down to us through living tradition) and sound learning (or interaction with the modern world and its discoveries) are 'bound together'. It is when they are torn asunder and elaborated systematically in isolation that you have the distorted ideological systems: biblical literalism (fundamentalism); blinkered traditionalism infused with uncritical nostalgia; and arrogant rationalism that subjects the mystery of Christian revelation to its own narrow analytical criteria. But when bound together and held together in a community life of prayer, study and service, the three vital ingredients of the Anglican appeal interact – stimulating, criticizing and modifying each other in a real and living synthesis. (Avis 2000, pp. 47–8)

Martyn Percy has described Anglicanism as 'a commonwealth of belief and practice', and this captures it well:

Much of the doctrine of the Church comes from hard-fought struggle which is, of course, ongoing. But there is usually an eventual convergence, a common and directional plurality in which people of differing views and integrities move together towards God's future. (Evans and Percy 2000, p. 187)

The parish communion movement is a reminder, though, of the centrality of worship to this process. It was the evolving life of worship itself that lead the different traditions of Anglicanism to interact in this way. This can be put (more concisely) in the traditional Latin phrase, 'lex orandi, lex credendi' (as we worship so we believe). It certainly describes the foundation of the Church of England, when Cranmer did not produce a confessional statement or *summa* of belief but concentrated on compiling and publishing a book of services which, along with the English Bible, became the main way in which Reformation theology spread through parishes up and down the country. The book went through a number of editions, and the 1662 book is different from the 1637 book, let alone that of 1552. Since then other editions have been used in different provinces and the notion that Anglicanism is united by a single book 'emerges as a matter of ideology rather than a description of actual practice' (Irvine 2008, p. 5). Yet, as the source of a set of services which have formed Anglicanism and created the way that Anglican life and discipleship is *held* by worship, and worship of a certain liturgical kind based on scripture and tradition, it has a fundamental significance across the communion. Furthermore, according to the papers of a recent international consultation, it has resulted in contemporary worship across the Anglican Communion still shaping the life of its churches in, for example, fostering a heightened sense of social responsibility in wider society, and facilitating greater biblical literacy through using a lectionary in the reading of the Bible in worship (*ibid.*, pp. 8–9).

Today the Book of Common Prayer is not generally used in worship, but the lesson of the parish communion movement is that worship still has the capacity to form the unity of the church. While, then, Anglicanism has only a few fundamental marks which run through its different traditions, and while it has a diverse and fractious current life that lacks a central authority structure to resolve disputes, its history shows that over time, through the interaction of its different traditions, above all through its evolving worship, under the influence of the Holy Spirit through the *consensus fidelium*, it finds a surprising unity of life that also points forward to the coming of a wider ecumenical unity of all God's people.

Further Reading

Anglican Communion (2008), 'Chicago-Lambeth Quadrilateral' at http://www.anglicancommunion.org/resources/acis/docs/chicago_lambeth_quadrilateral.cfm
Anglican Communion Office (2008), 'The Anglican Communion' at www.anglican-communion.org

Anglican Communion (2009), 'An Anglican Communion Covenant', final text, at www.anglicancommunion.org/commission/covenant/final/text.cfm

Avis, Paul (2007) *The Identity of Anglicanism: Essentials of Anglican Ecclesiology*, London: T&T Clark.

Chapman, Mark, ed. (2008), *The Anglican Covenant*, London: T&T Clark.

Doe, N. (1998), *Canon Law in the Anglican Communion*, Oxford: Clarendon Press.

Irvine, Christopher, ed. (2008), *Anglican Liturgical Identity: Papers from the Prague Meeting of the International Liturgical Consultation*, Norwich: Canterbury Press.

Ramsey, Michael (1990), *The Gospel and the Catholic Church* (first published 1936), London: SPCK.

Bibliography

Abbott, Evelyn and Lewis Campbell (1897), *The Life and Letters of Benjamin Jowett, M. A., Master of Balliol College, Oxford*, London: John Murray.

Anglican Communion (1888), 'Chicago-Lambeth Quadrilateral' at http://www.anglicancommunion.org/resources/acis/docs/chicago_lambeth_quadrilateral.cfm

—— (2004), *The Windsor Report* at http://www.anglicancommunion.org/windsor2004.cfm

—— (2009), 'An Anglican Communion Covenant', final text, at www.anglicancommunion.org/commission/covenant/final/text.cfm

Anglican Communion Office (2008), 'The Anglican Communion' at www.anglicancommunion.org

Arnold, Matthew (1885), *Discourses in America*,

Atkinson, David (2003), 'Gospel and Bible People', *The Church Times*, 19 September 2003.

Avis, Paul (2000), *The Anglican Understanding of the Church*, London: SPCK.

Avis, Paul (2002), *Anglicanism and the Christian Church*, revised edition, London: Continuum.

Avis, Paul (2006), *Beyond the Reformation? Authority, Primacy and Unity in the Conciliar Tradition*, London: T&T Clark.

Avis, Paul (2007), *The Identity of Anglicanism: Essentials of Anglican Ecclesiology*, T&T Clark.

Badham, Paul (2009), *Is there a Christian Case for Assisted Suicide?: Voluntary Euthanasia Reassessed*, London: SPCK.

Bartlett, Alan (2007), *A Passionate Balance: The Anglican Tradition*, London: Darton, Longman and Todd.

Bebbington, David (1989), *Evangelicalism in Modern Britain: A History from the 1730s to the 1980s*, London: Routledge.

Book of Common Prayer (1662) with amendments of 1964, 1965 and 1968, standard edition, Cambridge: Cambridge University Press.

Booker, Mike, and Mark Ireland (2003), *Evangelism – Which Way Now?*, London: Church House Publishing.

Booty, J. E., ed. (1963), *An Apology for the Church of England by John Jewell*, Charlottesville: University Press of Virginia.

Booty, John and Stephen Sykes, eds. (1988), *The Study of Anglicanism*, SPCK.

Buchanan, Colin (1976), *What did Cranmer Think He was Doing?*, Cambridge: Grove Booklets.

Buchanan, Colin (1980) 'Holy Communion', in *Anglican Worship Today*, ed. Colin Buchanan, London: Collins.

Butler, Joseph (1856) *The Analogy of Religion, Natural and Revealed, To the Constitution and Course of Nature* [of 1736] . . . *and Fifteen Sermons* [of 1726], London: Henry G. Bohn.

Bradley, Ian (1976), *The Call to Seriousness: The Evangelical Impact on the Victorians*, London: Jonathan Cape.

Bradley, Ian (1990), *The Penguin Book of Hymns*, Harmondsworth: Penguin.

Caird, Edward (1908), *Lay Sermons and Addresses delivered in the Hall of Balliol College*, Glasgow.

Cameron, Euan (1991), *The European Reformation*, Oxford: Oxford University Press.

Carter, Joseph (1741), letter to Charles Wesley, November 1741, in the John Rylands Library, University of Manchester, Early Methodist Vol. No 17, transcribed by Sally Spencer.

Chadwick, Henry, ed. (2010), *Not Angels, but Anglicans: A History of Christianity in the British Isles*, revised updated edition, Norwich: Canterbury Press.

Chadwick, Owen, (1971), *The Victorian Church*, Vol. 1, 3rd edition, London: Adam and Charles Black.

Chapman, Mark (2006), *Anglicanism: A Very Short Introduction*, Oxford: Oxford University Press.

Chatfield, Adrian (2007), *Something in Common: An Introduction to the Principles and Practices of Worldwide Anglicanism*, revised edition, Nottingham: St John's Extension Studies.

Cowie, Leonard W. (1973), *Religion*, London: Methuen Educational.

Cragg, Gerald R. (1966), *The Church and the Age of Reason 1648–1789*, Harmondsworth: Penguin.

Cray, Graham *et al.* (2004), *Mission-shaped Church: Church Planting and Fresh Expressions of Church in a Changing Context*, London: Church House Publishing.

Cross, F. L. (1997), *The Oxford Dictionary of the Christian Church*, 3rd edition, ed. E. A. Livingstone, Oxford: Oxford University Press.

Crowe, Philip (1967), *Keele '67: The National Evangelical Anglican Congress Statement*, London: Falcon Books.

Cumming, Geoffrey (1983), *The Godly Order: Texts and Studies Relating to the Book of Common Prayer*, London: Alcuin and SPCK.

Daniell, David (1994), *William Tyndale: A Biography*, New Haven: Yale University Press.

Daniels, Louis W., 'The Ornaments Rubric: Its History and Force' at http://anglicanhistory.org/liturgy/daniels_ornaments.html

Darley, Gillian (2004), 'Hill, Octavia (1838–1912)', *Oxford Dictionary of National Biography*, Oxford: Oxford University Press.

Davie, Martin (2008), *A Guide to the Church of England*, London: Mowbray.

Doerkson, Daniel W. (1997), *Conforming to the Word: Herbert, Donne and the English Church Before Laud*, Bucknell University Press.

Duffy, Eamon (1994), *The Stripping of the Altars*, New Haven: Yale University Press.

Duffy, Eamon (2003), *The Voices of Morebath*, New Haven: Yale University Press.

Elford, R. John, and Ian S. Markham (2000), *The Middle Way: Theology, Politics and Economics in the Later Thought of R. H. Preston*, London: SCM Press.

Elizabeth I (1574), 'Prayer at Bristol' at www.luminarium.org/renlit/elizaprayer.htm

Evans, G. R. and J. Robert Wright, ed., (1991), *The Anglican Tradition: A Handbook of Sources*, London: SPCK.

Evans, G. R. and Martyn Percy (2000), *Managing the Church? Order and Organisation in a Secular Age*, Sheffield: Sheffield Academic Press.

Fagbemi, Stephen (2005), 'Understanding Akinola', *Church Times* 27 May 2005.

Fletcher, Joseph (1966), *Situation Ethics: The New Morality*, London: SCM.

Forbes, Duncan (1952), *The Liberal Anglican Idea of History*, Cambridge: Cambridge University Press.

General Synod (1998), *Stranger in the Wings*, GS Misc 532, London: Church House Publishing.

Green, T. H. (1881), 'Liberal Legislation and Freedom of Contract', in *Works, Volume 3*, London: Longman, Green and Co, 1890.

Grimley, Matthew (2004), *Citizenship, Community and the Church of England: Liberal Anglican Theories of the State between the Wars*, Oxford: Clarendon Press.

Hague, William (2008), *William Wilberforce*, London: HarperCollins.

Haigh, Christopher (1993), *English Reformations: Religion, Politics and Society under the Tudors*, Oxford: Clarendon Press.

Hastings, Adrian (2001), *A History of English Christianity 1920–2000*, 4th edition, London: SCM Press.

Herring, George (2002), *What was the Oxford Movement?*, London: Continuum.

Hill, Jonathan (2004), *Faith in the Age of Reason*, Oxford: Lion Hudson plc.

Holloway, James, ed. (1989), *Old St Paul's: Three Centuries of a Scottish Church*, Edinburgh: The White Rose Press.

Hooker, Richard, *Laws of Ecclesiastical Polity* (1593 onwards), in Arthur Pollard, ed. (1990), *Richard Hooker Ecclesiastical Polity*, Manchester: Carcanet Books.

Hunt, Stephen (2004), *The Alpha Initiative: Evangelism in a Post-Christian Age*, Aldershot: Ashgate.

Hylson-Smith, Kenneth (1989), *Evangelicals in the Church of England 1734–1984*, Edinburgh: T&T Clark.

Hylson-Smith, Kenneth (1997, 1998), *The Churches in England from Elizabeth I to Elizabeth II*, Vol. 2 and 3, London: SCM Press.

Iremonger, F. A. (1948), *William Temple, Archbishop of Canterbury: His Life and Letters*, Oxford: Oxford University Press.

Irvine, Christopher, ed. (2008), *Anglican Liturgical Identity: Papers from the Prague Meeting of the International Liturgical Consultation*, Norwich: Canterbury Press.

Jacob, W. M. (1997), *The Making of the Anglican Church Worldwide*, London: SPCK.

Janz, Denis R., ed. (1999), *A Reformation Reader: Primary Texts with Introductions*, Minneapolis: Fortress Press.

Jowett, Benjamin (1907), 'The Interpretation of Scripture' (first published in *Essays and Reviews*, 1860), in *Scripture and Truth*, with an introduction by Lewis Campbell, London: Henry Frowde, reprinted by Bibliolife.

Kaye, Bruce (2008), *An Introduction to World Anglicanism*, Cambridge: Cambridge University Press.

Lake, Peter (2003), "The Anglican Moment'? Richard Hooker and the Ideological Watershed of the 1590s', in *Anglicanism and the Western Christian Tradition*, ed. Stephen Platten, Norwich: Canterbury Press.

Lambeth (1948), Report IV, 'The Anglican Communion', *The Lambeth Conference, 1948. The Encyclical Letter from the Bishops; together with Resolutions and Reports*, London.

Law, William (1728), *A Serious Call to a Devout and Holy Life*, at http://www.ccel.org/ccel/law/serious_call.toc.html. Also available in the edition edited by Halcyon Backhouse (1987), London: Hodder and Stoughton.

Livingston, James C. (2006), *Modern Christian Thought: The Enlightenment and the Nineteenth Century*, 2nd edition, Minneapolis: Fortress Press.

Luther, Martin (2003), *On Christian Liberty*, Minneapolis: Fortress Press. See also Janz (1999) above.

McAdoo, Henry (1992), 'Richard Hooker', in Geoffrey Rowell, ed., *The English Religious Tradition and the Genius of Anglicanism*, Ikon 1992.

MacCulloch, Diarmaid (1996), *Thomas Cranmer: A Life*, New Haven: Yale University Press.

MacCulloch, Diarmaid (2000), *Tudor Church Militant: Edward VI and the Protestant Reformation*, London: Allan Lane.

MacCulloch, Diarmaid (2001), *The Later Reformation in England 1547–1603*, Basingstoke: Palgrave.

MacCulloch, Diarmaid (2003), 'The Church of England 1533–1603', in Stephen Platten, ed., *Anglicanism and the Western Christian Tradition*, Norwich: Canterbury Press.

MacCulloch, Diarmaid (2003b), *Reformation: Europe's House Divided*, London: Allen Lane.

McGrade, A. S. (1988), 'Reason', in Stephen Sykes and John Booty, *The Study of Anglicanism*, London: SPCK.

McGrath, Alister E. (1999), *Reformation Thought: An Introduction*, 3rd edition, Oxford: Blackwell Publishing.

McGrath, Alister E. (2007), *Christianity's Dangerous Idea: The Protestant Revolution: A History from the Sixteenth Century to the Twenty-first*, London: SPCK.

Maurice, F. (1884), *Life and Letters of F. D. Maurice*, 2nd edition, London: Macmillan.

More, Paul Elmer and Frank Leslie Cross (1935), *Anglicanism*, London: SPCK.

Morris, Jeremy (2005), *F. D. Maurice and the Crisis of Christian Authority*, Oxford: Oxford University Press.

Morris, Jeremy (2007), *To Build Christ's Kingdom: F.D. Maurice and His Writings*, Norwich: Canterbury Press.

Mursell, Gordon (2001), *English Spirituality: From 1700 to the Present Day*, London: SPCK.

Newman, John Henry (1833), *Tract 1*, at http://www.newmanreader.org/works/times/tract1.html

Noll, Mark (2003), *The Rise of Evangelicalism: The Age of Edwards, Whitefield and the Wesleys*, Leicester: InterVarsity Press.

Norman, Edward (1998), 'Authority in the Anglican Communion', lecture to the Ecclesiastical Law Society, at justus.anglican.org/resources/misc/Norman.

O'Donovan, Oliver (1986), *On the Thirty Nine Articles: A Conversation with Tudor Christianity*, Exeter: The Paternoster Press.

Paley, William (1802), *Natural Theology; or Evidences of the Existence and Attributes of the Deity, Collected from the Appearances of Nature*, in the edition of 2006, ed. Matthew Eddy and David Knight, Oxford: Oxford University Press.

Percy, Martyn (1999), *Introducing Richard Hooker and the Laws of Ecclesiastical Polity*, London: Darton, Longman and Todd.

Percy, Martyn (2000), 'A Theology of Change for the Church' in G. R. Evans and Martyn Percy, *Managing the Church*, Sheffield: Sheffield Academic Press.

Pereiro, James (2007), *'Ethos' and the Oxford Movement: At the Heart of Tractarianism*, Oxford: Oxford University Press.

Pickering, W. S. F. (2008), *Anglo-Catholicism: A Study in Religious Ambiguity*, 2nd edition, Cambridge: James Clarke and Co.

Platten, Stephen, ed. (2004), *Anglicanism and the Western Christian Tradition*, Norwich: Canterbury Press.

Platten, Stephen (2008) 'One intellectual breeze: Coleridge and a new apologetic', *Theology*, No. 867, pp. 323–35.

Podmore, Colin (2005), *Aspects of Anglican Identity*, London: Church House Publishing.

Preston, Ronald H. (1981), *Explorations in Theology 9*, London: SCM Press.

Procter, Francis and Walter Howard Frere (1951), *A New History of the Book of Common Prayer*, London: Macmillan.

Rack, Henry (1989), *Reasonable Enthusiast: John Wesley and the Rise of Methodism*, London: The Epworth Press.

Ramsey, Michael (1990), *The Gospel and the Catholic Church* (first published 1936), London: SPCK.

Redfern, Alistair (2000), *Being Anglican*, London: Darton, Longman and Todd.

Reynolds, David (2009), *America: Empire of Liberty: A New History*, London: Allan Lane.

Rowell, Geoffrey (1983). *The Vision Glorious: Themes and Personalities of the Catholic Revival in Anglicanism*, Oxford: Oxford University Press.

Rowell, Stevenson and Williams (2001), *Love's Redeeming Work: The Anglican Quest for Holiness*, Oxford: Oxford University Press.

Sanders, E. P. (1991), *Paul*, Oxford: Oxford University Press.

Sheldrake, Philip, ed. (2009), *Heaven in Ordinary: George Herbert and His Writings*, Norwich: Canterbury Press.

Singer. Peter (1983), *Hegel*, Oxford: Oxford University Press .

Skinner, S. A. (2004), *Tractarians and the 'Condition of England': the Social and Political Thought of the Oxford Movement*, Oxford: Clarendon.

Steer, Roger (2009), *Inside Story: The Life of John Stott*, Leicester: InterVarsity Press.

Stevenson, Kenneth (1994), *Covenant of Grace Renewed: A Vision of the Eucharist in the Seventeenth Century*, London: Darton, Longman and Todd.

Stott, John (1999), *Evangelical Truth: A Personal Plea for Unity*, Leicester: InterVarsity Press.

Suggate, Alan (1987), *William Temple and Christian Social Ethics Today*, Edinburgh: T&T Clark.

Sykes, Stephen W. (1978), *The Integrity of Anglicanism*, London: Mowbray.

Sykes, Stephen, and John Booty (1988), *The Study of Anglicanism*, London: SPCK.

Taylor, Jeremy (late 1620s), 'On the Reverence due to the Altar' at http://anglicanhistory.org/taylor/reverence.html

Taylor, Jeremy (1650), *Holy Living* at http://www.ccel.org/ccel/taylor/holy_living.html. A scholarly edition is available edited by P.G. Stanwood (1989), Oxford: Clarendon Press.

Temple, William (1929), *Christianity and the State*, London: Macmillan.

Temple, William (1941), *Malvern 1941: The Life of the Church and the Order of Society*, London: Longmans, Green and Co.

Temple, William (1950), *Christianity and Social Order,* Third edition, London: SCM Press.

Turner, John Munsey (2002), *John Wesley: The Evangelical Revival and the Rise of Methodism in England*, Peterborough: The Epworth Press.

Vidler, Alec (1948), *The Theology of F. D. Maurice*, London: SCM Press.

Ward, Kevin (2006), *A History of Global Anglicanism*, Cambridge: Cambridge University Press.

Warner, Robert (2007), *Reinventing English Evangelicalism, 1966–2001: A Theological and Sociological Study*, Carlisle: Paternoster Press.

Webster, Christopher (2003), *Temples ... Worthy of His Presence: The Early Publications of the Cambridge Camden Society*, Reading: Spire Books.

Wesley, John (1944), *Sermons on Several Occasions (44 Sermons)*, London: The Epworth Press.

Wilkinson, Alan (1998), *Christian Socialism: Scott Holland to Tony Blair*, London: SCM Press.

Willey, Basil (1980), 'Samuel Taylor Coleridge' in *Nineteenth Century Studies: Coleridge to Matthew Arnold*, Cambridge: Cambridge University Press.

Williams, Rowan (2004), *Anglican Identities*, London: Darton, Longman and Todd.

Wood, Thomas (1986), 'Anglican Moral Theology/Ethics' in *A New Dictionary of Christian Ethics*, ed. John Macquarrie and James Childress, London: SCM Press.

Worrall, B.G. (2004), *The Making of the Modern Church: Christianity in England since 1800*, third edition, London: SPCK.

Yates, Nigel (1975), *The Oxford Movement and Parish Life: St Saviour's, Leeds, 1839–1929*, York: Borthwick Institute of Historical Research.

Yates, Nigel (2001), *Buildings, Faith and Worship: The Liturgical Arrangement of Anglican Churches 1600–1900*, Oxford: Oxford University Press.

Yates, Timothy (2004), *The Expansion of Christianity*, Oxford: Lion Publishing.

Index